GUINEA PIGS OF THE NEW WORLD ORDER

GUINEA PIGS OF THE NEW WORLD ORDER

BLACKMAN THE ENDANGERED BREED

ONYEAKOR, JOACHIM

Library of Congress Control Number: 2012919407
ISBN: Hardcover   978-1-4797-1496-4
                 Softcover   978-1-4797-1495-7
                 Ebook   978-1-4797-1497-1

This book was printed in the United States of America.

To order additional copies of this book, contact:
Xlibris Corporation
0-800-644-6988
www.xlibrispublishing.co.uk
Orders@xlibrispublishing.co.uk
304462

CONTENTS

THE NEW WORLD ORDER

A one-world government and one-unit monetary system, the New World Order is under permanent non-elected hereditary oligarchs who self-select themselves from amongst their numbers in the form of a feudal system as it was in the Middle Ages. It is a system to be implemented through the use of human population control, the means ranging from stopping the growth of human societies through reproductive health and family planning programmes, which promote abstinence, contraception and abortion, or intentionally reducing the bulk of the world population through genocides by mongering unnecessary wars, through plagues by engineering emergent viruses and tainting vaccines, and more . . .

It is a worldwide plot being masterminded by an extremely powerful and influential group of genetically related individuals at least at the highest level, which include many of the world's wealthiest people, top political leaders, and corporate elite whose goal is to create a one-world totalitarian government, stripped of nationalistic and regional boundaries, which is obedient to their agenda. Their intention is to impose and achieve complete and total control over every human being on the planet and to dramatically reduce the world's population to a figure desirable to them.

A guinea pig is a form of an experimental animal.

In time to come, if the black man as he is called does not begin to produce what he consumes and also consume what he produces and in the process also develop a supportive culture to engineer a mini-system to survive in this New World Order that is already in force, he will be the guinea pig of the New World Order and will become endangered in time to come, for any man who has nothing to call his own, not even identity, is not worthy to be called a human being no matter the circumstances that place him where he is. Life is a continuous struggle; hence, the black man must rise up today to reshape his destiny and protect his future or be ready to be displaced from this only world that he knows . . .

Message from the Author

As I write this book, I say we should not generalise on those who have tapped into their potentials and done the best but on those who still have not learnt to rise above themselves and change their ways of thinking, those who do not believe in themselves, and those who do not believe that they can ever achieve anything and live a better life.

This is a power-packed book, an empowerment, practical and positive philosophy, a liberation chant. It is written in depth though presented in the simplest form of English. Ensure that you are not a prejudiced or narrow-minded person to read this book. This book is written to invoke what I call mental curiosity in the minds of the readers (to make the readers think critically and 'out of the box'). This book will do well for intellectuals, mostly the free thinkers in their midst.

As you read this book, take note that I am at war with a concept that I call mental slavery and the affected victims that I call mental slaves who are found predominantly amongst Africans or the black community; hence, pay special attention to where the battle is going on. This book is written to bring to limelight the problems that plague the black man, engineered by mental slavery and possible solutions to these problems. Mental slavery has turned the African continent and its people into consumer breeds. A lot of ugly assertions have been made about African people ranging from the way they look to their colour and their pattern of thinking, including their belief system. None of those ugly connotations give me concern more than why the African continent has been mentally enslaved yet being called humiliating names. Why will the world create a slave race out of harmless people yet always connote them in a pejorative manner? Why Africans were called 'blacks' in the first place?

The lack of mental curiosity and poisonous information fed into the mind of the black man through faulty religious doctrines, faulty education by the colonial masters, societal conditioning, and superstitious beliefs which include those concocted by his forefathers for control purposes have contributed immensely to enslaving his mind. Hence, in as much as the problem of the black man is related to mind, it is both internal and external. This book is intended to address all of these issues so as to enable the black man to think and function properly like a normal human being, capable of harnessing the earth's resources to survive like others. The humanity of the African people who are classified as the black race is being questioned in these present times because they are seemingly unable to produce what they consume or to consume what they produce. They import everything, including God. They are losing their self-identity and may become an endangered human breed.

As an author, I do not necessarily teach, but I intend to make the reader think. This book is provocative and powerful. The information contained in it is like a journey to understand what I intend to make you achieve.

The information contained in this book is presented in the simplest form of English for easier and wider reading and to avoid ambiguity, confusion, and misunderstanding. This book is a blend of inspirational motivation and simple poetry including African wisdom and sayings. This book can only be helpful if it is read with an open mind. I wrote this book as an activist, a free thinker, and a motivational speaker. The use of the word 'God' in this book represents the universal God, though at times I see other types of god(s), imaginary ones created by diverse religious institutions of the world; as evidently felt in the Pentecostal Christian community that is splitting into untold numbers as if God has varieties. The lack of understanding of the universal God and the real purpose of life on this planet has created many problems ranging from wars and series of inhumane actions against fellow humans, but the sooner mankind begins to think out of the box and appreciates that the universal God is not a god of any particular religion or any race, the better will our lives be for God is either for all or for none.

DEDICATION

I dedicate this work to all the living and fallen heroes of Africa; to all the freedom fighters,activists,intellectuals,nobles,and great achievers who have made ineffaceable imprints on the stones of African history. Most especially, I recognize the selfless sacrifices of Great Kwame Nkrumah, Great Patrice Lumumba and Great Nelson Mandela in their relentless struggle to end all manner of oppressions and ugliness perpetrated against the African people by the colonialists. I applaud the bold revolutionary effort of Jerry Rawlings which improved the political face of Ghana.

I recognize the efforts of powerful women and great achievers like Oprah Winfery, Dr.Wangari Mathaai,Winnie Mandela; Great and noble men like Martin Luther King, Malcolm X, Marcus Garvey; Extraordinary and highly endowed intellectuals like Prof. Phillip Emeagwali, Prof. Barack Obama (American President), Prof. Wole Soyinka, Prof Chinua Achebe, Ngugi wa Thiong'o, Cyprian Ekwensi, Dr. Ave Kludze; Great Artists like Bob Marley and Mutaboruka; Great sportsmen like Mohammed Ali and Kanu Nwankwo and more just to name a few. I thank them immensely for proving that Africans are equally intelligent humans capable of higher thoughts, higher arts and unlimited higher achievements.

I dedicate this work also to all the children of Africa at home and the Diaspora who have been victims of all manner of oppressions, slavery, brain drain, foreign diseases, apartheid, racial segregation, colonialism and neo-colonialism. Today we fight a greater war—Mental Slavery. Let every African take up his mental armor, spears and shields so that we can collectively annihilate mental slavery, the invisible enemy, the enemy that devours the mind, the worm that is fast feasting on the fabrics of African renaissance, awakening and development, the greatest enemy of the African continent. The enemy that is about to transform Africans into Guinea Pigs of the New World Order, prone to endangerment and possible extinction.

Behold the time of Awakening, Arise Africa, for this is the time. Let the battle begin!

THE BLACK MAN, THE ENDANGERED SPECIES

An endangered species is a population of organisms which is facing a high risk of becoming extinct because it is either few in numbers or threatened by changing environmental or predation parameters. Technically speaking, African natives are facing serious predation parameters, which most of them know nothing about and it seems that the New World Order since its creation and inception designated the African natives (that they call blacks) as guinea pigs that will be used in its operations and to advance its cause. Black man has faced cruel slavery, colonialism, forced dominance and subjugation, and neo-colonialism, and he is now also facing mental slavery, a far more dangerous situation. A situation not recognisable with the naked eye, yet it exists and poses more danger than all of the former, creating a cloud of mental slaves who are moving in the wrong direction, applying the wrong life operational parameters. Development is extremely slow in the African continent, and the advanced nations have ceased that opportunity to transform the continent into a huge market for their finished goods, in the process also fuelling mind slavery using religion and neo-colonialism to impair same development. They hypocritically condemn the African continent as incapable of self-governance, resource control and management and self-sustenance, but it has never occurred to anyone that if Africa stands up today economically and development wise, those advanced nations will lose their huge market having also contributed immensely in fueling economic slavery and over dependence on foreign goods in the African community while creating their market. In exchange, directly or indirectly, for the rich natural resources of the African continent, the advanced nations have fuelled wars and mental slavery in the continent while still condemning the continent. In exchange for material wealth, cures to diseases like HIV-AIDS that are ravaging the African continent and its people are not invented rather treatment. Man has stepped his foot on the moon and landed his creations on mars yet claims that HIV-AIDS and other deadly diseases like TB have no cure; I beg to disagree.

I will not delve into the involvement of the illuminati organization and the Freemasons in the formation of the one world government since I know virtually nothing or better say I have no reliably conclusive information about the two above mentioned organizations but what I know is that there is definitely a move towards a one world body to be governed by a one world leadership structure. This arrangement will favor those at the top and not those at the bottom. It will be like a pyramid where by the strongest sits on top of the strong who in turn sits on top of the weak and so one. It will be like a food chain. A strong eat the weak kind of arrangement. The master servant relationship, the predators versus the prey. The lions versus the other lower animals. The marriage between the strong and the weak will ultimately favor the strong. The weak if not loved will be victimized. Africans are not loved; they are apparently not accepted in the world as equal humans hence the formation of the New World Order will not favor Africans. I asked a good friend of mine how the colonialists could give them heaven and at the same time HIV, a virus which ultimately leads to death has no cure if the world loves them that much. I asked him whether those who understand HIV virus do not know demographically the continent and the breeds that it will affect more. I also told him that if HIV was killing more of Europeans and Asians, it would have had a cure now. I also asked him why the black man has not capability to invent a cure for HIV-AIDs. He wants to go to heaven when he dies, yet he fears death. Yet he fears HIV virus, a death resulting virus. I asked how a man who finds you unfit on this planet as a human species or better say a man who thinks you must interact with other humans as a low breed, finds you fit for heaven, a place meant for good people. I wanted to know whether if a place like heaven does exist, Europeans and the Jews will not grab it all and hold the key unto themselves. My friend gave me no answers.

You see, the progression of the New World Order will result in Africans being used as Guinea pigs and over time, they will become endangered. I wonder why Africans have not learnt some lessons from what happened in North America leading to the formation of USA; what happened in Australia, New Zeland and Southern Africa. It was not a plot to bring races together to cohabitate peacefully, rather one of displacement and forced dominance. A word is enough for the wise.

Unfortunately, the same mercenaries of the new world government who enslaved the African people in the past and who also forcefully colonised them have engineered a form of government prevalent in the African continent, which impedes development of the continent one way or the other, while at the same time they classified African natives to be of lower breed incapable of achieving anything that requires serious and hard intelligent work and thinking. I stand to completely oppose the conspiracy theory that the black man is close to the apes and did not inherit intelligence hence cannot partake in higher arts leading to scientific innovations and technological developments. I also stand to partially agree that during the days when the pharaohs built the pyramids of Egypt and also the Ethiopians built the axioms, the Europeans were also leaving in the dark.

Without slavery, forced dominance, colonialism, neo-colonialism, false religions, weak education, and mental slavery in general, the African continent would have developed in its own ways and style just as their languages evolved and developed being fully functional human beings. But in these present times, the black man is becoming endangered since he is a victim of all forms of oppressions and subjugation—spiritual, economic, and political. His lands are forcefully taken away from him, his children enslaved and taken to strange lands, and his culture destroyed, impairing economic evolution. The perpetrators of these acts have not seen anything wrong in their actions, hence proving their fabricated facts that the black man is of a low breed. Having noted all that have been happening to the black man even in his own lands in these present dispensations, it is evident that he will be used as a guinea pig in time to come by the New World Order and also that he will become extinct in time to come. The world does not see African natives as fully functional human beings though some Africans are helping to fuel this belief by their thinking and actions. African natives are seen as unintelligent breed. Even though great African scientists like Phillip Emeagwali and great Poets like Wole Soyinka are proving this notion wrong, the world has not change their stands rather they will find a way to also erase any opposition to this conspiracy theory and plot to make Africans look like lower humans and in extreme cases they are systematically making Africans themselves to accept the notion that they are low breed. Africans unfortunately have not learnt from the event of the natives of India, South Africa and Australia. They ignorantly breed a generation of slaves that will live their entire lives depending on other people for everything including God. The only thing that can prevent this from happening is if the black man unites and also spiritually withdraws from the world and embarks on African renaissance enabling him to reshape his destiny and recreate his future. It might sound strange, impractical but we must all remember that someone landed a robot on the planet mars, this thing may have been considered a dream or a mad thought if someone said this 100 years ago that someone will step his foot on the moon and also that man will place a search object on mars. No one will believe if we are told 50 years ago that the Indians will own TATA a wonderful car brand. Africans are not holding unto big dreams and designing programs for the longer future. This is also one quality that I admire about Europeans, the ability to envision things and make them happen. The ability to dream big and work hard, making massive action to make it happen. The ability to think beyond the normal only for such abnormal thoughts to become reality with time. Though Africans may have equally been great without the ugliness of the past but it is time that they start copying the strengths and pattern of thinking of Europeans for the future of their generations. Africans must start thinking about the future of all of these children they have in these present times and the future of the generations that these children will give birth to. Unless they develop this kind of mind attitude, they will remain the way they are, chasing little things like children and living close to nature, depending on other people's creations and living almost like basal beings. I told someone that animals have their own children, they feed them and reproduce, animals are controlled entirely by humans so it is time that Africans know that if their entire world is under the control of others even the God they worship then that justifies why the world is treating them like slave animals. The world may have designed an ugly faith for the black man in the past but it is time that the black man takes control and redesign the blueprint for his future and rewrite his destiny. The black man must most especially appreciate his roots and embrace his heritage. He must begin to produce what he consumes and to consume what he produces. In the past, Africans were taken to strange lands as slaves, but today they submit themselves to slavery to the same people that perpetrated such acts in the past. The worst nightmare that has befallen the African continent is a wave of leadership which does not look inwards but outwards. It is a neo-colonial form of arrangement that is only interested in maintaining the colonial status quo and nothing else, ushering in a form of leadership that impairs development and a leadership that promotes backwardness, perpetuating economic slavery of the African people. This is the worst nightmare the African continent is facing, and it must be rooted out for Africans to see the light of the day.

European racist propagandists would wish to create and impose a belief system enshrined in non-factual or better say fabricated facts and knowledge-based assertions aimed at positioning the Caucasian race as fundamentally superior human beings, hence called whites, just to find reasons for dominating others whom they perceive as inferior; they acquire land and natural resources and in the process get away with the guilt. It must be known that at some time in human history the Greeks who developed philosophy acquired knowledge from the ancient Egyptians in Africa, though there have been serious efforts to destroy all such evidences and erase any such historic records. It is unfair to classify people of other continents as inferior so as to possess their natural heritage. A lot of this and other ugliness has transpired in the African continent engineered by Europeans, who have also refused to pay reparation or admit their guilt just to sustain the belief that the black man is fundamentally less human than them and hence can receive any treatment fit for animals. The earth was not designed in such a manner that humans all over the planet must look the same. There is no evidence to prove the fact that humans of a race should have dominion over humans of other race. The Bible tried to prove that the pharaohs of Egypt enslaved the Israelites yet the same Bible tells us that the Noah's ark sailed across a flood that affected the whole planet. How can a flood happen in Iraq and someone in California could see the same flood when the earth is spherical and when obviously someone in Australia can never see what is happening in Lagos without a satellite or a telescope that were not availavble then. We need to prove whether in reality the pharaohs enslaved the Israelites and whether any truly black African empire has championed the cause of enslavement of other people of other race. Without the creation of gadgets that permeate other geopolitical zones, Europeans will not see Asians and Asians will not see Africans and vice versa hence people would evolve and develop in their economic and cultural activities naturally according and in accordance with their environment, needs, and other natural life around them. African culture and evolution was destroyed by slave masters and colonialists who also brought a form of knowledge hence a teacher will always be the master but our teachers have called us black monkeys and are treating us like one and we are almost also acting like one. My problem is that the Chinese and Indians learnt from the teachers knowing also that in the past the same teachers learnt from African, the ancient Egyptians but the black man of today has refused to learn and better his life but have decided to maintain the slave status. This is one reason why in no distant time to come, drugs and other substances will be tested in the bodies of Africans considered as lower breed before other better humans can consume them, and that is what happens to a guinea pig. The population of the African natives will be drastically reduced and their natural resources including lands will be taken away from them completely. The remaining ones will become full-blown slaves and guinea pigs. I agree that Europeans have a great and valiant advanced civilisation, for which, of course, I give them kudos. Let all men know today that civilisation is a force that came into being naturally to put man in a phase where he can understand nature and control nature to an extent. It is a force for good and not one of evil that will be used to subjugate and displace others as it is almost happening today. Science evolutionary theory and varying religious doctrines are trying to explain the origin or creation of man with limited information and none of these institutions will be able to give accurate account of how man was created for the intelligence that made man manifest has not revealed such information to any mortal. Religious institutions claim knowing, yet what they know vary from one religion to the other making such knowledge an inconclusive proof of man's origin. Science claims knowing yet from time to time, scientific information keep on changing. All of those theories and beliefs are full of flaws as they contradict one another; hence, how come a human being stands armed with these flaw-filled theories and beliefs to create a system that is gradually transforming Africans into guinea pigs and exposing them to endangerment?

A lot has been done by the advanced nations to put down Africans while at the same time they criticise and condemn the continent and its children. This book is not going to deal extensively with all of that ugliness but will treat a phenomenon called mental slavery or mind slavery which is prevalent in the African continent, resulting in the reason why the black man as he is called is incapable of doing anything for himself in the only world he knows. Africa is the centre point in this book since they are the most risk-prone species, incapable of doing anything for themselves except consume. They are now labelled as the consumer race, and they brazenly ignore this ugliness; not even their leaders know what it means for a human being to be given such a label. Of all the continents of the world where the forces of development and civilisation have crept in, it is only in Africa that mental slavery, economic slavery, underdevelopment, ugly leadership, and backwardness thrive. It may amaze you to know that a country like Nigeria, the oil giant, the self-acclaimed giant of Africa, an unproductive human population-fuelled giant, cannot boast of stable electricity yet they boast of supplying electricity to a few neighbouring countries in West Africa. Industries are vacating to neighbouring Ghana because of lack of electricity. It is a country that is one of the largest oil exporters in the world yet cannot refine their own oil, reason being that the refineries cannot be maintained, hence the crude oil has to be refined offshore and resold back home. It is a country where the leaders fail to understand both the physical and philosophical meaning of light. It is a country in darkness. Someone will ask if there are leaders in that country at all or are the leaders the ones stage-managing the downfall of the country. Some of these shameless leaders who cannot do anything but come into power to seek wealth and fame are the reasons why Europeans have called us all sorts of name and depicted Africa as a continent of apes. It takes a fully functional, sensitive, creative, and concerned human being to understand human needs and lead other human beings. As they say, the leaders should learn to look into the mirror, and when they do so, they must see the people they serve and not themselves. The African continent is filled with leaders who seem not to be concerned about the plight of the citizens, as Nelson Mandela put it, 'There are no keener revelation of a society than the way it treats its own people.' The African continent needs creative, visionary, educated, sensitive, and pragmatic leaders and not leaders who are also suffering from chronic ignorance and mental slavery like their subjects.

Africans are not helping matters either. They submit themselves to the same system that enslaved and colonised them as slaves unwittingly. Africans have failed to dream big. Their vision end in meeting their human needs like food, shelter, raising children, health care, self-gratification, education and more. Their vision does not go beyond those needs. Only a few Africans have purpose in life and only a few of those few have purpose directed towards African emancipation from all the ugliness that plague the continent. We bear children everyday yet we are blind to the ugly reality that a new wave of capitalists, a bunch of chronic and mindless materialists are ever ready to provide more drugs for the treatment of death threatening diseases present and more to come that we begin to wonder wether they are the ones engineering those diseases themselves. Africans must think out of the box and remove themselves from shallow mindedness. They must begin to think as humans should do. The world is engineering the African mind to act and think like an animal to see justification to treat Africans they way they are being treated just like to give a dog a bad name just to hang the dog. Yet Africans do not notice these things. They chase base things like basal beings incapable of higher thoughts and higher arts. They dream like little children, chasing only things that are short lived. Their politicians attain position of power only to abandon service to humanity in pursuit of material wealth. In these present times, our artists are deployed in the promotion of imoralitiy and mental slavery, our clergies are deployed by politicians to provide us false hopes and stage managed miracles and also brainwash us destroying also our zeal to resist injustice. Where do we start from ? We go overseas only to seek basic necessities of life like cars, houses, money, husbands, wives, show off items etc. and not to dream big and make our dreams come true. I am not even sure that an average African in this present time knows what a life of purpose is all about. If we are not building castles in the air, we are building liabilities and show off empires that can only be used to oppress one another. We arrive easily and when our achievements are measured, only liabilities are seen. We do not think about the collective future of our continent. I know that the world has a hand in this right from the origin when we are enslaved, made to starve and die like animals but is it not time someone removes the blindfold and see clearly. What I am saying is that we are assisting the world also in their oppression of reducing Africans to the level of lower animals. We can do better if we change our thinking and follow it up with massive actions.

Generally, the black man is suffering from mental slavery, and the African continent is raising a cloud of mental slaves. A mental slave is one suffering from mental slavery. We shall be discussing about mental slavery extensively in the following chapters of this book, hence enabling the reader to understand how mental slavery is leading the African continent into an era where Africans shall become an endangered human breed and also how they shall be used as guinea pigs of the New World Order. To throw a little light on the subject of mental slavery, take for instance someone travelling to Australia; if he boards an aircraft knowingly or unknowingly heading to New York, of course he will arrive at New York and not Australia. The same thing happens in the mind of the black man in his everyday life through false religion, misinformation, faulty education, superstitions, mind control using audiovisuals, etc. If a person's mind is held motionless or drifts to the wrong course using information, then the person is suffering from mental slavery. Mental slavery is a result of mind arrest or mind diversion using information. It happens in the mind which is the centre of intelligence, thinking, feelings, creativity, enthusiasm, will, and all other emotions. Those suffering from mental slavery or mind slavery are mental slaves. In this era, information has become a great tool of slavery. In the days of physical slavery, chains and locks were used, but today an invisible chain is used which is information. Superstitions, false religions, mind control using audiovisuals and other gadgets, twisted education, and reverse modern-day colonialism are some of the causes of mental slavery. Any form of information generated and transmitted for deceitful purposes or for the purpose of diverting a person's mind to the wrong course can lead to mental slavery.

We are already in the era of the New World Order, an era when information has become so powerful that it could be deployed as a tool of mind control and mind slavery. The black man as he is called will face a drastic reduction in his population by all means available in time to come due to mental slavery, which has made him weak and defenceless against anything, even hunger and diseases. It may amaze you to know that in some African countries, they import food, identity, and God. The New World Order is already in full swing. The forces of globalisation, the United Nations, World Health Organisation, so-called incurable diseases like HIV, and all the global institutions and structures like the Internet are just a few of the tentacles of the New World Order. There are more, and they are now in full force. The weaker breed will be grossly affected and victimised. Their blood shall be used to fuel the engine of the New World Order. Africans having accepted to be called blacks; hence the black race, the dark race, will soon become useless in the world as all evidence points to the fact that the dog was given a bad name to hang it, and it seems nothing good will ever come out of that name black.

Most of the biblical aphorisms about the New World Order, the end time, and the Antichrist are already happening today, and I begin to wonder whether the writers of the Bible truly saw the future of mankind or whether the creation of Bible was engineered by the forebears of the same people masterminding the New World Order, considering so many conspiracy theories and plots existing in the world of information that we receive today politically and religiously. I must state that the Bible's view about the New World Order is almost exactly what is happening in these present times except that the numbers 666, the person of the anti-Christ, the beast, Satan and many others used in the book of Revelation of the Bible have not been clearly defined and identified hence making such views inconclusive, unacceptable to other religious faiths, unacceptable to skeptics and critical thinkers and also seeming as if the same creators of the New World Order may have told us in the past what they will do, which is all happening now using the religious books, so that when such things happen we will accept them as human fate when they may have actually been stage managed.

Due to the advancement of various mind control mechanisms and sophistication of information-based systems in the world today, humans are evolving faster and are exhibiting features like robots as if controlled by electronic chips in their brains. Also these days, due to the quest for material acquisitions, people vacillate between right and wrong, hence no longer understanding what conscience means, though they notice what is wrong when it happens to them and not when they do wrong to others. Man has advanced in intelligence so much that I am wondering if there are aliens in our midst in human form. The level of scientific advancement of today clearly shows that something out of the ordinary is in control and definitely something out of the ordinary will be happening. I hope that scientists engineer life on Mars, otherwise African people will be cleaned out and the continent will be taken over completely. Sometimes I fail to understand why Africans cannot challenge popular beliefs that they are incapable of higher thoughts. If biological viruses and strange diseases are being created every day, then Africans are at risk. Man is looking for land and natural resources and has created a jungle-like 'survival of the fittest' kind of world. Africans must wake up before they become extinct as they have already become guinea pigs of the New World Order.

I will not delve deeply into the creators and the creation of the New World Order as it is out of this context, but would like to throw a little light on the meaning of the New World Order. There is a worldwide plot being masterminded by an extremely powerful and influential group of genetically related individuals at least at the highest level, which include many of the world's wealthiest people, top political leaders, and corporate elite, whose goal is to create a one-world totalitarian government, stripped of nationalistic and regional boundaries, which is obedient to their agenda. Their intention is to impose and achieve complete and total control over every human being on the planet and to dramatically reduce the world's population to a figure desirable to them.

The common theme in conspiracy theories about a New World Order is that a secretive, powerful elite group with a globalist agenda is conspiring to eventually rule the world through an authoritarian world government—which replaces sovereign nation states—and an all-encompassing propaganda that ideologises its establishment as the culmination of history's progress. Significant occurrences in politics and finance are speculated to be orchestrated by an unduly influential cabal operating through many front organisations. Numerous historical and current events are seen as steps in an on-going plot to achieve world domination through secret political gatherings and decision-making processes. It is a one-world government and one-unit monetary system under permanent non-elected hereditary oligarchs, who self-select from amongst their numbers in the form of a feudal system as it was in the Middle Ages.

According to Prof. Johan Malan, University of the North, South Africa, Since 1989 when the former Soviet Union disintegrated into 15 independent republics, thereby greatly decreasing the threat of communist revolutions, the cold war between the capitalist West and the communist East made room for a common ideology—the new world order. This development not only brought the First and Second Worlds closer together, but the struggling Third World (particularly Africa) is rapidly uniting itself while asking for bigger aid packages from the international community and inclusion in a new world order.

World leaders have embraced the idea that the various nations should be united to such an extent that they grow into a world state, thereby superseding and eliminating the conflicts and differences of the past. The process of globalisation is gaining momentum while steadily moving away from the biblical principle of sovereign and self-sufficient nations towards a new world order in which a world government will eventually gain full control over all nations. That will set the stage for a world dictator to institute a global reign of terror.

It is not the first time in history that powerful global structures are created, thereby allowing a world dictator to control all nations, exploit them economically and subject them to domination by a false world religion. Various world governments in ancient times, of which the Babylonian, Greek and Roman empires were the best known, established structures of this nature. All these empires utterly oppressed the nations under their control and eventually all collapsed. That will also be the fate of the end-time empire of the Antichrist, which is already taking shape as the new world order.

The views of this professor is tenable to an extent but we must be sure that it is not the same New World Order creators that wrote the same Bible.

Conspiracy theorists believe that the New World Order will also be implemented through the use of human population control in order to more easily monitor and control the movement of individuals. The means range from stopping the growth of human societies through reproductive health and family planning programmes, which promote abstinence, contraception, and abortion, or intentionally reducing the bulk of the world population through genocides by mongering unnecessary wars, plagues by engineering emergent viruses and tainting vaccines, and environmental disasters by controlling the weather. As I stated from the beginning, the essense of this book is not to dig deep into the New World Order and who created the New world order rather to awaken Africans to an ugly reality that will hit them real hard as the New World order is gaining strength. We shall be dealing more with Mental Slavery which is the primary problem facing the black man in this time in human history. The black man needs to wake up and see clearly as it seems he is too long asleep and is turning to a consumer breed as he is been branded everywhere in the world.

Man in evolving the New World Order has created a system whereby only the fittest survives. A force will sweep away all those who are operating on weak emotions and low life energy to make way for the so-called 'better humans' who will be under the control of a few who are running the New World Order. Africans are not proving that they fit into the passing world; hence, they may not be deemed fit into the new world. That is why they are endangered.

The black man is making serious efforts and preparations to migrate to heaven when he dies, yet he does not want to die. He makes great use of inventions more than those who invented them, yet he turns away and condemns science and technology. Africans will be most affected when the New World Order is in full force. Many will die of diseases known and unknown, but the few that will remain will be used as guinea pigs for the survival of others. The African continent will become the continent of guinea pigs, having also been a slave continent all along. With the full evolution of the New World Order, the entire world will see no need for Africans as they are classified as a consumer race, incapable of achieving anything in life. They will be completely displaced from their land just like the natives of India and the aborigines of Australia in the past.

The economy of most African countries relies solely on natural resources, yet they fail to know that any economy functioning under such a parameter is not a true economy. Granted that the colonialists contributed immensely to the destruction of the entire evolution of the African continent and its people, but is it not time that Africans adopted the same strategy of the Chinese and Indians (copy/clone syndrome) and improved their lives? It is becoming evident that they are incapable of achieving self-identity and self-sustenance. If Africans cannot utilise the technological and scientific parameter on ground to build a life for themselves via copy/clone syndrome and if Africans cannot spiritually withdraw from the world now and begin to reshape their destiny, in time to come they will face out of this earth as they are already guinea pigs of the New World Order.

The only thing that is making the African continent and its children become the guinea pigs of the New World Order is mental slavery. African people are living close to nature and having nothing to call their own, except natural resources which of course the world out there needs to fuel their technology which Africans have invented none in this present time hence, they will be the worst hit by the effects of the New World Order. Civilised man has taken control of nature; Africans are making use of the tools of civilisation, yet they have decided to live under the control of nature, believing in pseudoscience or miracles. Africans have become part of nature which the civilized man is controlling and this is dangerous to the survival of the African generations that will perpetuate human life on the continent. Africans must rise up and take charge of their lives, embrace their heritage and redesign their future.

Africans are unable to either produce what they consume or consume what they produce. They suffer from chronic mental slavery incapable of thinking like fully functional human beings. They are almost being reduced to the level of animals. Africans import God, culture, education, food, and almost everything. They suffer serious identity crisis. They import God and religions. They import food and life styles. Africans are gradually by omission or commission or by the design of the New World Order creators, failing the humanity test.

Understanding
Mental Slavery

A slave is a person held in bondage, in thrall—a person in physical, moral, and (or) mental captivity. Mind is the human consciousness that originates in the brain and is manifested especially in thoughts, perception, emotion, will, memory, and imagination. Information is the food of the mind, and it is an ordered sequence of symbols, data, instruction, mental stimulus, perception, representation, meaning, pattern, communication, or knowledge that transmits a message. The human mind is the powerhouse of the body, and when the mind is arrested or functionally disabled with any form of information, then the person is incapacitated.

A mental slave is someone who suspends his intellectual faculties and subjugates himself to the will, beliefs, and attitudes of another person or group. Mental slavery is the inability to view events, or one's self, objectively. A mental slave will not apply his brain to evaluate what he is being told, to discover what is true and rational; mental slaves are in the habit of accepting and believing what is told to them, whether it makes sense or not. Often the mental slave does not even stop to ask himself whether what is being said makes sense or not; what is important is that my side said it.

If you want to comprehend the meaning of the subject 'mental slavery', think about the yearnings for freedom as experienced during the slave trade era. Also, think about physical incarceration or when you are locked up in jail and your physical freedom is denied of you. In these instances, physical tangible elements like keys, chains, locks, people, police, government, and jail are deployed. In the case of mental slavery, information is the tool deployed. Information is an invisible non-physical, non-tangible device, and information works on a human mind situated in the brain. When information is the tool of slavery, the mind is held bondage and therefore the person suffers mental slavery, hence a mental slave.

Mental slavery is a situation whereby a person's mind is either drifted to the wrong course, held still (motionless), or fed with poisonous (damaging) information. A mental slave is one who is mentally held captive with deceptive information or a person whose mind is held motionless. Back in those days, Africans were captured, some bought and taken on slave ships to strange lands, where through their hard labour, pain, blood, and sweat, great nations were built, but today another form of slavery, a more dangerous one unseen to the naked eyes, plagues the African continent and its people.

Generally, mental slavery is primarily a result of misinformation, weird superstitions, unhealthy and standstill traditional beliefs and cultural practices, faulty and weak education, misuse of religion and maladministration of religious doctrines by untrained individuals, reverse modern-day colonialism (neo-colonialism), and summarily, any form of mind diversion that is intended for deceitful purposes.

Anyone suffering from mental slavery or anyone who acts upon or holds firmly and conscientiously in his mind information that cannot be proven in any manner scientifically or logically, or information intended for deceitful purpose or mind arrest, is a mental slave. False religious teachings and abuse of religious tools have contributed a lot to mental slavery, especially in the African continent. The African continent has more churches than factories in these present times, yet the crime rate in the continent keeps rising and there is no development in the continent. Africans worship God more than any other continent of this earth, yet they suffer the most from poverty and diseases. Common sense has disappeared in the African continent and God has become a commodity or a commercial entity in Africa. It is time that Africans begin to wage war against mental slavery which is the primary problem and disease that plagues the continent.

Mental slavery is the king worm feasting especially on the African continent and the future of the children of Africa, both at home and the diaspora. Mental slavery has given birth to numerous other worms (problems) that are more evident in the continent. Mental slavery is a disease of the mind that must be treated today for people (mostly mental slaves), especially Africans, to see the light of the day so as to be able to develop like other human beings and also develop like other continents of the world and take active part in this present-day cycle of civilisation. This book will help you independently identify mental slavery and destroy the invincible chains in your life so that you can attend a state of mental freedom, ignite your creative potentials, take full control of your life, and become the lord of your life.

I am at war with mental slavery and not with any individual, sect, or any institution. Most people especially from Africa are under the scourge of chronic mind slavery (mental slavery), yet they do not notice it. The chains and locks of slavery have become invincible. They have been modified and repositioned from hands to minds.

The sooner Africans accept the fact that if there is any being or person called God, he is definitely for all religions and all of human race, the better will their lives be as they are not only divided into numerous tribes and ethnic groups but it seems as if God is also divided within their respective religions and nationalities. Africans must scrutinise the kind of education they are acquiring in schools to find out why they are not yielding the desired results; it is rather making them polished slaves who can neither invent nor create to fulfil their needs. They must learn to appoint for themselves visionary and creative leaders, not incompetent leaders and puppets who champion the cause of neo-colonialists and mind enslavement of their own people using religious tools and others.

When a man's mind is fed with the wrong kind of education, superstitious beliefs, or religion, then he also becomes a mental slave. The kind of education in the African continent lays more emphasis on theories, passing of exams, and acquisition of certificates without in-depth practical experiences and knowledge, which has resulted in a breed of university graduates in the fields of science and technology who are not able to develop physical models, having gone to schools only to be fed with theories and given shiny papers called certificates. Those who are not allowed to ask questions even when what they are told makes no sense to them or does not add real values to their lives are mental slaves. Africans suffer from chronic mental slavery (mind slavery), and this has given birth to numerous other problems suffered by the continent and its people. Mental slavery has paralysed human, industrial, and infrastructural development in the African continent. Mental slavery has created a wave of weak and ugly leadership in the continent, destroying African evolving cultural values

It may amaze you to know that in some African villages they still worship and fear trees, snakes, mountains, rivers, etc. There are lots of myths surrounding these things, enshrined in fear, and the people are psychologically compelled to fear and worship those things. This is chronic mental slavery. The invasion of the continent by colonialists was done alongside with religious tools introduced forcefully with guns and other ammunitions, and Africans were not fully sure if they were going to welcome such religions if the force and weapons used were not there in the first place. This is forced mental slavery. Africans have failed to identify mental slavery, but it is the primary problem facing the continent.

Lack of mental curiosity is also another form of mental slavery, but this time around, an individual enslaves his mind indirectly. Mental curiosity makes one to develop the tendency to ask questions all the time. It makes one to crave to know, to be curious. Remember that I have said that Africans have the same capability as other people in the world, but their inability to utilise these capabilities now makes the world out there think that we are less human or that we do not have the same capabilities. The reasons for colonialism, slavery, forced dominance, and more are enshrined in the web of beliefs that Africans cannot achieve anything since they may be genetically unequipped to achieve anything. I have disproved these conspiracy theories by making references to people like Phillip Emeagwalli, whose immense works contributed to the invention of the Internet. He was a student of advance computing, whereby they refused him access to quality computers for his research works. He gathered abandoned computers, whereby he performed a calculation that has turned the world around. We all share the same genetic codes and DNA with him. He was not a good mathematics student when he was studying in his hometown prior to his going to America for studies. You see, it was all about environment, encouragement, and opportunity to gain good education. What about Dr Ave Kludze, the NASA scientist, and other great scientists of African origin? What about Imhotep who designed and built the pyramid of Egypt and who was noted as the first scientist in human history? You see, European propagandists and conspiracy theorists will design a belief system based on 'artificial' facts that will aid them in achieving their goals of dominance and economic colonisation one way or the other—theories like making the African people look like animals incapable of achieving anything just to show justification for treating them like animals.

Back to mental curiosity, whenever I watch TV, what run in my mind is how people are moving around inside that box and the principles behind the transmission of motion picture information from a distance to me through that box. I ponder about that and many more technologies around. When I watch a millipede crawl, I ask how such an animal moves like a train. What about a bee with a big belly and tiny wings? I ask how this bee lifts itself up and how it produces wonderful honey. That is part of mental curiosity. We must learn to ask how, why, and what questions about everything, and we must seek answers; we must seek to know. We must learn to read, seek information, travel, interact, and question everything. That is mental curiosity. Even Christ did say, 'Seek and you shall find.' Africans seek miracles while the advanced nations seek inventions. Sometimes people wonder why Africans are not producing what they are consuming and why they are economic slaves. I attribute this to mental slavery. Africans want to believe that a prayer can make a house appear; they want to believe that HIV/AIDs can be healed through prayers. They live superstitious lives and believe in false doctrines that cannot be proven practically, yet they make greater use of the products of logic, science, and reality. They have transformed themselves into a consumer breed. They are economic slaves because they depend on others for products of science, technology, reality, and logic while clinging to quasi-miracle-filled religions and pseudoscience. Someone holds a microphone which is a product of science and technology and speaks to a congregation of Africans in a manner that he can remove blindness merely by closing his eyes and uttering some words. I asked one of them a question that got no answers but aggression: 'What about an amputee?' Of course, if you can heal blindness merely by praying, then you can also restore the missing part of an amputee's body. The congregation will not question such an individual and his confused doctrines because of fear and the involvement of God. But I always tell them that God is a practical and a logical universal God and not a God of illusions and strange magic. Most African leaders encourage the proliferation of false and weak religious doctrines in their respective countries simply because most of them are ideologically bankrupt and want to remain in power; hence, they deploy all available tools to hold the people mentally captive. Religions in Africa have become a political slave tool and a tool of business and money making. It has completely lost every iota of truth and spirituality.

The primary reason that the African continent suffers and wallows in abject poverty, diseases, and economic slavery is because most of us are not thinking or our minds are filled with the wrong thoughts. Africans do not want to accept the reality of a dynamic world driven by ideas, inventions, science, and technology. We want to cling to superstitions, religious dogmas, and old beliefs that add no values to our lives, yet we are the greatest consumers of the products of ideas, inventions, science, and technology. This is the reason that we are economic slaves, and it is caused by lack of mental curiosity. Sometimes I wonder how Africans can produce what they consume and in the process also consume what they produce when everyone in the continent seems to be scientifically, mentally passive. I am not saying that Africans do not think; of course they do, but what they think about most of the times are mundane things, even though they are fully capable of higher thoughts and higher arts. Most African politicians are in power to amass wealth and fame and nothing else. Evidence of their presence in office can be felt by their overseas wealth deposits mostly in Swiss accounts and the lack of development of any form in their countries. Africans seem to be thinking only of self-gratification all the time.

Sometimes I also ask how Africans can produce what they consume when most African nations are still under indirect colonial rule without full control of their lives, minds, natural resources, and their land assets. As I said earlier on, in the cause of finding solutions to mental slavery in Africa and economic paralysis that has enveloped the continent, Africans must take full responsibilities. They must also not welcome hypocrites who do not really want Africans to wake up mentally and economically. Europeans are not qualified to criticise Africans as they contributed to 70 per cent of our problems, having developed a pattern of belief that permitted them to frazzle the lives of Africans through domination, slavery, and colonisation. Today we are facing economic domination and another form of neo-colonisation. Look at South Africa, for instance; they are fighting for food in their own land, yet the next generation of the same people who seized the land and natural resources call South African natives all sorts of ugly names. Sorry to say that but Europeans have turned the world into a jungle due to racial discrimination; hence, they are not qualified to discuss African future and they are not worthy to criticise us as they are not really keen on helping but want to see us plunge further down. If we develop economically and technologically, Europe and Asia will lose their market; hence, only Africa can save Africa. It was the Europeans who introduced Christianity into the African continent, but all evidence on the table shows that they are not Christians by practical lives. So they are not practicing what they are preaching. Christianity was only a tool of mind control while they plundered the rich natural resources of the African continent.

The support of voodoo priests who engage in magical tricks and worthless rituals instead of paying attention to herbal medicine, church clergies and pastors who concoct false miracles to gain the attention of their unsuspecting audiences, the kind of theory-based education in the African continent which pays attention to certificate acquisition, the creation of deities in African villages to control the minds of the people, colonialism and the influx of colonial religion designed to enslave and slow down people's creative thinking disguised as a moral and salvation tool, fear and superstitions found in traditional and religious practices, any form of misinformation leading to mind arrest and mind diversion, wrong influence of audio and visual devices, and more are the causes of mental slavery. Mental slavery has to do with mind and information, and when information has been used to divert the mind to the wrong cause, it results in mental slavery.

We live superstitious lives; we do not want to face the reality of time, and it is strange that with all our institutions of higher learning, knowledge and intelligence are not improving to the level of putting Africa to the position it should be. The world is trying to prove a theory that some people are more human than the others, yet we do not notice this. They call us names like monkeys, apes, baboons, slaves, yet we do not want to do anything about these ugly stigmas by rising up to the challenges of the time. We import god(s), food, languages, clothing, culture, and education. We import everything. They say that civilisation began in Africa, and I demand to know whether there was any form of civilisation in East, South, and West Africa. Yes, there was in Timbuktu in the historic times when they had fantastic medical colleges, but what is wrong with most African minds in these present times that they cannot do anything for themselves and depend on others? Are we animals pretending to be humans? No, we are humans, but we suffer from one major disease—mental slavery, which has given birth to all other problems in the continent. Today we fight mental slavery, the most dangerous enemy of Africa.

Today, as Africans who crave true liberation and mental freedom, we must examine what we feed our minds with. We must table all our beliefs and question all of them. We must try to establish the truthfulness and usefulness of all our beliefs. We must also know that God is universal and not a product of one particular religion. This will make us true soldiers in this war against mental slavery.

I see a problem with the use of the words 'blacks' to denote children of Africa and 'whites' to denote Europeans. The meanings of those words according to the original creators have to be made crystal clear to the people because nobody's skin colour is white and nobody's skin colour is black; hence, we would like to know what the originators of those words 'black' and 'white' had at the base of their minds so that we can truly understand what answering a 'black' or a 'white' person truly means. The creators of the words 'whites' and 'blacks' as used to denote a particular group of people must reveal to us the technical meanings of those words. I believe that we should simply be addressed as Africans and not as 'blacks' because this word has been used to denote ugliness, darkness, and evil in many instances despite the fact that we say to ourselves that 'black is beautiful'. In as much as I see a problem with the use of those two words, I only have a major concern with the naming of Africans as 'blacks'. Europeans can call themselves 'whites' for all I care, but what right do they have to call Africans 'blacks' when there are a lot of ugly connotations to this word 'black'? It is just like giving a dog a bad name just to hang it. The calling of Africans as blacks enslaves our mind subconsciously and it reduces our worth since those who created the names and their progenies will forever look down upon us, knowing the true meanings of what they created.

In fulfilment of the prophecy of the late Bob Marley, that 'none but them shall free their own minds', I write this book to break the chains of mental slavery in our continent Africa. In doing so, I hope that African nations will see the light of the day and develop like other developed nations of the world. Children of Africa must free themselves from mental slavery as it is gradually transforming us into inferior human beings who cannot think out of the box, and the world is almost drawing sad conclusions about our humanity. In this book, I have demonstrated my anger extensively against all the ugliness which our colonial masters (slave masters) have shown to the African continent, which they visited in the past, but I must also state that Africans in these present times are also helping them to achieve all of their lingering intentions. Some of our leaders are now puppets of a new form of colonialism known as neo-colonial. They are granted excessive power and wealth while the colonialists plunder our rich natural resources and also enslave us economically.

I used to wonder that Africans thought that the God of someone who treats them as an enemy and an inferior human would ever answer their prayers if that God was truly in existence. I also wonder how a poor wretched voodoo priest can make a poor African rich through witchcraft and magical tricks. Africans were told to look up in the sky and pray to a god that dwells in the sky (heaven) and they agreed, but it has never occurred to them that the same people that gave them that advice are busy tilling the earth every day and plundering African rich natural resources found only on land and not in 'heaven'. Sometimes I wonder what we do with our thinking faculty. I have asked someone how he ever thinks that someone who does not find him fit in the only earth (world) he knows will willingly grant him easy and free access to a better world called 'heaven'. Africans are not learning any lessons from the scourge of HIV, mental slavery, and other diseases that will soon erase their presence from this planet. Africans must know today that the New World Order is designed to use and displace the weak. The weak will be cleaned out. Africans must begin to live in reality and shun superstitious beliefs and false religions. They must embrace creativity, science, and technology. They must know that God is universal for the entire human race and all religions. They must know that God is either for all or for none.

You hardly see an African read except at school or during examinations, but he will spend all his other spare times thinking about sex and alcohol. If you send him to school he will join gangs, and the women will abandon their studies and search for stray men to open their legs for. They will never make efforts to understand what they are taught in schools in depth; rather they read only to pass exams and become unproductive and unemployable afterwards.

Africans wear European made clothes when they can actually make African clothes and wear them and be proud of that and in the process economically empower those making the clothes. Africans eat European food when we have our own traditional healthy, non-synthetic, non-biotechnologically engineered food.

Africans complain that Europeans perceive them as inferior human beings, not knowing that they are themselves bestowing superiority to the Europeans and bestowing inferiority upon themselves. The females style their hair with chemicals to look like Europeans, which will never happen, and in the process, they confirm that the hair that grows out of the natural body is not the right one. Some Africans tone their skin with chemicals to look like Europeans, which will never happen. 'Coconuts' will try as much as they can to fake their accent to sound like Europeans. Is that not telling someone that you feel inferior to the way you were created naturally?

This is the time for a serious mind revolution in the African continent. This is also the time for a shift in human thinking in general as humans have lost the touch of humanity. We have misunderstood individualism to mean insensitivity and capitalism to mean greed and selfishness in the name of wealth acquisition.

Man pursues wealth with aggressive animal instincts and in the process creates a lot of problems for other humans, yet when we depart from this earth, we depart with nothing, not even a single hair on our bodies. Humans create diseases and create their cure; they make computer viruses and make anti-viruses. Maybe we also make biological viruses and make their anti-viruses. This is also the time for Africans to appoint for themselves qualified, creative, visionary leaders who understand leadership and not colonial puppets who enhance the spread of mental slavery in their respective countries just to achieve control. This is the time for Africans to know that the physiognomy (facial appearance) and skin colour of a man do not determine the weight of his intelligence, for one of the most intelligent men on earth today is an African—Prof. Phillip Emeagwalli, the Internet genius. The first scientist in human history was an African called Imhotep who designed and built the great pyramid of Egypt for Zoser, the best Egyptian pharaoh.

I do acknowledge the obvious fact that there are quite a good number of people in the world today, including a few good religious institutions and politicians, who are making reasonable efforts for the benefit of the African continent and humanity in general. For the sake of those few, I plead for clemency, having made a lot of general statements in this book which may be considered provocative.

Permit me also to say that it is time that we start questioning all the stories told to the Africans that are not helping them deal with the tribulations they face in their day-to-day lives—stories that are beginning to look like fabricated stories and tools of mental slavery; information and stories that have kept Africans in the dark and held Africans mentally captive while making the continent a continent of economic slaves; beliefs and stories indoctrinated into African minds that cannot cure malaria, HIV, and poverty no matter how long we hold on to them; beliefs that offer hopes only 'when we die'; religious banks that never give back in return to Africans no matter how long and how much we give to them both in monetary terms and time. Rather all we get is 'after death' hopes, captivating stories, and stage-managed miracles. There are political arrangements that perpetually keep the African continent in debt so as to make their sufferings linger and paralyse development in the continent. Strange institutions pay no attention to the sufferings of African children all over the globe; institutions fail to notice the cry of children of Africa in war-ravaged Sudan, crisis-ridden historic Zimbabwe, poverty-soaked 'oil-rich' Nigeria, poverty—and abuse-ridden 'rich' South Africa, AIDS-ridden 'rich' Botswana, troubled and war-torn 'mineral-rich' DRC, and other countries of Africa. Institutions pay no attention to poverty, diseases, and HIV-ravaged nations of Africa. Strange and pre-arranged miracles and brainwashing scheme-filled belief systems and institutions claim to have solutions to all our problems, yet we cannot find those solutions; rather we constantly build castles in the air.

Permit me to forgive the imported man-made imaginary God that seems to be battling with the universal God. I ask for clemency if it is a mistake that I have chosen to embark on this expedition again from the known to the unknown, and I shall also pardon all the strange institutions and strange religious and imaginary God(s) for allowing me to dwell so much on the unknown, abandoning the known in the only world that I know. I shall also pardon you for allowing theories that conflict one another to rule the lives of human beings on earth, most especially Africans and for allowing religious stories and scientific theories to conflict each other, yet men must believe both and not strive hard enough to find out which of them is the right theory. I pardon you for allowing the scientific theory of evolution and the religious stories of creation to conflict, yet they both rule the lives of humans on earth. I pardon you for the way and manner they said that God created man, created sin, created a choice-free world, forgetting that most men would make the choices that would make you angry. I pardon you for not leaving man with one absolute manual for living. I pardon you for allowing people with faulty minds, lunatics, and slaves of money to create evil to destroy your so-called greatest of all creations—'Man'. I pardon you for so many oversights, knowing that they say you are omnipotent and omniscient, hence cannot be held accountable for mistakes. Most importantly, I pardon you for not appearing to everyone simultaneously, hence erasing all the controversies surrounding your existence. I pardon you for not announcing one religion, hence erasing all the controversies in most religions that have divided mankind, creating hostility everywhere.

As a free thinker who functions without prejudice, I only have a problem with the administration of religious teachings by untrained minds and conmen. I have a problem with the creation of God in religions also as man should not and cannot create God because God is universal. I am against the splitting of churches into fragments as if God has varieties. I am against the transformation of religious institutions into banks; party grounds; and tools of violence, extortion, and mind diversion. I am against the 'God chose some people' syndrome and the 'God will strike or kill you if you ask questions' syndrome as it becomes disempowering when one cannot question religious concepts and religious beliefs that are not well understood. I am against the enshrining of religious teachings in strange myths that cannot be proven or questioned, hence creating a cloud of mental slaves.

I am against the selling of false dreams and false hopes and the selling of God and salvation to innocent people who crave spiritual food and the knowledge of the one true universal God. I am against the falsification of miracles in churches, yet those false pastors have refused to walk on water just like the Bible said Jesus Christ did so that we can be evidently sure that the miracles they perform on stages are real. These hungry souls and mercenaries of deceit and mental slavery have ended up making the works of Jesus Christ look unreal to most hard thinkers and critics. I believe that with the power of the one true Universal God wonders happen as scientific wonders are happening today as they said that sufficiently advanced technology is not to be distinguished from magic. When false prophets position a crippled man on a church stage before a large unsuspecting audience and make the cripple walk while there are dozens of cripples in front of the gates of those same churches asking for the same divine healing, then we begin to have a problem with the entire arrangement. Christians claim that Jesus Christ healed miraculously, and we are forced to believe this information even though we were not there to witness them happen due to the position in which Christianity placed Christ and the myth surrounding him, but it would be wise for the government and the entire Christian community to verify the authenticity of miracles happening in churches today before critics begin to think that the whole affair from the beginning was stage managed.

I reacted angrily when someone told me that the Bible is a fraud, but I managed to hear him out when the dispute calmed down. The Bible may have been twisted during the course of revising, and also in these present times, the Bible is now used by conmen to extort money from innocent people who crave spiritual food. They now hold the Bible in their hands, making use of the power of evil to deceive people. When you fake miracles on stage, you are using the power of evil (illusion) and not the power of the universal God. Pardon the god(s) that these people call their name(s) every day when they carry out all of these evil acts because I am not sure it is the true universal god of justice and god of logic.

As someone who is awake to the realities of our present-day existence, I believe that any practical and good religion is welcome in Africa if it could address the problems we face in our day-to-day lives and deal with the known as well as the unknown in the only world that we know and if religious institutions and religious warlords could stop acting as if there are many gods which are racist and intolerant towards one another and must fight to control and dominate the earth and humanity using them as mercenaries. Nobody should ever claim that his own religion is better than that of another as this is one of the major causes of religious crisis in some African nations. Africans must shun pseudoscience (superstitions) and miracle craving. They must live practical lives.

Fragmentation of churches in Africa must stop because our universal God is not confused; hence the governments of African countries should institute regulatory bodies to control the splitting of churches and also to stop the sale of God and dreams using prearranged miracles which I call religious illusions in most churches. I was born into a Christian family, my friends are Muslims, Buddhists, and of other religions, and my mother holds other beliefs. I believe that the true God is universal irrespective of one's religion and he (though we do not know the gender) is one and only one God; hence, I have no problems with diverse religions so long as their teachings emphasise upright living, service to humanity, and love for the supreme universal Godhead and not their own imaginary self-created God which they are now selling to their blindfolded members and enslaving their minds also.

As there are genuine religious institutions in Africa that are helping to improve the lives and moral standards of the people in our society today, I also ask for pardon for generalising my statements regarding the scourge of mental slavery (mind abuse), which is caused mainly by mind diversions originating from the abuse of religious tools by hypocrites. Today we must learn to ask questions about teachings which do not make absolute sense to us or teachings which we do not understand fully, and we must also ensure that the answers we get are credible answers with facts and not mere stories. We must also raise our children with curious minds so that they grow up strong to face the challenges of today and the future. I am not at war with any human being or any institution but with faulty concepts that have enslaved the minds of the people in this world, mostly Africans—concepts that are turning Africans nuts day after day and fear-based concepts that give us no liberty to ask questions. I am at war with the proliferation of false and expired doctrines in the African continent, generating a cloud of mental slaves.

Africans must begin to adopt exactly the same style of education prevalent in the developed nations, and we must also begin to copy science and technology in their true and original contexts to develop our continent, since they say that Europeans copied the same process from Africa during the ancient civilisation, improved upon it, and brought it back to enslave us with the same tool. Africans must today appreciate their heritage, embrace their roots, begin to produce what they consume, and also consume what they produce to be free from economic slavery and the invasion and importation of strange diseases into the continent. We must also know that if God be God as we conceive him in our minds, then he is definitely one universal God for all humanity.

The essence of this work is to make the reader fight mental slavery by developing mental curiosity, and in doing so, he or she will be able to independently understand himself, his immediate environment, the society at large, his country, and our continent Africa. The reader will also be able to join us in this on-going struggle to liberate our people from the scourge of mental slavery and economic slavery. The archive of African heroes as added in this book will help to remind Africans of the labours of their heroes which seem to have been forgotten. Every chapter of this book deals with empowerment, addressing of injustice that is happening in the lives of Africans by external and internal forces, abuse of the mind, and abuse of religion. Africans must know today that without producing what they consume and consuming what they produce, they will never be free from economic slavery. They will remain 'guinea pigs' and also endangered human species, and the continent will remain a slave continent.

Let it be known to Africans all over the globe today that the only choice we have in these present times is that we are left with no other choice than to do what we have to do, having claimed that we are equal humans in this world of humans. This is a vital mission at least if not for us but for the unborn and the generations to come who will again live to inherit the struggle of proving their humanity in the only world they shall know if we fail to do something now. For Africans who claim that they have lost a battle, let them rise again for there was no battle announced in the first place. For Africans who claim that the 'black man' has no hopes in life, let them rise again, for even a cripple is never a victim of a battle announced in due course. Fear is human nature just like every other emotion, but even fear of death does not avert soldiers from going to war. How long shall we fear? How long shall we live in fear? How long shall we make others fear just to justify our own fears? A coward dies many times before his real death. How long shall we live under the absolute control of other human beings like us in the only world we know or are we not human enough like them? This is the time of awakening. Arise, Africa, for this is the time!

Some people live their entire lives achieving nothing but doing exactly what lower animal species do every day. This category of human beings feed, search for food (strive to survive), excrete, mate, reproduce, and please their senses just like all other animals do. But these people do not think beyond all these things. They never think about what they can offer to the entire humanity and towards the improvement of the society at large. They continue in this manner until they pass away with no legacy. They care about no one else but themselves, their children, and their immediate family members. These are the ones that I call 'basal' beings, narrow-minded in nature and not quite different in thinking from a cow.

Do you know that the African continent has honest and visionary potential leaders who could redesign our future if encouraged and given the right opportunities? Do you know that if our present leaders could become more mature and creative and stop seeing politics as a moneymaking trade, we would collectively reap the dividends of democracy? Do you know that Africa has both human and natural resources enough to sustain our existence if properly harnessed, managed, and equitably utilised? Does it ever occur to you that our value system has collapsed in most African nations ushering in a new type of system, a disordered system? It is also a system, one which works directly against the people. It has no ingredients of a normal system and works in the opposite direction, a type of crazy system that has no respect for the dignity of mankind; it promotes crime and 'get rich quick syndrome', has no plans for the future, has no respect for justice, does not produce but encourages consumption, impoverishes its own people, and in all abuses fundamental human rights. It is a crime-filled lawless and disordered system with neither a vision nor a direction, favouring only a few narrow-minded hungry souls (sycophants, political prostitutes, and 'nepots'), who in turn perpetuate and prolong such a sick system. It is a system fuelled with illiteracy, ignorance, widespread corruption, political prostitution, mental slavery, sycophancy, nepotism, ethnic bias, elitism, idiocy, lunacy, witchcraft, false religion, pseudoscience, police corruption, mental slavery, lack of mental curiosity, narrow-mindedness, total moral collapse, lack of creativity, and lack of productivity.

This is a call for African nations to soberly reflect on the future of our children, the unborn, and the generations to come! It's also a call for African leaders to look in the mirror of today and see the pain, poverty, hunger and starvation, infrastructure collapse, lack of productivity, lack of development, and all the hopelessness in the minds of their subjects! Let them look into the mirror of today and see the youth who are the future. This is also a call for Africans to stop pointing accusing fingers only at their leaders or colonial masters when they are also vulnerable, but to learn to develop patriotic spirit and support visionary leaders! This is a call for African people to begin to utilise their common sense for it seems that common sense has gone into hiding in Africa!

This is an activism to force Africans to begin to produce what they consume, consume what they produce, and also to pay attention to agriculture and the economy at large or remain perpetually a 'guinea pig continent' and a 'slave continent'. This is an important call for Africans to invest in their youth and also begin to live practical lives; having accepted the products of science and technology, they cannot live lives of false religions and superstitions. Whatever problem the African continent is facing, it has solutions, and the solutions lie in the hands of the people of Africa. Let us stand up today and reshape the destiny and future of our continent and the future of our children and the generations to come. Let us begin this struggle by unleashing a peaceful mind revolution against mental slavery in Africa.

The entire world suffers today because man is turning science away from spirituality. Life should be both scientific and spiritual. Man definitely created religion and politics but spirituality and science seem to be natural, and man also may have discovered and shaped them in his search for the truth and the unknown. We live in times when humans create diseases and create their cure. We live in times when leaders whom we appoint to manage our affairs abandon the cause to pursue self-interest, most particularly ego and wealth. They forget that our concern should be for the good we do for the society and mankind when we are alive, for the good we do for ourselves dies with us but the good we do for the society and mankind lives forever for this earth is a shrine. No one departs here with anything, not even a single hair on his body. We live in times when family values and moral values have gone into extinction (collapsed) and humans have also become stereotyped, behaving like robots as if driven by chips in their brains and acting as if they do not possess feelings or remorse and conscience when dealing with others but will always expect others to exercise feelings, remorse, and a sense of right and wrong when dealing with them. This is the time for Africa to wake up.

The Liberation Chant

A cripple is never a victim of a battle announced in due course. Africans are faced with a war which they know nothing of in terms of its origin. Many of us own up that we have lost a battle, but it seems that majority of us are not able to see any battle going on. I have personally observed the invisible war going on and the weapons used in this war, and I want Africans to see this war and the weapons also.

Africans have failed in areas of self-governance. Africans have failed to command their economic freedom. African economy relies solely on natural resources, which is only a stepping stone to a self-made grave. What if there is no longer a use for fuel as the world is developing alternative sources of energy, as some cars made in Japan and other parts of the world today could be powered by electricity? Africans have failed to use their common sense. They have externalised God, yet not embraced the universal God. Some African leaders do not believe in their subjects; hence, they loot the resources of their countries and hide overseas. They send their children abroad; hence, they see no need for infrastructural developments. Most times when they invigorate crisis in their home countries, you will find out that only the poor dies as their own children are living in luxury abroad not partaking in the crisis. Mosquitoes do not bite their children, so they see no need for eradication of mosquitoes. Their children are not food-starved, so they see no need for food production, and poverty alleviation is of no concern to them. Their children study in the best schools almost, so they do not mind the dilapidated schools all around the countries. Africans are almost failing the humanity test. We import everything including God. Africans believe in superstitions and crave miracles from Pentecostal church pastors. Africans believe that you can turn one dollar into a million. In some countries of Africa, people still worship trees, snakes, mountains, and more. The problem that I have is that Africa has become a

---

41

dumping ground for the products of science and technology. They boast of purchasing the latest Blackberry phones in the market; they boast of the best cars, yet they have never given a thought about how Chinese people managed to copy European technology and creativity style. Africans will watch TV all the time but will never ask how someone can talk inside that box called TV, not to talk of asking how a TV is made. This chapter will elaborate on the reasons why Africans exhibit such attributes. Africans are fully functional, intelligent human beings on this planet, but one reason has kept them in the dark. That reason is mental slavery. Having understood what mental slavery means in the previous chapter, let us go ahead to show how it truly happens and how the people of Africa can escape mental slavery.

I remember a story I was told when I was a child regarding the existence of the paranormal, ghosts, spirits of the ancestors, demons, Satan, Lucifer, etc. It took a lot of reconditioning to relieve my mind of the reality of those perceptions, and in the conditioning period, I never saw any ghost, spirit, or demon. But you may be surprised today that some Africans even until the age of eighty years still cling to the belief that there are ghosts and spirits of the dead hovering around, and they instil their fear-based beliefs in young minds without giving any concrete and tangible proof to the existence of those things.

I was told that in the cemeteries dead people wake up at nights, and this story ruled my mind for decades that I even feared passing through cemeteries. But some day, I decided to sleep in the cemetery just to prove a point. I slept there for three days, but I saw or felt nothing. I went out and bought food and came back to the cemetery. I ate, slept, watched, marched on those graves, and even used one of the graves as my bed for three complete days and I did not even hear a whisper.

We have lived with the belief that there are places called 'hell' and 'heaven'. I do not dispute the existence of stars, planets, galaxies in the universe, and other celestial bodies, since they have been proven to exist scientifically, but those places which are assumed to exist where no one has been to and come back to give an account of and of which there are no scientific ways of proving their existence make me doubt; places that are accessible to only Africans when they die make me doubt.

We were told in the Bible that Saul visited a voodoo priest to invoke the spirit of Samuel; hence, I ask how Samuel's spirit appeared to an idol worshipper in the first place when Samuel was the prophet of the living God when he was alive. We were told that during the days of the Noah's ark, the entire earth was flooded; hence, I ask how someone could have seen an entirely flooded spherical earth because if you are in Iraq you cannot possibly see what is happening in Chicago considering the shape of the earth. What about the dinosaurs that lived millions of years back? If you calculate their time of existence and the time they said Creation was done in the Bible, you can see that someone is not telling us the truth. My mother who is a self-acclaimed prophetess of some kind of spirits used to hide her money in a shrine that she held in our house; she created a lot of myth around the shrine until one day I went in there and took some money, but nothing happened. You see, mental slavery is a dangerous thing, and it is even more dangerous than physical slavery. The former you do not see, but the latter you can see.

We have to find a means of attesting the existence of whatever we are told in this present time. As I have stated in the beginning, we have chosen to give a name to the Infinite Intelligence or Universal Creator as God because, since we as human beings create every day and all that is not of nature has been created by man, it implies that man could not just have surfaced from nowhere; it implies also that every other thing that is natural could not just have surfaced from nowhere. There must be a form of force or power infinite in wisdom, intelligence, and energy which has made all things, and that we have chosen to call God not because he told us his name or gender, and of course, this being will have no gender since it is not of a human form.

Born into a Christian environment, I was told from childhood to pray whenever I had a problem for solutions to those problems, and I always did. They told me that prayers could move mountains without explaining the kind of mountains prayers could move. On one occasion, I went to a preacher who claimed he could heal the deaf, dumb, blind, and all kinds of diseases. In fact, this man claimed that he could heal everything in the name of God if one had faith; then I went to his place of worship which I would prefer to call a bank. I went there because I had a broken tooth, and I managed to show him the broken tooth and asked him to help me restore the tooth to its normal shape. This clown stretched his filthy hands, placed them on my forehead, and started to shout and pray for me, but after the whole drama, I left without my broken tooth still not having been restored. I asked the fake priest what I should do, and he told me that I should go home and starve (fast) for seven days from 6 a.m. up until 6 p.m. This I did, and after seven days, the tooth was not restored. I went back to his shrine and lied to him that the tooth was restored, and I saw surprise on his face (as I am sure he knew that it was impossible to restore a broken tooth with prayers). I later explained to him about how I felt about everything he was doing and threatened to expose him if he did not return my money because you normally pay those people for the dream and 'God' they sell to you. Africa must rise against all these outrageous acts and the institutions that enslave the minds of the people with dreams and illusions.

Deceptive information from televisions, Internet, and other visual and audio devices may cause false images to be planted in our minds, and this may lead to mental slavery. Another example is our habits. We have to learn to acquire positive habits, and if we must copy, let us copy the ones that will build us positively and not the destructive ones.

A dog which does not eat faecal remains must not be allowed to follow one that does, as the one that does not would soon begin to eat the same, for birds of the same feathers flock together. Today, as Africans who crave true liberation, we must be strong to resist habits that damage our minds and personalities. Also, we must be careful of the company we keep or else we may end up adopting energies that we would live to regret in the course of our lives. We must be careful of the kind of information that we allow to dwell in our minds as they result in mental slavery if they is unhealthy information.

It baffles me that in some African countries proper education is not taken seriously, and I wonder how there could be growth and development when people are illiterate. Illiteracy is another worm that is eating deep into the African societies. By proper education you will understand your environment; you will enrich and improve your creative mind, and you will be able to empower yourself as true empowerment exists in the mind. You will be able to think critically and sceptically. You will be broadminded. It also baffles me that some African leaders are not educated, hence do not value education, and I wonder how such leaders will promote education. I implore African leaders to make education free at all levels so that people will not find excuses in acquiring one. I implore the African leaders to use part of the huge money from their natural resources to educate its people at all levels since the people have no ways of directly benefiting from these natural resources.

I implore the African governments to ban the sale of alcohol to underage groups in the society; rather they should make education affordable, if not completely free but at least cheaper than alcohol; completely abolish the use of guns by ordinary people apart from the law enforcement agents; and ensure that the police, doctors, and teachers are well taken care of as they deal directly with people. Proper education could assist someone gain employment so as to build a better life. It could equally make one creative and empowered in the mind to be self-sustaining; hence, one could be able to create jobs instead of working for others all the time or remaining unemployed after going to school. I implore all African leaders to make proper and quality education a priority at all levels. They should also examine our academic institutions and find out why they are not yielding the desired results. We should find out whether African students are actually learning what those in the advanced nations are learning at the same academic levels, and if it is the case, then what exactly is going wrong with us, and if it is not the case, then what should be done to introduce the right kind of education. African leaders should pay more attention to serious matters and stop acting as if power is food, abandoning vital issues.

Low quality of education is a huge problem in Africa. If you visit most African countries, you will be amazed at the state of their schools. In my own opinion, I think that the wages of teachers, doctors, and policemen are unimaginably meagre in Africa, and in some instances and in some countries, they are have not been paid for months. These groups of people are directly important in our day-to-day lives as they deal with people directly and their activities are highly sensitive and in direct need of the people. The police deal with crime and our safety, doctors deal with our life and health, and teachers deal with information and our mind. A poor and miserable policeman would be prone to corruption, conspiracy with criminals, and bribery; a poor and miserable teacher would not teach efficiently in classes. Sometimes he would abandon classes and sometimes collect bribes from students to excel them in their courses. In most cases, he would concentrate on the sale of handouts and manuals to students just to make money, and you would be likely to fail his courses if you do not purchase those materials. A poor and miserable doctor would abandon a surgical blade in someone's tummy due to frustration and lack of concentration.

Back to the issue of low quality of education in most African schools; serious emphasis is placed only on students passing exams, and I wonder if that is the primary reason for one going to school. These institutions provide the kind of education which emphasises mainly exams rather than empowerment and development of creative abilities, and at the end of the day, there is no positive improvement in the graduates' lives who have gone to school only to acquire a piece of paper in the name of a certificate. Some clowns even go ahead to buy those certificates, and others pay their ways through corrupt teachers and lecturers to acquire them. Some get them through exam malpractices. Students should be empowered in the mind so that they do not come out as half-backed graduates. They should be able to create jobs for themselves when they graduate, and the government should be able to support them.

As Africans who crave true liberation, we must revamp and improve our academic institutions. Also we must ensure that our leaders are properly educated so that they can transmit same culture on to the people. Adult education is another aspect which should be introduced into the African society so that those who were not fortunate enough to acquire education in their youth days could also benefit from the programmes at their later age.

Skill acquisition even while in school should be a vital integral tool of an African student's life to enable African graduates build sufficient capacity and also be able to create employment for themselves and others when they come out of schools since there are limited job opportunities.

Our belief system is another major worm causing mental slavery and backwardness in our continent. I wonder why we choose to believe untrue concepts, doctrines, and information. I wonder why we do not take time to establish the existence and truthfulness of what we believe. We choose to live in a world of illusions. Most African tribes are under the crunch of God(s) and gods which do not exist. As Africans who crave true liberation, we must question all our beliefs. I had once seen a 'ghost' when I was young, but after thorough analysis, I discovered that what I saw was a figment of my own imagination. I believed so strongly that I would see a dead friend of mine that when I came across his burial place I looked back and saw 'his ghost'. I did not attend his burial ceremony, but I was told the kind of clothes he was wearing when he was buried. As I passed his burial place, out of deep emotion energised by fear, my mind gathered together all the information I was provided coupled with the visual image of my late friend and formed an image of him. I looked back and saw my dead friend's 'ghost'. I must tell all Africans that this enigma was all in my mind, and it is one of the attributes of the human mind, which is the formative power of the human mind and the limitless power of the mind to subjectively create and form anything.

It is only the eyes of childhood that fears a painted devil; ghosts do not exist, and I am not sure that there are tangible spirits of our ancestors anywhere or whether there are tangible 'gods' somewhere. I am not sure either if there is a demon anywhere; rather your mind could create one for you. The African problem is in the mind just as all of these pseudo beings mentioned exist in the African mind. I am not saying these without expecting anyone to prove me wrong; hence, if any African has seen spirits, ghosts, demons, etc., let him invite me to see one. There is God, and I believe in God. I believe in the universal God and not any imaginary man-made God. Though man gave a name to the supreme force, energy, or power that made the universe and all that is in it, we must acknowledge that the word 'God' was created by man to depict this infinite being. The shape, colour, gender, or nature of this infinite being cannot be established by man as no man has seen, touched, or heard directly from him. We feel the energy of this being, and by rational thinking, we know that man cannot just appear in the universe without a grand designer or grand creator. There is God, but his name is not God as man cannot name his creator. A cell phone cannot name his maker neither can a computer name his maker. God is God and God is definitely one and only one God, and man cannot rationalise him, though by rational thinking we know that such a being does exist. Do not ask me who created God.

I would like to thank Michael Faraday who invented electricity, Isaac Newton who put together the laws of motion, Albert Einstein for his laws of relativity and efforts in nuclear physics, and Bill Gates for his great works in software. I would not like to fail also to thank the late Martin Luther King, the late Malcolm X, and the late Marcus Garvey for their strengths and courage; I would not like to fail to thank Prof. Phillip Emeagwalli who has made Africans proud in the field of Internet. I thank also Chike Obi, the great mathematician, and Chinua Achebe and Wole Soyinka who together have ended up proving that Africans are equally great in the art of writing. I give thanks to the great Nelson Mandela for his strength and courage in fighting a liberation struggle which gave birth to the new South Africa. Can we not learn from these people for God's sake and stop living in a world of illusions and fantasies?

The business of God with the unknown is known to no man, so do not be deceived. Our beliefs in the existence of 'spirits' and 'gods' in Africa cannot be proven at all, so let us concentrate on that which we can prove. I have tried to search for spirits. I have been to several nations of Africa looking for 'spirits', but all I saw was illusions and all I heard was stories and myths. In my search for the existence of the paranormal, I ran into a man who claimed to be a psychic. He told me that I could see mermaid spirits in the Indian Ocean. I did not hesitate to fly him to Durban, South Africa. When we arrived at Durban, we lodged at Protea hotel, and by twelve midnight, he woke me up so that we could go and see mermaids. He thought that I would be afraid of following him, not knowing that life to me was less important than proving that which had tormented my mind from childhood. I wanted to know if there were mermaid spirits anywhere since my mother claimed having one in the house she worshipped. We went to the Indian Ocean. Firstly, he told me that on arrival he would make some incantations and we would find ourselves in the home of the mermaids. I followed him, and when we got to the ocean, he brought out the horn of a goat and pointed it to the top of the sea. To my greatest surprise, nothing happened and we did not disappear. He tried several times, and afterwards, he told me that the mermaids did not like me because I had a lot of doubts in my mind. I said, 'OK, what do we do?' He said that we had to go back to Johannesburg to my house and that he would make another incantation in my shadow, then the mermaids would appear. I had doubts. Then I had to put this clown into a bus while I flew back to Johannesburg. This clown forgot that if I could fearlessly allow myself to disappear with him into the world of the mermaids, it meant I was serious with my quest. Finally, I allowed him into my house after a long time of thinking. He spent three days in my house eating my food and drinking a lot of beer with two girls that he came with to perfect his illusions. Those girls were around merely to distract me and perfect his scam. Finally, I did not see any mermaid after all that this guy did. He made me drink a lot of concoctions so that I had to stop drinking before I got killed with a poison, since he realised that I had busted his tricks. Out of pity, I allowed him to go, but after a week, my house was robbed and all my things stolen.

As Africans who seek true liberation, I ask that you stop stealing from one another and stop playing illusions in the minds of one another. Stop selling dreams to one another. Learn to respect one another and also learn to render selfless services to the society and mankind in general as it is a progressive way forward. False prophets and fake preachers must also stop deceiving Africans and selling dreams and God(s) to them.

I did not stop there. I went to Molanje, a remote valley between Mozambique and Malawi, in search of the paranormal again. I made sure that I visited all the voodoo priests in that strange village. I cannot recall all that happened there, but on one occasion, I asked the voodoo priest what my name was, because I chose to go to a different voodoo priest who was not known to the 'agent' who was taking me around (the agent is a syndicate usually known to the voodoo priest, and if you examine properly, the person who tells you about the voodoo priest is linked to this 'agent' if you are not approached directly by this agent). Be careful because the person spreading the rumours and advertising the voodoo priest and the agent together with the voodoo priest are running a properly networked scam business, and they share their loot at the end of the day. Whatever you tell the other two goes to the voodoo priest's ear, and that is what he repeats when you come to him no matter the fear-based illusions you see in his shrine. Africans must be warned also that fake pastors and false religious institutions are doing worse than these voodoo priests in the name of 'God'. On getting there, I insisted that the fake priest tell me my name. He got upset, and I immediately demanded that we leave the place. I have to confess that I went to more than twenty voodoo priests, and at a point, I found out that they do the same thing. They have the same formula and act the same way, but sometimes some of them have more serious illusions that if you have not been to the others you may fall for them. But be careful. Some even have registers, invoices, and receipts.

The most amazing one was when I went to a voodoo priest in Molanje, where I saw seven dwarfs running around in a circle. They put me into a pot, poured water in, put vegetables and all sorts of things, and started boiling the pot. When the pot started getting hot, I demanded to come out because I did not know their intentions. For all I cared, they could be cannibals, but on the other hand, the agent asked me to remain there so I trusted him though with caution and mixed feelings. After a short while, they asked me to come out; I did, and they gave me something to drink, and I recognised that most people who drank that concoction were all lying asleep under the heavy Mozambique heat. I demanded to know what the content of that liquid was, and the voodoo priest got angry. At a point, I remembered a story my mother used to tell me—that they would mix all kinds of hallucinatory drugs and place you in front of a mirror with a candlelight or keep you under the hot sun so that with the heat of the sun you would certainly hallucinate. I refused to drink the mixture and demanded to leave, and when I wanted to go, they asked me to pay. In fact the 'secretary' to the voodoo priest brought out a register and an invoice. I laughed. I ended up paying in order not to incur their wrath.

I came back to South Africa, and someone took me again to Pretoria to see another one who according to the agent was Godsend. I got to his place, and there he had a shop. I walked out immediately because this guy was so rude and arrogant, not even caring to perform illusions or speak to us, but you could see spiritual belts and their prices; you would also see King Solomon's oil with their price tags on them. I saw such a lot of weird items that I just decided to walk out because I did not need a prophet to tell me that this guy was a thick conman.

Finally another one came who said he was from Malawi. In fact, this one came to my house, and on noticing that he was hungry and desperate, I first ordered a McDonald's burger meal and he cleaned out everything in no time. I bought beer, and he drank without mercy. I went further and brought a bottle of brandy, and this clown drank it all. I intentionally put on a cartoon movie, and he started laughing like a fool. Then I called a taxi and asked the taxi to drop him off at the bus station.

I travelled to Nigeria, where I went to see a man in my state, who they said was a living spirit. This crook man forced his right hand into the chest of a living chicken and forced the heart out and started making incantations. But before he had finished, I had already started my car and driven off. I stopped searching for the paranormals because I was convinced that whatever existed in the physical realm is physical, scientific, and logical. Most of these so-called mediums operate with fear and illusions. There come the fake churches.

A fake church is one that is run with the sole intention of making money using excessive entertainment and prearranged miracles as major tools. If you walk into that kind of a church, you will find out that their pastors excessively pay attention to money and tithe paying, abandoning spiritual motivation. Their pastors are so low in character and will easily get close to any rich guy in the church. The churches look like party grounds. Their pastors are not intelligent enough; hence, they cannot stand a good public speech without unnecessarily referencing to the Bible and making references that people already know. They repeat themselves all the time; they are always performing prearranged miracles. They are always prophesying to the people; they make a lot of noise because they have less information to give out; hence, they get physical. Sometimes they beat up people; they preach exactly what suits the ears of the audience. They behave like prostitutes and can mortgage their pride whenever they need money; they beg all the time and you can always see those hungry and craving traits on their faces. They are conmen. A good church is the one that applies strictly the principles of Christianity according to the teachings of Jesus Christ. When you see their pastors, you will know by their behaviour and seriousness. They are very few but you'll find them if you are a Christian. Hence, you should run from slave churches that are only after your money, which I call religious banks.

Fake preachers found in some churches are not different from voodoo priests. They claim to know God, but I confess to the whole world today that most fake churches are banks. Illiterate, ill-informed, broke young men set up their own fake churches and send out their female agents to go hunting for people who only come to the churches to donate money to 'God', and after six months, the pastor buys houses and cars and marries the most beautiful female members of the church.

For those women who are unable to conceive children, please go to the doctor for proper advice as you may end up in bed with some of these fake pastors. One of my pastors preached so much against association with 'sinners'; he used to tell us that going to clubs was a sin, but one day I saw him with a prostitute in a morally unhealthy condition. I had to sneak out because some of them are dangerous and may pose a threat to your life if they find out that you saw them for fear of exposure. Please take note that there are very good and honest churches out there, but learn to look before you leap because the false ones advertise themselves and their pastors are chronic materialists. Also when you visit churches, do pay attention to inspirational teachings and practical motivations and not miracles.

As Africans who crave true liberation we must learn to live in reality. We must also be strong and bold enough to question whatever we are told, including religious doctrines which we do not understand fully. My friend, Akpan, went to a church in Canada, and on getting there, he found only Caribbean people being led to 'heaven' and 'hell' by a Caribbean pastor. There was no single European in that church. He sat on the back seat and watched the pastor (mercenary of mental slavery) preach. Akpan watched the excitement on the faces of the innocent 'God seekers'. Finally the pastor asked if anyone had any questions. Normally one of the pastor's syndicates would ask the pastor simple questions that would not embarrass him. One of them did, and they clapped. Akpan was not satisfied; hence, he asked the pastor the following questions: 'Who is God and where does he live? When did God create Adam and Eve? Who created sin and why? Who created Satan and the serpent? If Adam and Eve gave birth to Cain and Abel and Cain killed Abel and ran away, where did he run to and whom did he get married to in that place since life began from the garden of Eden? If God created everything and knew that man would fall by sin then why blame man when he created sin also or did God not create sin and man? Is God not omnipotent, omniscient, alpha, and omega? Are there any other reasons why God created sin and man that humans are not made to know? Why should we switch from the Old Testament to the New Testament? Did God change? Why is it that there are so many killings in the religious books by God's advocates when the religious books say "thou shall not kill"? Is Solomon in heaven or in hell, as they said that he married 300 wives and 700 concubines and Christ came and said one man, one wife? Where is Sodom and Gomorrah? Where is the Garden of Eden?' The pastor asked Akpan to say the closing prayer as those questions would be answered in the next Sunday session.

In some of the strange churches today, you find women who cannot even keep their homes; those churches have become party places, places to show off and attract the opposite sex and even indulge in adultery. False religious bodies are not helping matters in the African continent as they are blindfolding people, building a population of mental slaves.

This civilised system is self-running and impersonal. It does not care about individual feelings; it does not care whether your belief system has turned you into a dummy. In fact, it even helps you to be displaced, for the system has no provision for dummies. The system wants to take absolute control of everyone, so anything that helps the system achieve this is welcome to the system, which accounts for why politicians do not want to do anything about the proliferation of false religious doctrines which are turning people nuts every day. The system has destroyed marital love and divided a man and his wife so that the only thing that exists between them is sex, a piece of paper called a marriage certificate, and money. Religion is perfectly healthy if well administered and not used as a tool of fraud; hence, I do not want anyone to misunderstand me in this struggle. I am only worried that religious tools are now moneymaking tools. Our fellow brothers have now turned into mercenaries of mental slavery, finishing off from where their European slave masters stopped. Good Islamic doctrines and Christian doctrines are welcome in Africa, and these two major religions must play developmental roles in the lives of the people and not a disempowering one mentally. They must also begin to worry about the material needs of the people, considering the harsh economic realities of the day. They have to go further to design empowering models for their members and also teach them to pay attention to agriculture. The two religions must also learn to coexist.

Africans have suffered untold difficulties due to multiple versions of slavery, and we are pleading on our knees to the world to stop now, for we know all their tricks. Why would the world not study what is wrong with our brains when they have succeeded in turning us nuts; when they are the ones who introduced fear-based and twisted religious doctrines with guns causing chronic mental slavery; when they are using their technological advancements to intimidate and oppress Africans physically, economically, and mentally; when they are plundering our resources every day, asking us not to worry as our treasures exist in heaven; when they are confusing our leaders every day and turning their minds against us; when they keep on waving their economic wands in our faces with threats of withdrawing them if we do not dance to their demands? What is the relationship between a gun and a Bible that our colonial masters had to invade our lives with guns and at the same time brainwashed us with religious stories? How could some people succeed in their 419 tricks if they are not aware of the workings of the human mind? Some teachings in the religious books are healthy, but most of the stories in them are used only for illustration purposes, and Africans must understand this today since they were not there in person as live witnesses. They have to absorb the good messages in religious books and not pay so much attention to stories and miracles.

I shall also emphasise that our ancestors played a major role in the slave trade era as I see no reasons why a man with genuine love in his heart would sell his own child to a total stranger, if he believed that he was human and also that his child was human like him. What if his child was going to be eaten alive in foreign lands by wild animals as food or used for scientific experiments? My problem with African-Americans is that they do not want to define their direction in life, and I tell them that they are not the slaves, but their ancestors were the ones who were enslaved and also that the Irish people were also enslaved. They are only products of the scheme, but I still understand their anger against native Africans, considering the fact that most of our ancestors were thinking with their noses when they sold their African brothers to European slave masters. What happened during the slave trade era was complete nonsense, and I must reprimand our ancestors wherever they are, if not in the grave, for their idiocy and coldness. Europeans on the other hand must tell us whether the story of the pharaohs enslaving the Israelites was used to perpetuate slavery. They have to start embarking on reparation also and the earlier the better, or else we will conclude that their concept of humanity and their laws are either racially tuned or mere deceptive sentiments. Today, as Africans who crave true liberation, we must join hands to ask the world to stop all forms of slavery as the chains of slavery have been repositioned from our hands to our minds, and these days our fellow Africans, traitors, and Judas amongst us are used as mercenaries.

Colonialism did a lot of good as much as it yielded a lot of negative results—the plundering of African resources, the blindfolding and brainwashing of African people, and many more. This is the time for Africans to identify with the positive attributes of colonialism and also bear in mind that Indians and many others were also colonised and today they are doing greatly. The development, civilisation, and education which colonial masters brought to Africa should be our major concern now and not the wrongs the colonial masters did to us. Faulty Western cultures and lifestyles are also contributing to diverting our minds from reality. Being developed and civilised does not mean that one should throw away his good culture and traditions; after all, the Chinese and Japanese are developed and civilised, yet they retained their good cultures and traditions. We have by our own hands bestowed inferiority on to ourselves by completely denouncing our values. We do not even eat our natural and healthy African food any more. Our good traditions and cultures must be preserved and the ones that impair our growth and development scrapped off.

Crime is negative application of creative energy, and I also consider it a waste of time. I tell the African brothers to examine their actions, and they would discover that the same amount of energy which they apply in perpetrating crime could be applied to achieve positive and productive goals in life. Crime is abuse of energy, intelligence, and time. I went to a dance club and had a deep conversation with a prostitute. I asked her why she was in the act of selling her body, and she said that she had children and family members to look after. She told me that if I could give her the funds she needed to rebuild her life, then she would quit. I was silent for a moment, but I later on told her that nothing could justify exposing her body to all sorts of men when she had children that would grow up to bear the shame and the pain of losing their mother to strange diseases like HIV, herpes, and other STDs.

Today, as Africans who seek true liberation, we must make use of our creative minds and seek alternatives to crime, for it is a waste of time and creative energy. It is a diversion from reality. Africa is a home to corrupt politicians, corrupt law enforcement agencies, and corrupt citizens such that sometimes I ask who would police the police. A corrupt leader cannot properly deal with corruption matters in his country because darkness cannot prevail over darkness but light can.

When will visionary leaders come on board African politics? My fear is that most of our money are in Swiss banks instead of being used to develop Africa—instead of being used to invest in research and quality education, poverty alleviation, and finding lasting solutions to HIV and malaria. Sometimes I ask how come the Chinese, the Japanese, and the Indians who travelled overseas returned to their lands to contribute to their nation's growth and development, while Africans returned with flashy cars and 'white' women if they ever came back. I remember a story about a dog and a tortoise that were sent to go and retrieve a message from the queen. The dog started with haste and great speed, but on the way, he was distracted by bones littered on the way to the queen's palace. The dog started eating the bones while the tortoise (though slow) steadily arrived and retrieved the message from the queen. The dog finished eating the bones and hastily rushed to the queen only to realise that the slow tortoise had already retrieved the message and gone. Africans are easily distracted by the bones littered on the streets. Eavesdrop on African youth conversation and all you will hear about are clubs, girlfriends, boyfriends, sex, alcohol, parties, etc. They dwell on mundane and shallow matters, never giving thoughts to serious issues in life. A word is enough for the wise. This is a wake-up time for Africa. Africans must realise today that mind poverty is even more dangerous than material poverty though both are not welcome. We must enrich our minds through education, skills, and experiences, for they say, seek knowledge for knowledge is power and all other things shall be added unto you. We must invest in capacity building and also invest in our youth. We must have research institutes, and African nations must pull resources together to develop a techno-research institution that can start copying and cloning technology via reverse engineering and others. Sometimes I wonder what our professors and universities are doing. We have to learn to think creatively, innovatively. We must learn to support the creative works of one another. We should utilise the available science and technology of today to improve our lives, hence attracting growth, development, and full civilisation to Africa.

There is a lot we must learn from the Europeans—team spirit, collective efforts, collective love for one another, and the ability to render selfless services. These are positive virtues which would help build Africa. Some politicians in Africa do not want to quit the seat of power so as to not expose their atrocities since the next opposition if genuine would likely question them. Team consciousness, discipline, persistence, perseverance, hard work, determination to succeed, attitude of never giving up, creative thinking and constructive creativity, quality education, selfless services to humanity, genuine love for one another, love for our continent Africa, courage, fearlessness, and purposeful living, all would contribute a great deal in the growth, development, and full civilisation of our continent.

Another problem we are having in Africa is our entertainment industry. It amazes me that in some African countries the kind of music people listen to can totally enslave the mind of a person. We idolise immorality and mundane things in music. Our entertainment industry is filled with artists who express their energy through rape, drugs, violence, and a lot of stupid and childish things. They say that a man whose house is on fire should not chase rats. These days we do not only chase rats, but we abandon the fire burning the house and look for cockroaches. Education, religion, and music if wrongly administered could lead to mental slavery. The youths of Africa do not behave as if they are the future of Africa, and I wonder why we hate the future so much that we do nothing about it at least to improve upon it for the generations to come. We hate the future so much that we do not even build our own future, not knowing that if we build our future, we would build the future of the nation and build the future of our great continent Africa. This is a wake-up time.

Lack of self-confidence and inferiority complex is also ravaging us deeply. Do not use the European concept of appearance to judge yourself, for they are from Europe and created or evolved the way they are and we are from Africa hence created or evolved the way we are. And there is no factual proof that intelligence did not evolve in humans found in Africa. So love yourself the way you are for you are perfect, handsome, and beautiful and learn to destroy low self-esteem, inferiority complex, and lack of self-confidence.

Malaria, tuberculosis, HIV, and AIDS are not helping matters. I do believe today that the sale of malaria drugs and HIV drugs seems to be more important than the lives of the people, and also the trauma of African people suffering these diseases seems not to be the concern of the world. It is time that Africans stood up for themselves. When diseases come, they kill us because we have no control over them. The solutions come from overseas; hence, we depend on others for everything. We depend on others for God, food, cultures, healthcare, religion, lifestyle, etc. This goes to apparently prove that we are low in nature. We are not low, but we have allowed ourselves to sink to that low level by abandoning our heritage; by not embracing our roots, not being creative, not embracing science and technology even though we make use of its products; by clinging to pseudoscience and false religions; and by building castles in the air and more.

We must not blame Europeans for all our problems though. In some parts of Africa, tribes are marginalised; some tribes feel that they are the only ones chosen by God to rule their nations. Most African politicians allow tribal matters to meddle in the affairs of politics. In some African countries, some tribes feel that they are the ones chosen by God to control the natural resources of their nations. Some tribes will always ensure that the other tribes are not in harmony with one another just to achieve control. Some tribes are always willing and ready to unleash genocide on other tribes simply because they are either greater in number or are in power. Some tribes think that they are better off than the others.

Anyone who ridicules you because you do not speak English like an Englishman and if that person is an African, tell him that you are an African and also ask him to speak his native African language, and if that person is a European, kindly ask him to speak any of the African languages. As a token of spiritual unity, I would suggest that Africans choose any African language and make a general language which all Africans could learn and speak in common while still retaining their colonial (slave) languages. This language should also be taught in all schools in Africa as language unites people.

Recent xenophobic hostility in South Africa created a huge problem, which in my humble opinion should be addressed as it seems to be erupting from time to time. They need to heal the wounds and the earlier the better. Africa is not happy with the evil that erupted on 20 May 2008, the desecration of our continent Africa, the burning of an African.

In my latest conversation with a South African friend whom I respected based on his corporate profile, his views on the xenophobic attacks were that he felt no guilt for what had happened, and I almost believed him. South Africans must realise that we live in a changing world and if the doors of other African nations are shut against them, they would be weak and vulnerable in the midst of their 'white brothers' in this prejudiced, changing, and unpredictable world where racism seems to be a perennial worm, unless they did not learn from apartheid. A word is enough for the wise. They must broaden their scope of thinking and know that when a man's corpse (dead body), starts to rot and smell, friends, strangers, and allies will run away but your brother will never run away. Your brother is never a stranger in your house.

A South African TV presenter told me that I was in his space when I needed him to grant me an interview on his programme even though the project would enhance the masses of South Africa; another told me that I am 'kwere kwere'. He meant that I was a foreigner. I could not imagine that a TV producer, a fellow African brother, openly called me a 'kwere kwere' in the midst of other artists just to put me on the spot and distinguish me from them. The other said that I am forcing myself on to the people. I heard such a lot of ugly remarks that I decided to stop wasting time in the country pushing my cause. In SABC, someone said to me, 'Hei, I know what you want to do. You want to be Steve Biko of Africa. It will not work in South Africa. Mark my words, it will not work.' I wish I had listened to him because I spent a lot of money; though I received powerful media exposure I achieved virtually nothing. This was a result of xenophobia which is happening in South Africa one way or the other even as we speak. Xenophobia in South Africa has various levels, but it is prevalent amongst the ill-informed and uneducated, impoverished class. I have faced several xenophobic hostilities and treatments from a few South Africans that I began to wonder how all of a sudden this group of people have forgotten the struggle of African nations for their freedom from apartheid and how they have forgotten all of a sudden that most schools in Africa were paying survival levy for their welfare during the period of apartheid.

Xenophobia is primarily a result of economic depravity and racism and also the metamorphosis of the nation of South Africa into a land of immigrants ('a rainbow nation' as Desmond Tutu put it). Racism is abuse of human dignity, and any abused person by psychological study is most likely to abuse a more vulnerable person if he is unable to abuse the same person who abused him. The invasion of South Africa by European settlers apparently opened the doors for the transformation of South Africa into a land of immigrants just as it happened in the United States of America after the subjugation of the natives of India who were the indigenous America. Xenophobia is caused secondarily by poverty (amongst the indigenous), unemployment (both indigenous and

African immigrants), crime (amongst some of the African immigrants), lack of will power, laziness, low self-esteem, and scarcity mentality (amongst the indigenous South Africans, which could all be attributed to apartheid, depravity, and subjugation). On a spiritual level, xenophobia is caused by mental slavery. I advise that since there are not much jobs for the indigenous, not to talk of African immigrants, the government of South Africa should ensure that they grant visas to Africans who will be constructively useful to them just as it is happening in countries like Canada. South African immigration officials in African countries should not accept bribes to grant visas to hooligans who come into their country to practice hooliganism. Additionally, the system doors should be opened to positive efforts of African immigrants as it is not all immigrants that are involved in anti-social behaviours. They should be part of the economic force, and also there should be economic empowerment of the South Africans via aggressive job creation and government support to reduce poverty, unemployment, and crime.

There should also be wealth redistribution in the country to institute an equitable and just order in the country.

South Africa is still a country in a struggle; hence, they must uphold a good relationship with the African continent and its people in general as we live in an unpredictable and constantly changing world. Nobody knows what will happen in the future. African immigrants on their own parts must become constructive in their economic endeavours. It is important that they do unto others as they will have them do unto them. I am not sure that any African will be happy to see South Africans migrate to their country to abuse their women and also pollute their country with drugs and other criminal activities.

In the entire southern part of Africa, history has changed the meaning and definition of who an African is. In this region, you will find native Africans and other Africans of European origin, Chinese origin, and Indian origin. Also you will find other Africans born by intermarriages between the natives and those of European, Chinese, or Indian roots, generally called coloureds. You also find those born by intermarriages between the South African natives and other African natives (immigrants). The identity crisis lingers on as there has been a long debate regarding who an African is. The natives are those whose ancestral root is Africa. In my humble opinion, anyone born in Africa is an African.

In the west, east, north, and central part of Africa, it is not a very common sight to see Africans of European, Chinese, and Indian descent. Hence, the question of who an African is becomes complex to answer. In my own opinion, an African is anyone born in the African continent no matter the root, but we may distinguish the two parties by saying that any African whose ancestral root is in Africa is native or indigenous. Also anyone born in Africa from other roots is also African but from those ancestral roots. This is closely related to the designation of an immigrant's nation of birth in his international passport if he acquires the citizenship of another country. If you are an African even from another root, then you must act like a true African in the spirit of love for our great continent and not like one who has ulterior motives to accomplish in Africa. Africans of European descent must learn to respect aboriginal or native Africans as they say 'do unto others as you would expect them to do unto you'. If you are an indigenous or native African from another country who finds himself in another African country that houses aboriginals or native Africans, it is important that you respect the aboriginals you find in that African country. If you look closely enough, you will realise that the identity crisis situation in the southern region of Africa is a result of mental slavery, ignorance, and misinformation. Africans of European descent have given themselves names to distinguish themselves from others. They call themselves 'whites', a racial connotation which actually depicts supremacy. In other instances, they call themselves 'Afrikaans'. They name African indigenes 'blacks'. African indigenes must acknowledge that they did not give themselves this name but the Europeans did. Some of the 'whites' as they are called in that part of Africa decided to extend their names from Africans to Afrikaans, and this is also to separate them from the indigenes so that I began to wonder what the intentions of their forefathers were in that part of Africa. Due to errors in human thinking, we are faced with serious situations whereby humans who I believe are naturally the same act as if they are natural enemies who must exploit each other physically and mentally to survive and dominate. I believe also that nature has a way of creating adaptive features which are not intended to create barriers amongst species but to enable them to adapt to some environmental conditions. For instance, in extremely cold regions, one does not need a dark skin, rather a light one, but in extremely hot regions, one definitely needs a dark skin for protection from natural radiations. I wish people could realise these obvious workings of nature. Indigenous Africans must start copying science and technology in their true contexts, at least to compete favourably with other people in the world and gain respect. Every African must join the creative train, for that is the only way we can achieve collective growth and development like other continents of the world.

If everyone born in Africa is an African, then let us join hands to develop the continent Africa. Let us stop living like cats and dogs in Africa. Africa is great; Africa is rich and has all that it takes to sustain all of us. Let us learn to respect one another. Let us learn to work for the collective interest and betterment of everyone in Africa. Let us destroy all forms of discriminatory tendencies in Africa. Let us strive to encourage and support one another. Let us strive to bring out the best in one another for the future of Africa, the unborn, and the generations to come. We most importantly need spiritual unity in Africa, by institution of friendly business and trade links and developing one unifying language, and also unity structures like AU are effective and not mere instruments of control. We also have to collectively unleash a war against mental slavery in Africa, for when a man is mentally arrested, his entire being is arrested. We have to also unleash a war against bad leadership in Africa, for the time has come when African leaders must realise that they are not leading cows but humans like them and also realise that they are employed by the people to serve and not to oppress and abuse power. The time has come when we have to unleash a war against sycophants and political prostitutes who encircle leaders, encouraging faulty governance for their own selfish gains.

There comes the huge question regarding the identity of African-Americans living in America. Though their case seems different because their ancestors were taken to America on chains and slave ships, but it is not far different from Africans of European descent found in South Africa whose ancestors came to Africa as colonial masters because the same identity issue is being debated.

This is why I have chosen to say that if you are an American of African descent you are simply an American but of African descent, and if you are an African of European descent, you are simply an African but of European descent. The use of the word 'black(s)' to denote native Africans also contributed to instilling inferiority in our minds not because the colour 'black' is an inferior colour but because 'black' has been used by the same people who created the word to denote things that are not clean, for instance, black magic, black book, blacklisted, and many more. In my humble opinion, African-Americans are simply Americans of African descent and European Africans are simply Africans of European descent.

People adapt to their respective environment, and in every part of this planet, the highest hierarchy of life is 'man'. And the mere fact that one does not exhibit similar features to another does not make him less 'man'. The world must learn to respect indigenous Africans as we cannot all look exactly alike. It marvels me that indigenous Africans would bleach their skin to look like Europeans; it has become a status symbol for indigenous Africans to lose their natural identity and be who they are not. Indigenous Africans exhibit 'coconut syndrome' without making attempts to copy the astuteness of those whose behaviours they imitate.

I ask: Why do we cry when Europeans treat us as inferior people? I am not sure that they treat us as inferior people because of civilisation which they advanced because I believe the story that they copied civilisation from Ancient Egypt in Africa. The only reason is that we have no true identity and we have no confidence in ourselves. We feel inferior about ourselves and the way we are naturally created, and they know this. We are bestowing inferiority on to ourselves by denouncing all our values and proving to the world that we are less human than them and that we should change our nature completely to be like them. I prefer to be a proud, creative, and civilised native African upholding my vibrant and positive cultural and traditional values. I am proudly African.

In this book, I have chosen to dwell more on the 'king worm' devouring the African continent, which is mental slavery. Mental slavery is a problem that has given birth to multiple problems in Africa, and if this dangerous 'parasite' is annihilated, all other problems of Africa will gradually dissolve, for when you have a disease, you do not pay attention to the symptoms of the disease only; rather you pay attention to the root cause of that disease while also alleviating the symptoms. My concern is that in Africa we treat symptoms of diseases (problems), abandoning the root causes of those diseases. All African problems emanate from mental slavery, and mental slavery is a fertile woman who is always pregnant, always conceiving after giving birth and always giving birth to multiple babies, who in turn multiply geometrically with time. This book has been designed to identify mental slavery, disentangle the chains of mental slavery, and empower Africans in the mind, for true empowerment exists in the mind and nowhere else. Mind over matter, all powers exist within. This book has been also designed to usher in an era of spiritual unity amongst Africans both indigenous and non-indigenous.

In reality, no one is absolutely sure if the controversial theory of evolution is true; also no one is absolutely sure if the strange story of creation as depicted in the Bible and other religious books happened exactly the way it is depicted as no one was there when the first item was created and no one was there to record it. We all live by theories and stories relayed by others, yet those controversial theories and strange stories are told with so much certainty. This is another cause of mental slavery in Africa. These two concepts contradict each other, and since we are not allowed to question them at all, we are chained mentally.

I believe in the universal God, though I was born in a Christian family. I choose to call myself a reformed Christian since I accept the philosophical teachings of Christ. I must state that no science or religion can state with absolute certainty who and when the first man or human being was created as no one was there to witness the process. I have also chosen to align with the cyclical nature of life and the universe. Everything in life, the universe and all within it, is cyclical and constantly in motion. The total sum of all forces in every situation equals zero; hence the equation of life balances. Life is continuous; everything is in constant motion whether we notice it with our naked eyes or not. Everything in life consists of energies whether we feel them or not. How would one comprehend the existence of electricity in the so-called non-living metal? How would one comprehend the existence of nuclear energy in uranium, radium, and plutonium? How would one comprehend a plant that closes up when touched and comes back afterwards? How would one comprehend the fact that a virus has 'children'? How would we comprehend that the moon revolves around the earth? How would we comprehend that the earth rotates on its own axis and also revolves around the sun? How would we comprehend that the sun's energy nourishes the energy in plants? How would we comprehend that when we give out carbon dioxide, plants breathe them and utilise them to produce food for us? How would we comprehend that we inhale oxygen which is also a by-product of a process in plants? How would we comprehend the fact that neither oxygen nor carbon dioxide finishes no matter how they are utilised in nature? How would we comprehend that the sun on its own revolves around a central galaxy (the Milky Way galaxy)? How would we also comprehend that the Milky Way galaxy on its own is in motion? How would we comprehend that atoms have 'people' that move around in definite manners in their cyclic 'homes'? How would we comprehend that a car is driven by fuel and that fuel is extracted from the ground?

Indigenous Africans must become broad-minded in these current times and develop mental curiosity to wage war against mental slavery. Mental curiosity can be understood in that if you drive a car every day, something should prompt you to ask what is making the car move and the principles behind the entire motion together with the conversion of petrol to energy that drives the car. We must develop the 'how', 'what', and 'why' mentality. It may amaze you to know that the invention of the airplane happened because someone out of mental curiosity began to analyse a flying bird. The submarines happened because someone out of mental curiosity started analysing the movement of whales in the ocean. Most gadgets have been invented out of mental curiosity. This is one thing Africans lack, which makes it easy for them to accept any garbage fed into their minds. They have failed to ask 'why', 'how', and 'what' questions.

Africans must also endeavour to understand the infinite powers that exist in our minds and stop living narrow-minded lives caused by expired teachings, strange traditional beliefs, and bizarre cultural practices. Africans must learn to delay self-gratification for it is one indispensable prerequisite for success. As the universe is infinite in its capacity, so also is the human mind infinite in its own inherent capacity; we only limit ourselves. Albert Einstein, Isaac Newton, Michael Faraday, Bill Gates, Phillip Emeagwali, Chinua Achebe, Wole Soyinka, and Chike Obi just to name a few are human beings like us. The only difference is that they are awake, knowing that the human mind is limitless in its inherent abilities, powers, memory, and actions. This is a point of awakening, and if any African, after reading this message, still sleeps in his mind, then I do not know when he is going to wake up.

Man created rockets, computers, TV, cell phones, and many other gadgets just to name a few. So if man created all these things, then what should one wrap up of the human mind: simply infinite, limitless in inherent powers, abilities, and actions. A friend of mine owned up once that he had poor memory, poor learning ability, poor this, and poor that. I understood that he limited himself and wanted others to accept his limitations and self-defeat, but I put it today that except morons and mentally disabled people, no one has poor memory or poor learning ability; we limit ourselves. You may choose to run away from realities due to laziness and fear, but I tell you that he who fights and runs will always live to fight the next day. As for me, for the sake of the generations to come, the unborn, and the future of Africa, I have chosen to embark on this expedition, to unleash a total war not against people but against a concept which I call mental slavery. I have chosen to start with the root cause of all African problems created by image implant, strange religious stories, controversial scientific theories, wrong conditioning, wrong image implants, abuse, faulty education, bogus traditional beliefs, bizarre cultural practices, and false religion spreading at a jet speed while growth, development, and civilisation of Africa is spreading at a snail speed. It is my mission to tell Africans that the universal God is a scientific God, a God of logic, a God of reality and not a God of pseudoscience strange miracles, magic tricks, or illusions.

Indigenous Africans also suffer today because our ancestors could not think deeply and predict the future. We even fight for basic needs of life in these present times, needs like food, health care, and shelter because our ancestors were narrow-minded not knowing that in life there are constant changes. Our ancestors were busy with fruitless rituals to non-existent gods that could not protect them during European invasion, gods that could not reveal to them through their diviners that there was invasion looming ahead and that advanced civilisation was being brought to Africa by force. Gods that could not even protect themselves talk less of protecting those who worship them. If we do not open our eyes now, our children will suffer more. Our children and generations to come will become guinea pigs in this unpredictable and changing world.

Creation is still happening as life is continuous; evolution or creation is still happening as we speak since it is a function of time. Man is a creative genius just as he was made by the universal God. We must also know that energy is never destroyed; rather it changes forms, and when we understand this, we would not need to worry why Eve was made from Adam's ribs or why amoebas and baboons decided to become humans after billions of years. We will not also fear death or worry about what will happen to us when we die. A computer has no capacity to question how it was made. A wine has no capacity to question how it was brewed. Can a meal question how the cook prepared it? So I wonder why man has decided to abandon his job and dwell on the mind of the infinite intelligence that brought him into existence. Let it be known to all corners of the world that both the biblical story of creation and Charles Darwin's theory of evolution are not clearly explained. Hence, without proper explanations they resort to nothing but mental slavery and total confusion. The biblical theory makes men superior to women, and Charles Darwin's theory makes some humans feel superior to others. How man was created would remain a mystery to man and also what happens to a man when he dies would also remain a mystery. The universal God has not revealed to anyone how he did his job, so let no man deceive you. No one can absolutely say with certainty that there is a beginning, and no one can say that there would be an end of time. People should stop deceiving others. My major concern is that Africans absorb all forms of information that is fed to their minds and never make reasonable efforts to question them or dig for the truth. Fellow Africans disseminate such information in a manner as if they are fully certain about them, hence spreading a virus that enslaves others in the mind. Why is it that Asians have been able to prove a point that all humans are creative and are fundamentally the same, yet we are stuck in one place? When are we going to wake up and reason like other human beings? Are we not seeing our growing population and children and the need to consolidate the future? The situation of Africa is so disgusting, and the irritation gets deeper when you see the ways those who should champion our cause, our leaders, are behaving as if they are confused or working for the colonial masters who think we are the conquered species. Our leaders must fasten their seat belts today.

Today native Africans must recognise the power of conditioning, beliefs, and religion in the lives of human beings. We must make sure that conditioning, beliefs, and religion do not constitute mental slavery in our lives, having understood what mental slavery means. Granted that most of us received weak upbringing, conditioning, and education due to many factors including poverty, religion, and our traditional belief systems and these have weakening effects on our psyche, but that does not mean that we have to function like lower human species. We can turn the clock around as long as we believe that we are fully functional humans with brain power like others and also begin to act in the same manner.

One serious problem I have which may offend a lot of people in the world is the use of the words 'black man', 'black people', 'blacks', 'black person' to denote native Africans. We answer out of ignorance, but we do not know the true meaning which the originators of these names had at the back of their minds when these names were created to denote native African people. I hate the use of the word 'black(s)' to denote Africans as it is easy to blacklist someone just to destroy him. Africans should have the power and capability to twist the mind of the world and change all dictionary meanings of the word 'black(s)', 'black people', 'black person', etc., to simply mean any person whose ancestral root is in Africa. If we cannot do that, then let no man call me 'black'. African-Americans chose to deceive themselves by saying that they are 'blacks' because black is the mother of all colours; black is beautiful. Black is this and that; what I am saying is that we did not give ourselves the name 'black(s)', so I can only answer 'black' if I am truly sure that what African-Americans have in minds in answering 'black(s)' is exactly what the creators of that word have in their minds when they call them 'black people'. Do not deceive yourselves living in a fool's paradise; learn to be real. If you look upon the sky, you would discover that nobody's colour is like that of snow and also nobody's colour is like that of charcoal. Africans must start thinking. When you hear any of the names: 'black magic', 'black book', 'blacklisted', etc., a feeling of something negative comes to your mind. They even said that Adam, Eve, and Christ were 'whites' while Satan and the devil were 'blacks'. And if you examine the Bible story properly, you will find out that most of the so-called 'good' people exemplified therein seem to be 'whites'. Why then do indigenous Africans boldly answer 'blacks' when they are called? This is what I am saying; Africans must be broad-minded and open their mind's eyes and begin to see things the ways they are in reality and also begin to question concepts they do not understand fully. They should also be able to distinguish between when they are told fables and when facts are presented on the table. One thing I love about Europeans is that they are quick to think, judge, and doubt everything until they are fully convinced with facts and figures and not stories. They doubt everything until you present facts. That does not imply that all Bible teachings are not true, but the Bible has been revised over and over again, and when a book is revised, something is either added or removed; hence, we demand the original Bible that was written before the introduction of the King James version, revised standard version and other versions. The world will always want to classify people based on race; hence, if native Africans must be classified racially then let us find a name for ourselves and not to be denoted with 'black(s)' as I am not sure of the true meaning of 'black' in this present times, and it seems Africans are not prepared to redefine the meaning of the word 'black(s)' and force the world to accept the new meaning. Whatever we answer today in the name of 'black(s)' holds the same meaning which the creators of the name hold in their minds, such meanings as evil, darkness, a dark race, ugly, uncivilised, savage, and many others.

Africans must also destroy fear completely because it seems that the world is using fear as a tool. When the world preaches freedom and love but do not practice them when dealing with African people, then I wonder. They said that Christ did say that when a man slaps you, turn and receive 77 × 7 more slaps; that means continue to forgive until that man kills you so that your treasure would be in heaven. When the World Trade Centre was blown, Americans would not turn, as they claim Christ depicted, to receive 77 × 7 more bombings. Africans must free their minds from teachings that transform them into weak and gullible people. They also claim that Christ said that the rich can only go to heaven if a horse passes through the eye of a needle; Africans must not absorb this message literarily. It is a mere allegorical statement intended to depict the ugly ways by which some of the rich people (not all) make their money. There is nothing wrong about acquiring riches via positive efforts. As for the issues of forgiveness, I forgive people when they offend me by mistakes and not the other way round. Before asking for forgiveness, I must be sure the individual deserves it and not ready to wilfully perpetuate such actions again only to come in the future to ask for forgiveness. This is because some people ask for forgiveness when they do not really mean it. Africans must realise today that a human being cannot forget anything unless he is dead as memory is independent of will. We must advise the world to stop thinking that our brains are like computer hard drives that can be reformatted at will and also the world must stop replacing our history as it is not helping us at all. We need to rediscover ourselves in this world and this is the time.

I wonder why in some African countries if you speak English or French with a poor accent your fellow native Africans will look down upon you, and in some places, if you ever open your mouth and utter a single word of your native African language, automatically you become out of place in the midst of your fellow indigenous Africans who speak the same native language. Why this sense of inferiority? Is it not time that native Africans choose one of the African languages without politicking on the choice and make it known to all native Africans all over the world and also ensure that it is taught in all African schools so that when a native African sees another native African, they would feel that sense of oneness and unity on being able to understand one another? Another problem I have is that most African leaders are busy amassing wealth and storing in Swiss bank accounts. They do not care about the future or the people; they do not care about anything but wealth acquisition and self-image.

'I want to be the leader at all costs whether I am qualified or not. I want everybody in the village to know that I am above them. I want everyone to notice me. I am ready to die if I am not made the leader. I am ready to die in power. I am the only one chosen by God to lead my people. If I become the leader, I would deal with this and that enemy. If I become the leader, I would repossess this and that land. Please, Pastor, pray for me so that I will become the governor (the fool also goes to the voodoo priest, 'sangoma', or witch doctor). Please, voodoo priest, perform any magic on earth and beyond so that I can become the governor of my state in this election. I am ready to perform any ritual or pay any amount of money needed. I can bring human head, human finger, human eye, etc. Can I please borrow two million dollars from you? If I win, I would award you a 100 million dollar contract and I don't care whether you execute it or not'.

These stupid, insensitive, cruel, and savage attitudes of most African leaders must change. We must copy from positive European leaders of what leadership should be because they taught us what we are practicing.

Sometimes I ask why the advanced nations disrespect Africa so much when they said that civilisation began in Africa and when they are plundering African resources every day. Is religion designed to keep us in check and in perpetual state of mental slavery? Why should the world constantly plant in the minds of Africans the concept of forgetting everything in the past completely as if our brains are computer hard drives that could be formatted at will?

People are becoming so insensitive because of material things that you begin to wonder if God was truly of our image as the religious books portray. What kind of a world do we live in? A world where you see a woman with a dog, and you would gladly think the dog is a pet not knowing that the dog is involved in a sexual relationship with the woman; where churches now wed same sex couples using the same 'holy book' in which a chapter therein condemns such an act; a world where children no longer respect their parents in the name of social freedom; a world where alcohol, guns, and drugs are cheaper than education; where most Africans can no longer pronounce a word of their native African languages; a world where the life of a dog is valued more than that of a human being. This is the climax of futility. Let this hurt anyone for all I care, but the truth must be told in this era for genuine liberation to take place. How come no one goes to jail in this world for accusing Africa of being the mother of the HIV virus? What did our leaders do about this situation? Is there no one amongst them that could find this negative stigma attached to us offensive?

Why is there so much hate amongst indigenous African people, amongst African tribes, and amongst African nations? Is it because of the divide-and-rule syndrome or is it in our nature to hate and not possess team spirit? In some African countries where mineral resources are excavated, I expected African leaders in those countries to ensure that the communities surrounding those zones enjoy infrastructures, but it seems not to be the case, and you are not allowed to speak as there is no freedom of speech in those red zones (just like the late Ken Sarowiwa of Nigeria saw death when he revolted). We only read about freedom of speech in books, but it seems it does not exist in Africa. Human rights are only heard about on radios and TV, read in books and newspapers, but do not exist in practice in Africa.

Why is it that the world keeps waving (tossing) their economic wands in the face of Africa with threats of withdrawing them if Africa refuses to dance to their demands, demands that would never be to the benefit of Africans in the long run, yet our leaders do not do anything about it? Is Africa a prey to world predators or a guinea pig continent where world mafias and scavengers must exploit without the slightest respect, dignity, and honour to put back equitably in return? Anybody who speaks of reparation faces strange death, yet the world talks of right and wrong, laws, rules but what about humanity? Why should Africa owe so much that they cannot repay until eternity, if the world powers are enriching themselves and fuelling their technologies every day with the resources from Africa? Why should the African continent be so poorly developed when most brains of Africa are in America and Europe contributing to the development of those regions? The colonialists destroyed our cultural evolution, erased our ways of life, enslaved us, yet they saw no need for recompense. Upon that they call us animals. How can you say we are animals when you found us with languages and ways of life that you eventually destroyed? How can you call us names when you are the one who is perpetuating our sufferings and backwardness one way or the other because you want to dominate and convert us to economic slaves? Is Africa a slave continent whereby its children are perpetually enslaved physically and mentally? Is it not mental slavery that makes us fail to recognise what the world is doing to Africa? Is it not mental slavery that HIV is killing native Africans and no one seriously questions the root of this 'worm'? Is it not mental slavery that causes us to relax and wait patiently for 'heaven', where every street is furnished with roses, gold, and diamonds where our job would be to enjoy, sing praises, and clap hands unto God? I tell Africans to watch out carefully for false religion as it is destroying the continent. Tomorrow they will brand me negatively because I have decided not to be a fool. Native Africans are forced to be 'good' so that when they die they will inherit heaven and abandon the earth in the hands of those who brought them those doctrines. But the question is: How are those who brought us the doctrines treating us? Today the earth is being inherited not by the meek but by the strong. Why has the world not taken time to find out whether Christ was 'God', 'Son of God', or 'Son of Man' as depicted in several instances in the Bible, and this controversy has stirred numerous divisions amongst the Christian community?

I must clarify one thing that when I say that the story of God creating Adam and Eve in Garden of Eden is strange, I do not mean that the Bible teachings are lies, rather that the stories used for illustrations are not to be absorbed literarily. Also they are not transmitted clearly enough in the context that less educated readers would understand the meanings which the writers had in their minds and which they wanted to pass across to the readers. The use of incredible stories also is beginning to distort the messages completely. Those who try to explain the messages to Africans happen to be a bunch of conmen, hungry souls, chronic materialists, and money seekers who did not even go to school. In the process, they concoct false miracles to gain power over the people. When you read this book, you don't need a dictionary; you don't even need an interpreter because people have the propensity to interpret things in their own ways. Everything you read in this book is clear, and you can feel my mind and what I want to portray.

Why should Africa be so poorly developed and poorly civilised when there are so many African-Americans in America who are less productive within their own immediate American society even with their knowledge and skills? How come African-Americans have forgotten their history completely? How come they have forgotten the sufferings of Africans in poverty-, HIV-, and war-ridden nations of Africa? How come they believe that we live on trees and that we are all chimps? All these issues make me question our thinking, and I attribute them to mental slavery, a new form of slavery and a more dangerous one. Granted that slavery may be morally unacceptable, but I must say that if the biblical story of slavery is true, which I am sure most African-Americans believe in, they should visit those chapters where Israelites were enslaved by Egyptians and understand that slavery may be human nature which you must also strive to fight against. Can they not see also that without slavery there would be no America and there would be no African-Americans? Do African-Americans need any Moses to free them from Egypt (America), if they are angry that they are Americans today because their ancestors were taken in slave chains on to slave ships? Is it the stories they are told every day about Africa or mental slavery that makes them forget their root completely or are we born with passiveness in our genes? I ask why African-Americans are still complaining in America when they have failed to remember their roots. Why are they not ready to accept the realities of present-day America if they do not want to remember Africa? Why they are not prepared to fight for absolute equality in America if they are not happy with the ways they feel things are in America regarding their status? Is it that only people like Martin Luther King, Malcolm X, and a few others were not deceived by the new type of slave chains called 'bling bling' in America? Is it only them that were not deceived by rap music, gangster lifestyles, drugs, pimp lifestyles, prostitution, and other distractions in America? I asked one American of African descent the name of the vice president of America, and to my greatest surprise, he did not know. But he knew the names of all the striptease clubs in the neighbourhood, and he knew the names of all the strippers, even to their last names. This is the core of mental slavery, and African-Americans must wake up today and start thinking in the proper direction for they are truly disgracing Africa. They are misrepresenting the African native breed, and they are making the world draw sad conclusions.

For all you mercenaries of mental slavery, agents of deceit, traitors, slaves of money, beware for you shall be caught up in your own tricks some day, and nothing and absolutely nothing would justify what you have done to the minds of Africans. This book is only meant to stir up mind revolution amongst children of Africa all over the globe to see the need to learn from their Jewish, European, Chinese, and Indian neighbours, the creative process which led to the advancement of civilisation. And in learning they must learn only the positive values that would uplift them. The deep seas, the seas above, the land, the air, even the microbial worlds have been fearlessly explored and harnessed by Jews and Europeans. With their minds, love for one another, and team spirit, they have invented devices that could be felt like magic to us, and we are proud consumers who do not even think about producing anything at all. Automobiles, aircrafts, submarines, war machines, rockets, cell phones, visual and audio devices, medical equipment, industrial machines, and industrial chemicals just to name a few have been mostly invented by Jews and Europeans, so if others like the Chinese and Indians have copied them, then let us copy also, and this is the time. Great minds have ventured into the strange worlds with their devices; they have discovered all the elements of the earth and found the connectivity amongst them. They have in their minute ways emulated the ways of the universal God; they have acted like gods on earth. They have advanced science and technology; they have explored almost all the nine planets of our solar system with their gadgets and are still searching further. They have landed on the moon, landed a robot in Mars. They have also ridiculed deities that some of us fruitlessly worship—deities that could only accept animal sacrifices and money from us but not protect us when slave masters invaded our lives, deities that have nothing to offer against HIV, deities that seem to be deeply asleep. Could you imagine that their 'gods' even swallowed our so-called 'gods' completely? Europeans and the Jews have done so many wonders, though I wonder why Haiti and Somalia suffer amidst all of these great achievements and why HIV has no cure up till now. I have copied a lot from them, most especially creativity and creative thinking, and I want Africans to follow also. They have no problems if you can copy whatever they have to offer, yet indigenous Africans do not want to copy creativity, but we choose to copy discrimination (xenophobia), same sex marriages, and foreign madness including 'coconut syndrome'. We prefer to complain, cry, and beg for love and sympathy when we can do things for ourselves. What does it take to dismantle a car and build all the parts from scratch and reassemble? What are our professors and professionals doing with their knowledge? Are they mental slaves?

Being creative makes one part of the universe's creative force popularly known as God in English. It also helps someone think out of the box; hence, freedom from mental slavery can be achieved. Being creative makes one a smaller god also. There is joy in creativity. Most of us are dead inside, empty, depressed, bored, and angry all the time because we are not creative. This is the time of awakening, for anyone can be creative.

When you read my book, I do not expect ordinary excitement, but I expect acceleration in your mind power. After reading my book, I need to see acceleration in your life. I need to see inspirational motivation. I need to see you move from point 'A' where you are to point 'B' and not to stop there but to continue to point 'C' up until point 'Z', where 'Z' is an unlimited state of mind, for there are no limits to the powers of the human mind. True empowerment exists in the mind and nowhere else. Mind over matter, all powers exist within.

One who is not empowered in the mind, no amount of money given to him would be useful, but if one is empowered in the mind, he could even create wealth for himself. A word is enough for the wise!

The more we talk about the issues the world has marked red, the better, happier, and closer we would become. When these issues are talked about, the closer we would get to finding solutions to our problems and also the easier we would forgive and 'forget' the errors of the past. Anyone who advises you to just forgive and 'forget' without purging out your emotions is asking you to become a moron, and I do not think the person is helping you, and it is also part of this mental slavery I am talking about. If the Jews are constantly talking about the holocaust, then I see no reason why we should not talk about faulty colonialism, apartheid, racism, xenophobia, mental slavery, fake churches that have become banks, and the plundering of African resources.

If you submerge a balloon in water by holding your hands on it, you are not helping yourself as your hands would eventually ache and the balloon would float again. The advanced nations must help Africa today and compensate us for all the evil of the past, but if they cannot do that, it is time they free our minds so that we can evolve as we should have if they had never come in with brute force and conspiracy motives. It is time that they remove the grip of mental slavery from the lives of Africans. Mercenaries of mental slavery, you are warned to desist from your activities, and false prophets, you are also warned to leave Africa alone.

I do not blame native Africans completely; it is partly because our concept of values has been changed with changing times. It is also partly because we have been made to believe that we have no powers to change some of our ugly (standstill) traditional beliefs and bizarre cultural practices. It is also partly because most of us are afraid that if we ask questions relating to God and religion, then 'God will punish us'. In one of my interviews with SAFM (Johannesburg, South Africa), I was featured alongside with a culture activist who told me that he throws bones in his process of divination. I asked him what he sees when those bones are thrown, and he automatically took a strong hate-defensive stance towards me without providing any definitive answers. I also suggested that instead of using butchers to carry out circumcisions, let them employ professional surgeons and still carry out the cultural ceremonies (fun, feasts, or merriments) that go along with the tradition. Few people were not impressed with that comment, but I must tell the Africans today that culture is the totality of socially transmitted behaviour patterns, arts, beliefs, institutions, and all other products of human work and thought. Culture is created by man and not God, hence subject to changes. Culture is dynamic and can be changed if need be. I encourage the preservation of good cultures and traditions. I also did quote a philosophical saying about culture, 'Are not the processes of culture rapidly creating a class superfluous infidels, who believe in nothing? Shall a man lose himself in countless masses of adjustments and be so shaped with reference to this, that, and the other that the simply good and healthy and brave parts of him are reduced and clipped away, like the bordering of a box in a garden?' Good cultures and traditions must be preserved and faulty ones scrapped away without delays'. Good European cultures like technology and science must be copied today, and the unnecessary ones like same sex marriage and unholy lifestyles thrown away without fear of condemnation.

When I made these quotations, I noticed a lot of prejudice; some were happy and others were not, but then I said also and I quote, 'The story that Sodom and Gomorrah was destroyed because men slept with men and wanted to sleep with "God's angels" came alongside with European culture (religion) into Africa as part of the colonial package, hence how come in the same churches and with the same Bible, same sex weddings are taking place, when it is said also in the same book that "God" burnt Sodom and Gomorrah because men slept with men and wanted to sleep with God's angels? Should this particular religious culture be scrapped away since it is contradicting science which is also part of the colonial package as no one could scientifically turn into a pillar of salt as we were told in the case of Lot's wife?' I also asked, 'Should this culture be scrapped away since Africans find it strange and also considering the fact that Europeans are itching for some of our cultures to be scrapped away, most especially those that they find unhealthy?' After this statement also, the people's reactions changed. I then concluded that we live in a prejudiced world. People want to support whatever favours their point of view. People live and think in the box. People and not only Africans are also victims of mental slavery.

A WAKE-UP CALL

Is it not time that African Americans accept the reality of America, establish their true identity and position in the American community, or return back to Africa just like they said in the Bible that Israelites left Egypt and returned to Israel after a prolonged period of slavery? African Americans are confused whether to be called black Americans, African Americans, or other names, yet up until now, they have not accepted any definite name. I believe that if they hate to be called 'blacks' and also hate to be called Africans, then let them embark on the struggle to attain absolute equality with their neighbours in the American community. This is done by being part of the creative process that brought America to the present state it is and not by wearing big chains and living lousy and unproductive lives.

The entire children of Africa at home and the Diaspora including African Americans must all commence an era of mind revolution in this present time. The New World Order, an era of the central world government, will usher in an era when unproductive human species will either be eliminated one way or the other or be subjugated and positioned as full-blown slaves and guinea pigs. Globalisation, formation of central world bodies like UN, World Health Organization, and many others including the invention of the Internet and other communication systems, which are making the world a global village, and strange diseases like HIV/AIDS are all signs of the the New World Order. This era will see the African continent and its children compete with the strong and highly advanced people who in terms of technology are 10,000 years ahead of African people. African people will be absorbed. Since the history of mankind, the strong has always sought for land and resources. The technology developed by the advanced nations need natural resources to fuel them. Africa has a lot of them which Africans have no technological capacity to transform them into better use. In time to come, the world will no longer wait for Africans to wake up. If they continue to behave like animals, they will surely be treated like one for anyone who has nothing to call his own, not even name, identity, God, religion, lifestyle etc., is not fit to be called human. Humans must possess rational thinking, intelligence and creative abilities. In the past, Man was under the control of nature, over time, man devised a way to improve his life, advancement set in. Nature did not stop anyone. Today man has controlled nature and Africans are gradually becoming part of this nature that man will control. Man, the intelligent humans will treat anyone who is not fitting intelligently as a lesser human. It will no longer matter in the future, what circumstances placed Africa and its inhabitant where they are today. China was colonized so also was India but it marvels me that up until this present time in human history, Africans are still behaving like little children that are raised with stories. Africans cannot feed themselves. It is shameful.

The world population is experiencing aggressive growth, and Africans seem to be the only part of this growing population that is not producing what they are consuming. We only breed and increase in population but produce nothing to take care of the growing population. We are competing with Indians and the Chinese in terms of population explosion, but we are not doing anything to ensure that the needs of the growing population are met. Can we not see that HIV and other forms of diseases will continue to manifest in the lives of Africans? If we must multiply in numbers, then we must also learn to produce what will take care of this growing population. Is it impossible or are we not endowed with the same intelligence as others? Were Asians not colonised the same way we were? What exactly is wrong with Africans that they cannot at least copy the strength and wisdom of others if they cannot invent or discover their own? What is going on in the minds of African leaders? What is going on in African learning institutions? What are we learning in schools? A country like South Africa and Nigeria has become a status symbol for someone to fake his or her behaviour and to act like Europeans to be accepted in the society. It has become a status symbol for someone to lose his or her originality just to be accepted.

If anyone does not see any serious problem in the African continent, then something is definitely wrong with that person. There are many mechanisms by which unproductive species are eliminated on this planet, and no matter how long we cry or how long we complain, if we do not do something about our situation, nothing will ever go right. If we do not justify our humanity and creative abilities embedded naturally in every human being, things would never go well in the continent. Heaven only helps those who help themselves.

I adore Africans like Mr Nelson Mandela who could sacrifice their freedom for others. I adore Great Kwame Nkrumah of Ghana for his effort in promoting Pan African philosophy and a fight against colonialism and neo-colonialism. I adore Steve Biko and Oliver Tambo. I adore great activists like the late Fela Kuti and Bob Marley who spoke their minds devoid of fear or prejudice. I adore great leaders like Julius Nyerere, Patrice Lumumba, and Thomas Sankara of Burkina Faso. I adore great scientists from African origin like Philip Emeagwali who took a major part in the invention of the Internet as we know today. All of these people and more instil confidence in me and also buttress the point that the solutions to the majority of our problems exist in our hands. Africans must know today that we are living in a competitive world hence no one can help them fix the problems that manifest in their lives except themselves.

Is it not time that African Americans cry unto the world to help Africa, their ancestral root, since they cannot be treated exactly the way they desire to be treated in the American community no matter what they do? Is it not time that they cry unto America and the world to help develop Africa or free Africa from the clutches of mental slavery and neo-colonialism to usher in development in the continent. Is it not time the world tells Africans the truth about religions they introduced into the continent for they say practice what you preach, do unto others as you will have them do unto you, love one another etc. Is it not time that African Americans remember Africa where their forefathers were taken away during the slave trade era and where resources were plundered and are being plundered every day and cry unto the world to cancel Africans' debts at least as a form of compensation since the advanced worlds have failed to return part of the loot from the continent which have enriched their continent. The world kidnapped, stole, and bought African children during the slave trade era, and with the labour of African slaves (many who died in the Atlantic crossing), America was built; the same labour sparked up the industrial revolution in Europe, yet instead of compensation for such bloody rip-off, they resorted to colonisation. The end of this bloody slave trade era ushered in another period of colonisation when the continent was divided into colonies for the sole intention of plundering their resources both human and minerals. Is it not time that African Americans start recognising their roots, for a man who does not know his root will always strive but will never arrive. Is it not time that they plead to the world to leave Africa and African children alone to discover themselves if they have nothing to offer them than oppressions, plundering of their human and natural resources, and mind diversion.

In this part of the book, I am going to compare between indigenous Africans and indigenous Europeans to bring out some differences in their character which has either made Europeans excel or made Africans fall short of expectations.

Before I proceed to make these comparisms, I will emphasize that all of them are sociological and not physiological. Sociological problems can be corrected but not what is genetic as we cannot change our DNA. African problems are not genetic; they are caused by so many factors which also include the destruction of African natural cycle economic and cultural development through slavery and colonization, foreign religions etc. Having known these, let us seek to change our ways of thinking and in the process change our lives as the situations that will be mentioned here are not permanent. Africans must know today that the skin color of a person or his physiognomy does not determine the weight of his intelligence. Some of the most intelligent men in the world today are Africans. Phillip Emeagwalli, Wole Soyinka, Wangari Mataai, Chinua Achebe, thabo Mbeki etc are all Africans hence Africans must rise up to command their destiny.

Both Africans and Europeans are wonderful people, and they both have some similarities and differences in character: both are creative people, but most Europeans would utilise their creative abilities for a collective interest of their own people, but most Africans would either prefer to let their creative abilities sleep or utilise them for a destructive purpose against their own people.

Africans seem to be more prone to emotional weaknesses than Europeans, which accounts for the reasons why people easily take advantage of them. We love to cry, complain, attract sympathy, seek love from wrong sources, and also crave pity from others. We cry every day, but we are also directly involved in the creation of most of our problems. We always want to completely blame others for our inadequacies, and we never want to take responsibilities for our shortcomings in life.

While Europeans are united as one strong force, supporting one another, dominating the earth, Africans are often busy strengthening barriers, strengthening tribes, and forming numerous unhealthy cults that can never coexist. We are consolidating our divisionary strategies. We are assisting neo-colonialists in fueling wars in our own countries.

Europeans invest in the future, while we invest in pleasures of the senses. We pay more attention to self-gratification. South Africa is a country that has been subjugated for centuries through apartheid and forced dorminance attempt by the Europeans, and now they have freedom, yet they cannot utilise it. I wondered whether Mandela (and his co-activists) fought for freedom and spent twenty-seven years in jail only for South Africans to be free to compete for spaces in drinking places and dance halls with Europeans, to compete with Europeans in the type of beer, wine, brandy, whisky, crack cocaine, heroin, and cocaine being consumed, to compete with Europeans on clothes to wear, cars to drive, make-up to wear, and other secondary needs. This is the time to wake up. We only want to indulge in pleasures of the senses and self-gratification forgetting higher thoughts, higher arts and the hard task of securing the future. Let it be known to all Africans that the ability to discipline yourself and to delay immediate gratification for a greater reward in the long run is the indispensible prerequisite for success.

Europeans sacrifice their time, energy, and lives for their unborn and generations ahead, but we would rather choose to mortgage the future for our immediate wants. Our leaders would rather hide our national reserves in Swiss banks. Most European leaders come to power to manage the wealth of the nation, to meet the needs of the people, but most African leaders come to power to convert the wealth of the nation and the people into their own personal wealth.

When an epidemic hits, we normally become major victims. Our professors and medical institutions would do nothing. We cry unto the world for their drugs, drugs that may even be more harmful than the diseases themselves. We are always vulnerable in such situations when we claim to have capable hands in the medical field; when we claim to have those in the field of pharmacy; when we claim to have professors in the field of science and technology; when we claim to have universities and research institutes in Africa. Europeans would quickly revolt against such problems and find lasting solutions and challenge whichever source such epidemic came from whether created by someone or otherwise. Africans must realise today the futility of breeding too many children when Africans are not yet in full control of their economic and political lives, when we are not even striving hard enough to survive, when we are chasing rats and cockroaches when our houses are burning. I am terribly angry that in this digital age, someone is still talking about spirits of our ancestors and someone is still throwing bones, deceiving people and trying to interpret their destiny and future with chicken bones.

Africans have not seen any need to start a revolution against HIV and AIDS even when they proclaimed that it came from green monkeys somewhere in Africa. No one, not even a single African leader, could challenge such blackmail. Europeans would quickly take decisive action to revolt against this for the sake of their collective image and reputation and also to prove that they are lords of their lives. I personally expected African leaders to collectively file a lawsuit against whichever criminal organisation that came up with the story that HIV emanated from green monkeys in Africa or even sue the World Health Organization, but they did nothing about this false assertion. Sometimes I begin to wonder the role of an African leader.

Toxic wastes were dumped somewhere in Ivory coast by a group of European lunatics who felt that Ivory coast was the best zone to dump deadly toxic materials which are capable of annihilating people in millions. Today, this issue is no longer discussed, probably because someone out there, a fellow African, may be one of those African leaders, the hungry souls, has been bribed to keep silent. But I tell you, Europeans would never keep mute over this kind of inhumanity. They would fight to the end to see that even if such an act is corrected, other similar ones do not happen. Nigeria has no stable electricity yet they claim to be giants of Africa, companies are departing, youth unemployment rising. But does it ever occur to you that perhaps someone has accepted bribes from the Chinese to ensure that electricity problems are not fixed in that country so that the Chinese can import their generators? This is what Europeans will not do.

Africans are not allowed to talk about slavery and apartheid, but holocaust must be talked about by the Jews all the time and up until now, Nazis are being arrested as a token of punishment for their crime against humanity. Africans must forgive and forget because they have no choice, they are beggars, and as they say, a beggar has no choice. They will be awarded prizes for forgiving and forgetting even when they forgive those who have not admitted guilt. How can you forgive someone who has not done anything wrong to you? How can you forgive someone who has not honestly asked for forgiveness? Is this not stupidity?

Europeans sold dummy to Africans in terms of religion while Europeans live in reality driven by scientific and technological principles. Africa has become a huge market for the products of science and technology yet Africans live in wired dreams and build castles in the air. Africans do not question religious teachings that make no sense but Europeans do.

In Africa, a lot of toxic wastes are being dumped in the minds of people and in their social lives and no one sees it, whether it is same-sex marriage, foreign habits and lifestyles, faulty and weak education, fairly used clothes, genetically bred food which is not compatible with our natural body system, false religious institutions that siphon our resources and keep us psychologically paralyzed at the mercy of the same people who introduced same religions. Where do we start from? Africans will never speak against any of this ugliness, but Europeans will impudently do so.

It may amaze you that average ten-year-old European kids may have more information in their brains than an average fifty-year-old African adult. Europeans start to feed the minds of their children with information at early age, They condition them to crave information at such tender age but we feed the minds of our children with fear and superstitions.

When Africans are oppressed, they adjust, but Europeans would rise and resist, even be willing to die in the course of this resistance, at least for the sake of others. I must confess that this courage is one reason why I respect them though I respect them more for the application of their creative intelligence in advancing civilisation which history has it that they copied from Egypt during the days of ancient civililzation. I will own up though that I am not at ease with the fact that they are now applying the same creative intelligence to oppress Africans while preaching love and forgiveness to them. Let it be known to all Africans today that the first university in the entire planet earth was founded in Africa.

This is a wake-up call. Poverty, hunger, and starvation are all easy to eradicate if we could learn to think in a proper direction as Africa has a vast land, and with all the land, it is unbelievable that we import food. Europeans will import our grain, process it, and export a new product made out of our grain back to you. They will also import our crude oil, refine it, and send back to us as refined fuel all in exchange for our money. We prefer to import everything, even God and religions, while exporting nothing to the outside world except natural resources. This is truly a wake-up time. Let no one get angry with what is being said in this book, but if anger could spur you to action, then be truly angry, but apply a practical and positive attitude towards that anger and come out with a concrete result.

African time syndrome is a phenomenon prevalent amongst Africans. I get irritated with anyone who does not keep time. If you arrange an appointment with an average European, say 7 p.m., he ensures that by 5 p.m., he has already started preparing for the appointment so that by exactly 7 p.m., he would be there. But an average African will start preparing for the same appointment by

9 p.m. only to arrive by 11 p.m. And when you reprimand him, he will tell you that we are in Africa and that he is maintaining African time. This is totally unacceptable to me.

You would rarely have an agreement with an African where he maintains the terms of the agreement, but most Europeans, except some of their politicians, would honour agreements. Apart from a few European politicians, their citizens stick to their words in your dealings with them and in your relationship with them, but most Africans will lie and cheat all the time in business and other relationship matters.

Mr Ndlovu, an African started a cyber cafe with twenty good computers. Mr Jabulani also a fellow African seeing that Mr Ndlovu's business was growing, abandoned his liquor shop and opened a cyber cafe opposite Mr Ndlovu's cyber cafe with seven out-dated computers and with limited expertise. Mr Ndlovu being the originator of the cyber cafe business and who understood the business well had no worries as it took no time for his business to blossom. Mr Jabulani who had just ventured into the business with no experience ran out of business even before he started. Mr Jabulani firstly arranged his friends who went into Mr Ndlovu's cyber cafe with forged incriminating documents, and on the assurance that they were all seated, he invited his police friends whom he used to oppress, steal, victimise, extort, and intimidate people. The cops came in, went straight to where those syndicates were seated, arrested them, and confiscated all computers belonging to Mr Ndlovu. Later on, Mr Jabulani went and exchanged those computers for some cash. He resold them and used the money to expand his own business. In a month's time, Mr Ndlovu managed to obtain a loan from the bank to start again but this time with ten computers. Mr Ndlovu had good business experience in the computer field, being an IT specialist. On the contrary, Mr Jabulani knew nothing about computers and computer business. He used to own a liquor bar stationed amidst poor unemployed Africans and young female prostitutes, and there were several shootings and killings around and inside his business premises. In one of the instances, a group of gangsters, who came to have their share of the daily alcohol abuse, lost self-control and no one knew that they had guns with them. All of a sudden, they shot and killed three innocent people on the spot. Afterwards, they reached out for the cell phones of the dead victims and ran into the streets, and, believe me, those phones were probably sold for nothing, not more than ten dollars each.

I am trying to make a point here. This man Mr Jabulani had no knowledge of computers and the computer business. All he knew was liquor business, and his choices of customers were young and unemployed (jobless) youths with no definite means of income and prostitutes who hang around to hunt for stray men to deceive. Mr Jabulani did not care about who came to his business premises. He had no age restriction, and he encouraged prostitutes to visit his business premises to attract stray men. The major category of people who patronised his bar were young and irresponsible kids and gangsters who would not have a second thought in killing someone for a cell phone they would probably sell for less than ten dollars. Mr Jabulani never went to school.

If you entered Mr Jabulani's cyber cafe, which I would prefer to call a computer bar, though there were enough computers there, you would wonder whether it was a cyber cafe or a club as the noise and the category of people you would find there would automatically put you off. But in the cyber cafe of Mr Ndlovu, who was an expert in the field, you would find cleanliness, sanity, and serenity, and you would see quiet and decent people. After a while, Mr Ndlovu revived his business again, and Mr Jabulani noticing such a development, arranged criminals again. This time they broke into Mr Ndlovu's cafe at night and stole all his computer equipment, and automatically Mr Ndlovu's business collapsed. When troubles escalated between Mr Jabulani and his criminal syndicates due to poor sharing of their loot, all that he did to Mr Ndlovu was exposed and Mr Ndlovu wrote an official report to the authorities for a thorough investigation into the activities of Mr Jabulani. The authorities monitored Mr Jabulani for a period of six months, and on raiding his residence, they discovered some of the items stolen from Mr Ndlovu's business premises. Mr Jabulani was arrested, tried, and jailed for seven years. This is the way and manner most of us compete in business. We love to pull others down. We do not want to pull our energy and resources together to build a gold mine which would sustain all; rather, we would want to live in our fellow man's pocket until we run him down completely. This is one terrible horror we Africans inflict on one another wherever we are gathered as so-called brothers. Most of us are doing this every day without any remorse for our actions. If you are one of those, do not think you are smart. You are a chimp.

On the contrary, Mr Gert, a European, opened a manufacturing business. Mr Johan went into the same business, but Mr Gert made grade A3 products and Mr Johan made grade A2 products, better than the grade A3 products. Mr Gert, realising that Mr Johan had made a better product, improved on his own products and came up with grade A1 products which are better than grade A2 products, hence the competition began. They continued to improve on the quality of their products until they started improving on the quantity since the products had assumed equal quality standards. After a while, they both started manipulating prices to attract more customers. Each party applied incentives, various promotional strategies to gain control of the market, and with time they had a closer understanding of how they could control the entire market at large, knowing that it is a free market economy where there are other competitors. They finally merged and became one large body and took full control of the entire market. That is how competition is done. You can now understand how Africans compete in business and how Europeans compete in business.

It is so sad that if you assist an African brother today, whenever you stop rendering such assistance to him or if any misunderstanding arises between you and him, all that you have done in the past become forgotten totally. Build a team with your brothers to pursue a creative goal, they will prefer to live inside your pocket feasting on your meagre resources until they drain you dry. We lack team spirit. We complain that Europeans came here and took us into slavery, but today fake preachers and false prophets have turned into mercenaries of mental slavery, propagating another kind of slavery even more dangerous than the one we experienced in the past, and yet we all act dumb.

A European would be so persuasive and polite to his customers, while an African would be so impolite and hostile to his customers as if his customers are his enemies, which accounts for the reasons why most of their customers never come back when they go. A European has a way of retaining his clients, as long as they bring money to him. The African businessman would always have a way to fall out with his clients, and in some cases, even engage them in physical fights, and yet they are the people who should bring money into his establishment. The African person puts ego first in all he does instead of putting the work or service first. The African businessman would always want his clients to know that he owns the business, that he is the boss. The European businessman has a way of fooling his clients by making them feel like the bosses, while he is the servant at that moment, and this helps him retain them to survive in business. Sometimes the way in which the African business owner approaches his customers is by implicitly saying 'please try next door'.

There is always this repulsive facial remark and repelling expression. But the European business owner would fake a smile (a plastic smile), and as soon as you pay him and go, he retains his posture. African business owners bring their family problems and frustrations to their business premises, and they go extra miles to let their customers who are bringing money to their businesses share in such family problems and frustrations.

By nature, both Europeans and Africans are created to think, act, and function properly. But Africans have been poorly conditioned from childhood to fear, live in superstitions, think, act and, function slowly. African ancestors did not have the culture of change in their traditional belief system. They did not want anything to do with change, and they transmitted this unto their descendants. We live in a dynamic world driven by science, technology, principles and rational thinking, and there is nothing we can do about it but follow. We need to throw away weird dogmas, beliefs, and superstitions and adopt what makes the world go round.

You need to see some Africans walk or think—always slow, but watch a European do the same—fast and focused. You also need to see some Africans at a place of employment—always slow at work, acting as if it is punishment to work and get paid. But watch the European. He executes his duties fast, making sure that he justifies his pay. Europeans were tormented by cold and lack of sufficient resources in their lands, and as they say, necessity is the mother of invention. They began struggling hard. They conquered their needs and fears, and over time, this survival spirit got implanted in their nature and they grew to become world giants. From birth, they transmit this nature unto their children. Europeans do not have sufficient natural resources but Africans do. Europeans discovered the vast natural resources in Africa and devised ways of harnessing and plundering them. Should we complain because of this, instead of learning or copying (cloning) technology from them as they are our teachers and bosses now? We must learn to adopt their creative thinking abilities and not only their behaviours most especially the vain ones. We must think exactly the way they think and not behaving like them as you can find in the 'coconuts' of South Africa. If most Africans have decided to turn into 'coconuts' (those who try to fake their behaviours), let them also copy the intelligence and thinking pattern of Europeans completely, which brought civilisation to this present state, and stop living fake lives.

Europeans desire material acquisitions a lot, and they strive to acquire them to gain comfort, power, and respect. They tend to live beyond beliefs which do not put food on their tables, but Africans adhere to beliefs which proclaim that it is more difficult for a rich man to go to heaven than for a horse to pass through the eye of a needle; beliefs that destroy one's enthusiasm to acquire riches and become as powerful as others; beliefs that help Africans to remain poor so that they could go to heaven when they die. Africans prefer to build castles in the air in this present time.

European families would limit the number of children they would have based on their income, but a typical African family believes that having more children is a blessing from God, even when there are no resources to take care of those children. In the past, Africans practised polygamy and also practised having multiple children when one has limited resources.

In the Bible, Christ said that polygamy should be abolished and people must practice 'one-man one-wife' (monogamy) style of marriage, but in some African villages, you will find an African chief with his six wives in the same church where the same Bible which teaches against such is also being used as a tool of indoctrination. Europeans believe in monogamy, and according to them, this principle demonstrates respect for both men and women since men are not comfortable with bigamy (a woman marrying multiple men at the same time) and should not expect women to be comfortable with polygamy (a man marrying multiple women at the same time). I strongly believe that men and women are born equal and all human species should complement one another. I also detest when people say that our world is a man's world, for the world is for everyone irrespective of gender. Some Africans also believe that women are inferior to men and that women are properties that men could acquire and discard at will. This is an erroneous belief and must be flushed out of our minds. I also detest when people claim that God chose them and in the process look down on others and treat others as unequals. If God chose you, the information should be revealed to all, not just you as one should not blow his own trumpet. Americans using the Bible to wed same sex couples in the church when the book of Levinticus chapter 18 verse 22 condemns it.

Europeans create laws and strive to strengthen the laws for their protection, but we rejoice over lawlessness and break the laws that should protect us. In fact African leaders are the greatest of all hypocrites as they break the laws which they are supposed to uphold.

A European feels superior about himself and the pigmentation of his skin, but most of us feel inferior about ourselves and our skin pigmentation, and this is not a healthy development. Some Africans bleach their skin, trying to look like Europeans. Some apply chemicals on all parts of their bodies, including their hair, to look like Europeans, and when Europeans treat them as inferior people, they complain not knowing that they have by their own hands created superiority sentiments in the minds of Europeans.

One well-travelled African, Akpan, told me that he lived in Canada and the UK for five years without hearing a gunshot or seeing people fighting on the streets. But in the United States of America, gunshots are usually heard amongst African Americans, and in South Africa life is so cheap amongst indigenous Africans (though this could be attributed to the horror and inhuman treatment they received from the apartheid era, but now that apartheid is over and South Africans must learn to value lives, throw away the guns, and embrace education, creativity, and positive values). We threaten, shoot, and kill one another at the slightest provocation. In Nigeria, fighting in public is such a common sight that sometimes when I see people fighting, I wonder what has gone wrong with their minds. It is good for Africans to realise today that violence of any form is an attribute of one whose intelligence has failed. Faulty minds, people who do not have the capacity to think, people who cannot control their emotions resort to irrational behaviours and sometimes violence. People who want to be feared impose fears because they lack the ingredients that can attract love and respect from others. A leader who has nothing to offer usually resorts to oppression and intimidation just to gain attention and control. But the question is, why one should be feared in the first place. You need to be respected and loved and not feared. Empty people attract fear to themselves just to appear relevant.

Europeans are confident of themselves, but Africans seem not to possess self-confidence. It seems that they are battling with a self-created inferiority complex. The behaviour of an African person exhibits amidst a European group of people shows the tendencies to merely gain acceptance or fit into a class. Africans are always battling with inferiority complex, but who made them inferior in the first place if not themselves? Who told them that the sizes and shapes of their noses are a fault? Who told them that the colour of their skin is a fault? Who told them that their languages are faulty? Who told them all the things that make them feel inferior about themselves are faults? You have to be yourself all the time, for in every part of this earth, in every continent of this world, the highest hierarchy of life is man and nobody is superior to another, neither is anyone inferior to another. So let no one instil inferiority in your mind. Europeans came from cold regions and must look the way they are, Indians must look like Indians, Chinese people must look like the Chinese, and the Latinos must look the way they are.

When most Europeans listen to music, they enjoy the music while grasping the message in the music, while most of us listen to beats only without any effort to grasp the message. Europeans read a lot to enhance their knowledge, for knowledge is power. They eat properly and also study very hard, for it is always good to feed both the body and mind. But as they say, put information in a book, you hide it from an African. We would prefer to gather and talk about people, which is gossip amounting to time abuse. We prefer to abuse alcohol, women, life, and sex. We enjoy laziness and idleness, yet when we become poor, we complain.

In as much as I am deeply angry with Europeans for introducing fear-based religious doctrines into Africa through the gun, I must confess that it seems that our people are comfortable with it as they enjoy listening to fables. They enjoy gathering in the new age churches that have turned into party grounds with no spiritual feel for no constructive reasons, to show off their best of clothes and perfumes. Some young girls come to entice pastors because of the pastors' power, wealth, and fame, while others come to entice rich guys. Broke guys come with their best clothes (sometimes borrowed) to try their luck on girls. Prostitutes, thieves, 419ers, ritual murderers, assassins, and corrupt police officers come to the fake churches so that the pastors will help them plead to God to cleanse their sins (which they must pay for). New age churches are becoming incredibly ridiculous in this present time. These churches deploy the best of melodies to smoothen their brainwashing, mind control exploitative games, and the pastors love whatever is going on there so long as you do not leave that church with the money in your wallet. You must give it to God. (That does not mean that there are no good churches or no good men of God, there are, but they are not as conspicuous and the excessively rich as the false ones. They can also be found among the every other religion of the world.)

A European seeks a duty no matter how tough it is, then he gathers courage and strength to execute such a duty, but an African will prefer a duty equal to his strength or duties that are not challenging. Europeans take up seemingly impossible tasks and end up making them happen but Africans are afraid of great dreams and tasks. Most African leaders do want to remain in power until their demise, but a typical European leader wants to give others a chance in the true spirit of democracy—at least if one person could do it then another person can do it also. (Though I have been wondering the position of the Queen of England in the new global democratic arrangement because it seems they are constantly fighting to destroy monarchs in other countries so as to institute democracy, yet theirs is the strongest monarchy in the world. The office of the queen is not democratic and there are no elections to replace the queen)

African leaders seem to think that they are sent by God; some think that they are God figures. Some think that they are messiahs to the people, hence they must remain in power until their mission on earth is over. They enshrine themselves and their position in myths creating a cloud of fear and superstitions to perpetuate their stay in office and also to enhance their control over the people simply because they have nothing tangible or serious to offer the people.

I know also that any European reading this book at this point would want to hear only positive information about them as it seems to be in their nature to be prejudiced. I also know that any African at this point is warming up to hear negative information about Europeans. I have always said thatthis book is not written to suck up to anyone rather to reveal the truth for posterity's sake. Europeans are not perfect either. Though they have contributed immensely in the advancement of civilisation, science, and technology, they have in the process introduced a lot of unthinkable, strange and inhuman ugliness that defy human understanding and violate moral values. Same-sex marriage, human cloning, and bestiality are just a few of such creations.

The idea of indoctrinating Africans into believing that there is a place called heaven where lazy and idle fools would go when they die instead of working hard to survive on this earth is wrong and must stop now. Every day the world is crying about the Nigerian 419 scams, but can you not see that there is no 419 greater than false doctrines which incapacitates a man mentally while the creators of those doctrines are busy marauding the victim's resources? Europeans will preach love and democracy; they will preach against crime, but if you dig deep, you will realise that in most times, they do not practise what they preach when dealing with the same people they are selling those doctrines to making it look like a tool of mind diversion. They will steal from you and be giving you little by little from what is originally yours, using the gun and religious books as weapons to keep you in check and perpetually afraid. They do not apply all the tenets of humanity while dealing with other races, but they will emphasise on humanity to those race to protect themselves from being hurt by others Europeans have demonstrated that they cannot live without enslaving others having considered themselves as a superior race and as I said in the beginning chapters, this has led to several wars and will lead to the end of the human race in this nuclear age.

Europeans have been oppressing African people from time in the past. From physical slavery that transmuted into mental slavery. From the plundering of African resources to colonialism which has yielded no sound results in most African countries but brainwash and underdevelopment. Is it neo-colonialism? Europeans advanced civilisation which from history began in ancient Egypt, but in pretence of coming to civilise the African continent and its people, they came and looted the continent of human resources and natural resources while at the same time introducing a religion that forbids such acts with a gun.

Is it not time that Africans realise that when Europeans invaded Africa, African gods could not even defend themselves, talk less of defending the people who worshipped them. In some cases, Europeans even stole those ancient gods engraved in masks. Is it not time that Africans wake up, or should the genetic makeup of our brain cells be changed before we would decide to wake up? I ask to know what African engineers, scientists, technologists, and professors are doing. Should we not task all our engineers, scientists, technologists, and professors of science and technology all over Africa including our African American brothers to build the first indigenous African car with funding from African governments? I believe that we can do it.

Europeans question everything in life, while Africans believe whatever they are told. I have personally questioned the entire African 'Gods'; I have questioned all religions in Africa. I have also questioned this religion that Europeans introduced with guns and religious books, and I see no reasons why Africans cannot question beliefs and events around them. I have asked all the so-called African gods and spirits of our ancestors to appear to me, yet I could not see any one of them nor did I see any signs. Europeans do not believe in spirits, ghosts, demons, etc., but we do strongly believe in these things without making any efforts to prove an absolute existence of them. Japanese believe in no God, yet they are one of the greatest nations in the world today. I am not saying that Africans should not believe in God, as I know that it is in their nature to believe in something and not themselves, but what I am saying is that if they must believe in God, let them make efforts to establish that such a God really exists and not just an imaginary God, a man-made God, or a 'sky heaven' God. I believe in myself, and I serve the universal God of justice, logic, principles, order, peace, and harmony. I have no time for man-made religious gods or imaginary gods.

Europeans understand the meaning of love for their kind, which accounts for their sense of collective pursuit and self-sacrifice towards one another, but Africans are confused totally. They misunderstand love with weak emotions.

We do not even understand the true meaning of love and self-sacrifice. We confuse love with weak emotions. We think that giving money to a beggar on the streets means that we love him. We do not see that if we rehabilitated and empowered one, then we have shown him true love. Give a man a fish, you feed him for a day, teach him how to fish, you feed him for a life time.

Africans seem to lack team spirit. Europeans encourage, support and promote success amongst one another, but most Africans rejoice over failure of others. We crave hearing that somebody has failed. Older Africans who have failed in life do not want younger ones to succeed so that their failures will not become evident. African leaders who failed in their times will continue to thwart the efforts of vibrant leaders so that their failures do not become evident. Most of us thrive on negatives; we crave reading news and hearing stories about ugliness, failures, and downfall of people. This is counterproductive and must stop; we must develop a positive attitude towards life. Watch an average African open the newspaper; he is searching for those kinds of negative information and not information about the politics, economics, and social well-being of the society. He will be quick to pick up porn material but not material on current affairs.

Europeans go through life each day, manifesting the wisdom and intelligence of the universal God made manifest in all man, including Africans, but we are busy transforming our continent into a greater market, a dumping ground for foreign goods, and a dumping ground for foreign gods, foreign religions, and foreign lifestyles. 'Coconuts' (those who try to be like the Europeans in character and not in thinking) want others to see that they are more European than African. This is not a problem if they are thinking like Europeans also. Michael Jackson, a son of an African man, kept on cutting his nose and bleaching his skin trying to be like Europeans until he kissed the grave. That is to tell you how some of us are. When we become rich, we become fake and stupid.

Europeans are busy breaking the atoms, inventing great machines, fortifying their existence on this planet, conquering other continents; we are waiting to die and live in a better world, a heaven which has been prepared by God for the poor, lazy, and idle people. Europeans embrace challenges, but we hate, fear, and run away from challenges. Europeans suffer for a better tomorrow, but we fear sufferings and chicken out when the going gets tough. It is easy to instil division amongst Africans, but it is easy to unite Europeans.

Europeans utilise failure as an energiser, but we fear failure and chicken out when the going gets tough. Europeans believe in themselves as lords of their lives, challenging the deities that Africans worship, while we believe in foreign religions and non-existent deities. We just want to believe in something whether it exists or not, whether it makes sense or not. We want to believe in stories whether they are true or not, and we do not want to believe in ourselves even if believing in ourselves would work for us.

Europeans created a system, and they are all in the system, but Africans have not thought of creating anyone. We are all with the system, and we have not taken time to know the difference between being with a system and being in it.

To all Africans, know you today that any house divided among itself would never stand, and any man who does not think is not human enough; he who fails to plan has planned to fail; the earlier we learn to live in reality, the better will our lives be, as any time we live in illusion is a wasted time. The war in these current times requires no physical weapon, but mental. The survival of the fittest displacement mechanism has no mercy for the weak. Watch out for the weapons, illusions and fantasies, alcohol, drugs and all forms of abuse, illiteracy, mind diversions, and religious diversions. Behold, the chains of slavery are no longer in the hands, but in the minds.

Beware of what you see and what you listen to. Beware of what you do; image implants and conditioning. Beware of what you put into your body and minds and energies you transmit to other Africans around you. Beware, as you may be an agent of mental slavery without knowing it. Seek and you shall find as Christ said in the Bible, for all powers exist within. Africa has greater resources than most continents of the world, so stop wasting time in illusions and fantasies. Stop thinking about heaven, hell, afterlife, and the unknown. Wake up and start thinking like a normal, fully functional human being which you are. Stop dwelling on what happens to you when you are dead. Concentrate on what is happening to you when you are alive at least for the future of our children, the unborn, and the generations to come. If you live right on this planet and there is an afterlife place for good people, surely you would be there. In that place called heaven, do you think the world would not shut the doors against you when they have shut the doors of life against you in the only world you know by not finding lasting cure for malaria, AIDS/HIV, genocides, neo-colonialism, and mental slavery that have ravaged the African continent? Know today, Africans, that heaven and hell if they do exist may all be here on earth, but let us not worry about where they are, let us develop our creative abilities so as to protect our future. Out of laziness, idleness, ignorance, and poverty, we have chosen to die so as to spend the rest of our eternal lives in heaven, a place they say we would enjoy all that we could not enjoy while on earth. False religious institutions are busy strengthening these beliefs in our minds while their originators are busy plundering our natural resources, building spaceships, going to the moon, and exploring other planets in search of other forms of life and civilisation. They are doing all of these things while diverting our attention to a sky heaven, making us build castles in the air. They are also making the African continent a dumping ground for foreign goods engineering economic slavery and over depencence on imported goods in Africa

Religious institutions are making billions of dollars from impoverished African countries promising them heaven and sending those who do not believe in their teachings to hell. I am shocked at the amount of money being siphoned away to the Vatican bank from Africa every year through the Roman Catholic Church. What about the Anglican Church and other religious bodies? What about the new generation of churches that call themselves living churches fragmenting into pieces every day with the only agenda of siphoning people's money? They are taking our hard-earned money away from us in exchange for heaven and salvation. The use of the name of the Bible, God and Jesus Christ to steal from the poor is a huge problem demanding attention in Africa. I ask the world and I cry every day that I have run out of tears. Can the world please have mercy on Africa? We owe so much foreign debts that we may not be able to pay until eternity. The world is looting African resources every day. The world stole African children to build most great nations; the world is selling AZT and many other anti-retroviral drugs in Africa instead of finding a lasting cure for HIV/AIDS; the world is selling all sorts of malaria drugs to Africa instead of destroying anopheles mosquitoes which cause malaria or engineering real cure for malaria and not treatment. The world is selling religion and God to Africa. The world is shipping billions of dollars overseas from Africa through the sale of false dreams, false hopesand God in the glorified name of salvation, when they cannot salvage our stomachs and our health. It is obvious today that new age churches in these present times have become banks; leaders of these churches have no slightest love for the people, and they do not even believe in God because by their actions we can see. They have become lovers of money, fame, power, and material acquisitions. They gather people together and infest them with twisted doctrines causing mental slavery.

Remember, men of the earth, the blood of innocent Africans spilt every day by AIDS/HIV, instigated wars, poverty, hunger, and starvation makes the spirit of Africa cry and the tears of Africa will continue to drop bringing curses upon this earth until the world removes their filthy hands and their mental slave chains from Africa.

The ozone layer is depleting every day, humans are becoming programs like robots as if driven by chips, family and moral values are collapsing completely, children no longer respect their parents, peace in families is gone into extinction, divorce rate is on the increase, yet man refuses to run away from his wicked ways.

What makes one think that the man who created the anti-virus of a computer does not understand or have a hand in the creation of the virus? And what makes one think that biological anti-virus creators do not understand the behaviour or have a hand in the creation of the same virus they are trying to fight? Who is fooling who?

Man in his quest for money, power, fame, and material acquisitions has veered below the level of a beast. Man has found no happiness amidst his wicked ways, yet he refuses to stop. Any man holding another man on the ground is holding himself and would only be free when he frees the man he is holding. Europeans must free Africans today, or he who is holding a pig begins to look like one.

It does not matter what false religious prophets preach and the fables and illusions they use to nourish their games. God is one and he is universal. Whatever you sow, you must reap one way or the other. I tell you today that the wind of change is around the corner. For all those Africans deployed to deceive fellow Africans, mercenaries of mental slavery, new age pastors, suicide bombers in the Islamic sect committing carnage in the name of Allah, you shall reap what you sow as traitors always pay in their own coins, and not even Judas of the Bible survived it.

Africa is great. Africa is the heart of the earth, but I am angry that the children of a great continent are acting differently. Considering the fact that they say that civilisation began in Africa, Africans should be the most advanced and civilised people in the world today, but look at what is happening.

Many people have said all sorts of things about me regarding my views, but I do not care for I speak from facts on the table. We must copy from the Europeans the real things which they truly possess and not the vain ones which they possess also. I must emphasise that I do not grovel to people, rather I speak my mind.

Granted that Europeans have proven to the world that they are wonderful people and have manifested the God in man by their creative resourcefulness, it must be known also that they play a lot of tricks on the minds of others. They use divide-and-rule tactics to achieve total control. Wherever they go, they align with the weak to conquer the strong. They have fixed their tentacles in Southern Africa to dominate the African continent just as it happened in Australia, New Zealand, and North America. They use mind and religious diversion to deceive others. Majority of them suffer from chronic selfishness, greed, and self-centeredness that sometimes I begin to wonder what they would do with all the wealth they are amassing at the expense of other people's lives, peace, and safety. They seem to be at war with every other person, and most of them are racist. They always ask you to forgive, but they believe in revenge.

Europeans live by enslaving others. They would encourage you to destroy your cultural and traditional values which they find unhealthy, but they do not want to destroy same-sex marriage, bestiality, and several forms of ugliness which you find unhealthy. They are oppressors and bullies when it comes to dealing with others, mostly Africans. They would always show the best of them on TV while exposing your griminess on the same TV. They will systematically make you a fool and call you a fool. They will applaud anyone who speaks great and wonderful things about them and will always frown at anyone who speaks the ugly truth about them. They welcome and praise singers, traitors, and hypocrites but will shut the doors at realists mostly if the matter in question affects them.

I implore Europeans to apply reparation, for it helps one to forgive and forget as memory is independent of will. I also implore them to deal with AIDS/HIV in Africa so that we could forget as it would be pointless to forget when something else may be happening under our noses which we do not know of. I implore Europeans to stop undermining the peace and happiness of Africans. I implore them to stop invading others, disrespecting them and their values, playing around with their lives, and making them and their generations forget all that was done.

Europeans have attained a state of technological superiority, hence I implore them to assist Africa if they can, as history had it that their ancestors learnt from ancient Africa the process of civilisation or if they cannot, let them stop looking down on Africans because if they did not come with violence, guns, and twisted religious doctrines, we would have been somewhere technologically superior, especially considering that the first scientist in the history of the world is an African. (Imhotep designed and built the first pyramid of Egypt and also Prof. Philip Emeagwali contributed immensely in the invention of the Internet that we know today.)

Europeans cannot find happiness when they supply arms to Africans to kill one another, while their primary motive is to loot their natural resources at the same time as it happened in Angola, DRC, and other African countries. You cannot find happiness when you are only interested in what you can gain from others without caring about what you could give back equitably in return. Europeans cannot find happiness if African Americans whose forefathers were enslaved in America are made to see Africa as a jungle and Africans as lower animals.

Europeans cannot find happiness when African nations are continuously ravaged by AIDS/HIV, poverty, hunger, and starvation while their natural resources are looted every day and all we get is a hope of an after-death 'heaven'—a heaven we can only go to when we die while they and their children occupy the earth. You cannot find happiness when you encourage Africans to wallow in faulty education while you have the power to change it. You cannot find happiness when all sorts of diseases are being manufactured and imported into Africa every day. You cannot find happiness when you feast on the weak like a prey. You cannot find happiness unless you start to put back into Africa at least to heal the wounds and pain inflicted on Africa and the children of Africa all over the globe. You cannot find happiness through excessive greed. You cannot find happiness by insensitivity towards Africans. I tell the Europeans that amidst all their greatness and material acquisitions, what is more important is peace of mind and happiness and all that could be achieved when they turn the clock around. I believe that they know what I am talking about.

We need to overhaul our thinking and education system completely. Europeans who came to Africa with their technology to harness our natural resources should realise that their technology without our natural resources is worthless, meaning that there must be equity and justice, but the reverse is the case, and in extreme cases, wherever resources are found, conflicts start amongst Africans, and civil wars start. This is inhumanity and injustice and must stop. (The case of DRC and the French people is a typical case.)

Europeans established the standards for right and wrong that live by today, but how come most of their wrongful deeds are not addressed? Is the concept of right and wrong meant to keep Africans under control? Is morality only for a so-called subjugate race? Does it mean those perceived to be the inferior race are subject to specific moral codes established by the so-called superior race to regulate their activities? Why the double standards and hypocrisy? Europeans are committing a lot of felonies in Africa and must be checked before they systematically transform us into cows in our lands, sometimes with stories of the afterlife, heaven and hell while plundering our natural resources. Europeans must stop all sorts of conspiracy plots and false propaganda used to manipulate and control Africans. They should stop helping us to go to heaven; rather, if they truly mean to help us without hypocrisy, they should help us restructure our academic system, develop our infrastructures and economies, design proper means of population control, and stop using short cuts (HIV and instigated wars); destroy mental slavery and also destroy the explosion of false religions which charlatans are using to steal from poor, vulnerable, innocent, and unsuspecting Africans.

Africans have been made to abandon the things of the earth. They have been made to abandon the resources of their lands and focus upwards unto the sky for heaven where there is no proof that oil, diamond, or gold exist. Rather the only proof we get is word of mouth from mercenaries of mental slavery, and on the contrary, the designers of these stories are busy looting our resources every day from the earth they have taken our attention away from. If the problem of mental slavery, faulty leadership, HIV and AIDS, poverty, hunger, and starvation is not eradicated from Africa soon enough, I bet you, we are prone for disaster.

The academic system in Africa polishes someone and makes him a refined slave and is not structured to spur creativity. There are many kinds of education spreading around Africa today, and we have to make sure that these kinds of education are channelling us to the Promised Land. If you want to go to America, you must board a flight heading to America and not the one heading to Australia. You must also be sure that the flight you are boarding is heading to America even if they write America on it. You must always scrutinise and ask questions to avoid being deceived.

Africans must know that the human brain synthesizes information, creates ideas, stores information as well as processes information and if a man created the microprocessor of a computer; if a man created a cell phone; if a man invented an airplane, that is evident enough that there are no limits to the powers of the human mind. Only we set limits to our own minds. We have by our own hands bestowed inferiority upon ourselves by completely denouncing our values, abandoning our heritage, and copying the wrong values from others, and now they perceive us as lower human beings. This is a wake-up call. Let us make this beautiful continent proud.

Is it not time that African Americans either get into a slave ship and return to Africa or stop complaining about their ancestors being enslaved in the past as the Irish people were also enslaved by their own European brothers? After all, without the same slavery, there would be no African Americans today. If you look deep down into this issue of slavery, you will find out that apart from what Europeans are doing to Africans in terms of religious diversion, which causes mental slavery, Africans are also enslaving one another. Who does not know that there is widespread child slavery all around African villages? People of Calabar, in Nigeria, up until this present time still give out their children to strangers as slaves in exchange for money. Who does not know that there is child trafficking and child prostitution going on around Africa? Who does not know that there is child labour going on in Africa? Who does not know that even during the time the slave traders invaded Africa, there was also buying and selling of human beings in the African villages (case of King Jaja of Opobo)? If we know all of these, then we must not just blame only the Europeans, rather we have to blame ourselves also. I was also a victim of chronic child labour and child abuse in Africa.

Today, we still struggle to survive; we still struggle for quality leadership in Africa when others are thinking of cloning human beings in the laboratory and also joining their alien brothers in other stars. We struggle with mosquitoes and TB when Europeans have advanced science and technology beyond human comprehension. Our ancestors never saw the need for the changes we see today hence we are suffering the consequences of their ignorance. Is it not time for this generation to open their eyes to the changing times and dynamic world? Is it not time that Africans acknowledge the obvious fact that the fittest survives this New World Order? Is it not time that we abandon the vain lifestyles of others and copy their knowledge since it is said that they copied our knowledge during the advent of civilisation in Ancient Egypt? Is it not time that Africans find a place in their hearts to forgive the errors of their colonial masters who should also find a place in their hearts to compensate Africans for all the inhumanity and injustice of the past? Is it not time that Africans begin to copy the good values Europeans came here with and utilise that to improve the lives and future of Africans and also ensure that there are no more atrocities being committed against them that they do not know of? Is it not time that Africans learn today that united we stand, divided we fall and that any house divided upon itself will never stand? Unity is strength.

Is it not time that fake witch doctors concentrate on herb business and stop throwing bones in this jet age and stop predicting lies to people? Is it not time also that Europeans realise that same-sex marriage is not an African thing; rather, we have problems that need attention. We are plagued with AIDS/HIV, hunger and starvation, bad leadership, false religions, and mental slavery. Today I challenge Europeans to prove their love for Africa. Today I also challenge all Africans who are of European descent to prove to indigenous Africans that we are united in one spirit irrespective of different roots and that there is no hidden agenda (like the dominating of the Australian continent and the takeover of America from the natives of India by the British and other colonial allies). If any man born in Africa is an African, then let us collectively rebuild the continent of Africa.

This is the time to move forward in Africa, a time for Africans to unite to pursue common goals, one which is the development of our great continent where civilisation began. Is it not time that our leaders start seeking solutions to the plights of the poor? Is it not time that our leaders start looking inwards to fashion out which way forward for Africa and stop amassing wealth and dumping them in nations where such wealth adds no value to the African continent? Is it not time that Africans start learning to appoint for themselves visionary leaders, men with genuine love and respect for themselves and the people, men who are ready to render selfless services and not men who do not know that a leader is actually a servant and not the opposite? Is it not time that African leaders know that politics mixed with tribalism results to total disaster? Is it not time that Africans learn that civilisation has come to stay and that it may have begun in their own continent? Is it not time that Africans know that the true one universal God is scientific and logical in his ways and also that the world is scientific and science and technology has given birth to the advancement of civilisation? Is it not time that Africans learn that if God be God, then he would definitely be one God for all human race; he would be of no race, gender, religion, tribe, or nationality. The world is laughing at us today because we import 'Gods', languages, food, lifestyles, culture, identity, education, and almost everything.

Is it not time that African leaders learn to invest in science, technology, and research to enable us harness our available natural resources to sustain our lives and protect our future? Is it not time that Africans destroy all doctrines that do not add values to their lives, doctrines which contaminate and enslave their minds? Is it not time that Africans foresee the changing trend of events in the world that if nations like Afghanistan and Iraq were under attack, then no place in Africa would be spared if 'they' see the need to. The serious and urgent need for true African unity and to emancipate Africans from mental slavery has been identified by concerned Africans, and this non-violent war against mental slavery is going on as you are reading this book.

We live in times when humans are becoming more of robots with no feelings, when artificial living is dominating natural living in the name of modern living, when individualism has been misunderstood as insensitivity. Africans have to wake up today, for we do not know who the next Hitler will be. We do not know which other deadly diseases worse than HIV are being 'manufactured' by scientists in the laboratories as we are fighting against the plague of HIV in Africa today.

Nobody came to this planet by accident, and we were not born into Africa by accident. We are all here for a purpose, and we all have to identify such purposes individually. Every man on this planet has a reason for being here. It seems that there are no reasons to some of us, because we have not taken time to seek, as Jesus Christ said according to the Bible, 'seek and you shall find', hence Africans must develop mental curiosity and begin to seek aggressively, for whatever you seek is waiting for you somewhere.

Thoughts give birth to ideas, and when the right actions are applied, ideas give birth to physical manifestations. Thought, ideas, actions, and their products are all interconnected. If Africans could understand this creative process, then we would be able to create our own mini-system to help us survive the harsh economic realities of today. We have chosen to bring genuine emancipation to the children of Africa all over the globe, to bring true empowerment of the mind, to destroy all forms of illusions and false hopes which have militated against the growth and development of the African continent, and to enable Africans appreciate the fact that evidence and facts rule the strong and wise, while illusions and beliefs rule the weak and ignorant.

The revelation of truth liberates men from bondage. The business of the universal God with the dead has not been revealed to any man. No man has seen God, and nobody is definitely sure if any man shall see God hence let us dwell on the events of this life and not that of the afterlife, for if one lives right and accomplishes his task on earth while alive, there will be no need for fear of where he goes when he dies, as I believe that fear of the afterlife is only for those who live negative, unaccomplished, unproductive, and fruitless lives.

This is truly a wake-up time for Africa. Mind over matter, all powers exist within. Deep in the innermost layer of the subconscious mind inhabits this power. We all have the power. From birth, the seed of creative intelligence has been sown in us. We are underutilising these powers because of the lack of understanding, laziness, mind slavery, idleness, ignorance, and the lack of creative thinking. The world is slowing down our minds the more because of what they stand to gain from our ignorance and stupidity. If we develop today, the world will lose a market. But men must know today that in this game of life, there are no losers and there are no winners. But let this not be misunderstood by Africans as we must positively strive to create wealth and riches to be comfortable. We must also positively strive for fame and power as they are perfectly good for a human being, but let these not be pursued with aggressive animal fortitude.

Africans must know that in as much as we shall all depart with nothing when we die we must think about the future of our children and generations to come, hence the process of building a better future for them should be the cause of our visit to this planet as Europeans, Asians, and Americans are doing. So if one thinks that he does not know why he is here on this planet, then I think he may have found a perfect reason now. We are here to make this place a better place for us, the unborn, and the generations to come. We are here to serve humanity—to work for humanity and not against humanity. We are not here to strive to go to heaven or hell after death.

An average European could put his creative mind to work any time because they have conquered their basic needs, but today, an average African is always thinking about basic needs (food, sex, procreation, shelter, health, etc.), and that kills the creative energy that dwells in everyone. When you conquer your primary needs, it becomes easier to conquer your secondary needs. Let us help our children conquer their primary needs so that they can develop the capacity to protect the future of this continent.

I must tell Africans that no one will help them but themselves, so this is a wake-up time. Anyone who thinks that he has failed in life let him rise today, for there is no failure in life. Anyone who thinks that we have lost the battle, let him rise, for there was no battle announced in the first place that we know about. Now we know of a secret battle: a battle of survival of the fittest, a secret battle of dominance. Let us rise and fight like others by being creative; let us first of all unleash a fierce battle against mental slavery; let us remove the blindfold so that we can see clearly; let us copy like the Chinese and if possible clone technology.

If Moses felt that there was no future for the Israelites in Egypt and that it was time for the Israelites to be free from slavery and he led them out of Egypt to Canaan as we were told, is it not time that African Americans, Africans in the Caribbean nations, indigenous Africans in foreign countries, and indigenous Africans in Africa collaborate in spirit and begin to free themselves from mental slavery which is the Egypt of our time? Is it not time that we stopped washing plates and dead bodies for a living abroad and look for Moses to liberate us from the shackles of mental slavery? Behold the Moses of our time, behold the liberation chant ! To all children of Africa all over the globe, behold, the time for change, behold, the wind of change, behold, the era of mind revolution, behold, the era of creativity in Africa, behold, the era of development and civilisation of the entire Africa, behold, the era of religious freedom. Today we fight a greater war: mental slavery! God bless, Africa, God heal the world.

RACIAL DISCRIMINATION: THE FALL OF MAN

There are no clear-cut facts and evidence to establish how man evolved or how man was created; also how humans from different continents developed varying physiological features has not been unravelled conclusively. Some claim that human life began somewhere in East Africa, and as man moved outwards, weather and other environmental factors he was exposed to as he migrated outwards modified his features. Others claim that man was created in the Biblical Garden of Eden yet they have no factual clue as to where that garden is located in exactness. If humans were created in a particular location whereby two people, a man and a woman, were created, there cannot be a reason for physical differences except if those differentiating traits are embedded in the human gene. These differences have given birth to racism and subsequently racial discrimination. We shall be dealing with racial discrimination in this context, which is the real problem of man resulting to racial crimes but not racism. Naturally, humans have developed seemingly varying physical features like skin colour, physiognomy (facial construction), and more; also behavioural and cultural variations have evolved in man and it seems as if racism cannot be put aside in human existence. It seems to be a form of natural occurrence. For this context, we need to establish whether there is naturally a superior race and an inferior race and if not, did man create these notions making some race put a tag on themselves as a superior race and others made to feel inferior. We also want to know the fate of those born by the coming together of different races like the 'coloured' or half-casts of South Africa. Do we rule them out of the human sphere since most races are not agreeing in the concept of human equality?

The greatest problem man faces today on this planet is an ideological belief that some humans are superior to the others by race, class (royals, the rich, etc.), religious creed, tribe, and gender – a belief that says differences amongst the various human physiological and sociological features determine cultural or individual achievements, hence instigating the notion that one is superior and has the right to rule the other, also sometimes creating hatred or intolerance of another. Human discrimination against one another has various faces, namely, race, tribe, religious creeds, gender discrimination, age discrimination, health discrimination, class discrimination, etc. We seek to know to what degree humans have to tolerate all of these various forms of discriminations. Of all of the discriminations that are seemingly inherent in man, the one that will feature well in this context is racial discrimination as it has made the world look like a dog-eat-dog jungle.

The Caucasian race who chose to be called whites all over the world has assumed racial supremacy over all the other races of the world. They have positioned themselves as a superior race and in doing so have also ended up exhibiting segregation, subjugation, apartheid, and racism to other races. India is also a country that experienced class racism in the past. Other forms of discrimination exist in African tribes where tribalism thrives. In Kenya, for instance, the Maasai, Kikuyus, Luo seem to have problems in coexisting; in South Africa, the Xhosas, Zulus, Twanas also have minor tribe issues here and there. Nigeria experiences strong problems of tribalism and tribal marginalisation. The Hausas, Ibos, Yorubas seem not to coexist as one people; hence, marginalisation at all levels thrive. Religions of the world exhibit discrimination and intolerance that has led to wars and other ugliness that I wonder if they are not serving the same God – xenophobia in South Africa, the rich discriminating from the poor, the healthy discriminating from the unhealthy. Leprosy victims suffer from discrimination and people with known contagious diseases suffer from chronic discrimination from the public, even to an extreme case, isolation. The good-looking are discriminated from the ugly. Those of the upper class discriminate from those of the lower class. There is a lot of discriminations that has developed alongside with human evolution. Discriminations seem to be inborn in man, but we need to know to what extent humans can tolerate certain social problems leading to discrimination that seem natural.

Racism is the ideology that humans are divided into separate and exclusive biological entities called 'races'. This ideology entails the belief that members of a race share a set of characteristic traits, abilities, or qualities; that traits of personality, intellect, morality, and other cultural behavioural characteristics are inherited; and that this inheritance means that races can be ranked as innately superior or inferior to others. Some definitions would have it that any assumption that a person's behaviour would be influenced by their racial categorisation is racist, regardless of whether the action is intentionally harmful or pejorative. Other definitions only include consciously malignant forms of discrimination. Racism and racial discrimination are often used to describe discrimination on an ethnic or cultural basis, independent of whether these differences are described as racial. According to the United Nations convention, there is no distinction between the terms racial discrimination and ethnic discrimination, and superiority based on racial differentiation is scientifically false, morally condemnable, socially unjust, and dangerous, and there is no justification for racial discrimination, in theory or in practice, anywhere.

In history, racism has not only been a major part of the political and ideological underpinning of genocides such as the holocaust, but also in colonial contexts such as the rubber booms in South America and the Congo and in the European conquest of the Americas and colonisation of Africa, Asia, and Australia. It was also a driving force behind the transatlantic slave trade and behind the states based on racial segregation such as the USA in the nineteenth and early twentieth centuries and South Africa under apartheid. Practices and ideologies of racism are universally condemned by the United Nations in the Declaration of Human Rights. Racism involves the belief in racial differences, which acts as a justification for non-equal treatment (which some regard as 'discrimination') of members of that race. The term is commonly used negatively and is usually associated with race-based prejudice, violence, dislike, discrimination, or oppression; the term can also have varying and contested definitions.

According to the United Nations Convention on the Elimination of All Forms of Racial Discrimination, the term 'racial discrimination' shall mean any distinction, exclusion, restriction, or preference based on race, colour, descent, or national or ethnic origin that has the purpose or effect of nullifying or impairing the recognition, enjoyment, or exercise, on an equal footing, of human rights and fundamental freedoms in the political, economic, social, cultural, or any other field of public life.

In the course of writing this book, I visited an African country in West Africa, name withheld, a country with more than 250 tribes experiencing the ugliness of tribal marginalisation, a country where capitalism-driven colonialism brought all the tribes together as one country. The country also harbours diverse religions including Islam, Christianity, African traditional religions, and more. Christianity in the country has numerous denominations. Gender equality is not talked about in the country, and age discrimination is the order of the day. Religious crisis erupting all the time because of members of an Islamic sect fighting for the reinstatement of the sharia law and the use of suicide bombers to carry out brutal carnage has become the norm. A civil war which saw a tribe defeated and subsequently marginalised brought the country into a state of paralysis, with a system that has almost collapsed, ushering in an era of corruption and chronic inequality. Tribal marginalisation is the order of the day. I left this country because I became allergic to mosquitoes and also due to the fact that the system collapse in the country engineered a corrupt and selfish wealth-craving political class that milked the country yet could not fix electricity problems in the country. The sight of mosquitoes could send me to the hospital even if I do not have malaria. I had to leave the country in search of a more environmentally friendly place to live where I will not experience religious intolerance, tribalism, xenophobia, racism, gender discrimination, and age discrimination, but I found out that my dreams may not be actualised as it seems discrimination is human nature.

At the point of departure from that country, someone who obviously could see that I was in a hurry to leave asked me why I was leaving the country, and I told him that it is difficult to exist in a land where everybody discriminated from everyone, leading to a situation of system collapse and to widespread corruption – where the youth have no jobs and hence they have made crime a profession, where parents send out their children into the wild to go and bring wealth home no matter how they go about it, where morality has been buried and hypocrisy has become a norm, where politics has become a moneymaking business and people no longer have common sense, where businessmen who have no understanding of leadership sponsor their friends into the seat of government to bring returns and profit, where 'god-fatherism', nepotism, sycophancy, man-know-man, and a lot of ugliness plague the seat of government, where seniors who should be role models to the youth are a bunch of criminals and law breakers, a country where God is sold for money, where churches have become banks and market places, a country whereby secret cult political cabals manipulate, brainwash, or better say use Muslim fanatics to massacre Christians in the name of instituting sharia laws while the ulterior motive is to make the country ungovernable by the ruling class. I told him that the only thing that can make a sane person stay in this country is if there is a hope for a change force towards the positive, but of course there is none but a force leading to collapse and possible crisis that will result in the splitting of the country into fragments. Everything is constantly drifting progressively towards the negative, and everyone seems to be happy with it. The country is collapsing, electricity has almost become extinct, industries have all vacated, and of course, there are no indigenous industries. It is a country where their role models are hardened criminals and members of secret cult cabals, where lunacy and idiocy is a norm, where the police are so corrupt and in connivance with criminals. I was saying all of these with so much anger that the man asked me to move on.

As I was about to hand over my passport to the immigration officer, someone else from his tribe waved at him and flagged him to proceed; this guy bypassed the queue and went straight to him, and he attended to him, abandoning everyone in the queue. I tried to alert everyone in the queue as to why such ugliness should prevail; unfortunately, everyone in the queue was from the same country, so they said that such a sight was common and quite acceptable in the country. As if that was not enough, another woman carrying a baby from the church of the same immigration officer also waved at the officer, and he flagged her to come. She proceeded with her baby, and they were attended to. After that, they squeezed some notes into the immigration officer's hand and left. A police officer proceeded forward with his sister who was travelling, and she was attended to also. Luckily, it was my turn, and I was reluctantly attended to after a few arguments had ensued between me and the immigration officer regarding the ugliness that was publically transpiring in a government office. I arrived in South Africa in the morning.

I took time to understand what apartheid, racism, and xenophobia meant by doing an intensive study of the situation in South Africa and embarking on tours across most of the provinces in the country. In some provinces, you will discover discrimination happening between whites and blacks (racial discrimination); in others, you will see discrimination happening between tribes, and in the others, you will experience the same between natives and those that they call foreigners (African immigrants). I also discovered a different class of South Africans, who have assumed the name coloured and their discriminative tendency towards the natives and African immigrants and also the discriminative tendency of whites against the coloured. I found a few classes that are natives but prefer to exhibit features of whites, generally called coconuts. You see, in South Africa there is a general problem of identity crisis. You see, South Africa will be used as a case study of racism as it poses a serious problem in the African continent most particularly when it comes to the issue of who an African is. This is a country where segregation and marginalisation still thrive. An average South African wants to be perceived as European while still at one point trying to maintain his African identity. South Africans faced apartheid which was the invasion of the boars (descendants from Holland), not necessarily a form of colonisation but subjugation and displacement of the natives for land and natural resources. South Africa also faced British colonisers, but due to a conquest that resulted in a defeat of the

British colonisers by the boars, South Africa was left in the hands of the boars resulting in the creation of a government of apartheid system. That South Africa is a country of numerous forms of discrimination, and segregation is a result of the historic past. South Africa is classified as a rainbow nation because it seems to accommodate different races and nationalities yet not living in perfect social harmony, I must say. You can hardly walk into a place without smelling one form of discrimination or the other, making the country though beautiful seemingly uninhabitable.

Apartheid was about the geographical separation of people defined through laws. As these laws do not exist anymore, the question arises as to what extent South Africa, ten years after the end of apartheid, has found a common space' as a nation?

It was as a result of racism and racial discrimination that South Africa still remains a third world country and also the original natives of South Africa are suffering from poverty and other ugliness today. Racial discrimination is the fall of man. What I believe is that in a system of racial discrimination, a particular race will want to dominate the other, and Europeans have done this. They conquered the natives of America and took over their lands. They conquered Australia and New Zealand and took over their lands; they want to conquer South Africa but did not succeed completely. All I am saying is that racial discrimination must be put to an end now as all the atrocities committed in the past have been known to all, and no one will tolerate such a debacle on this planet any more. The so-called creation of the New World Order is just to scheme a plot to protect the interest (to a greater extent) of a race. The entire world must be careful. As I said, Africa will suffer more. Europeans are looking for land, people to enslave and rule, resources, and more; hence, racial discrimination is a tool they have used to justify their actions and deal with their guilt, but how long will the entire human race allow the ugliness of racial discrimination? Of course, we know that with time natural resources and land will become limited as human population is growing, but can mankind not design a new frontier of coexistence and manage the earth resources equitably for everyone rather than a particular race craftily trying to take it all? Take it or leave it, the New World Order on a higher level is a racial conspiracy plot that will favour a particular race and jeopardise the existence of the others who are less strong in this present time in human history.

We live in a world where the universal God's manual of human existence may be with us, but we ignore it and claim that in life there are no rules, yet we give rules to others to follow which we do not follow ourselves. One thing

I must say is that man has distorted so many orders in nature. Europeans have not given a clear-cut factual proof as to how humans evolved on the planet. They introduced the biblical creation and the Bible to Africans, yet they do not live by the biblical codes. They live scientific lives. They see nothing wrong with that, having enslaved the Africans mentally, making them live low lives, and calling them low human breeds. There are no reasons in the first place for racial discrimination. You cannot discriminate, isolate, and marginalise a human being because of race. We have agreed that race is natural whether it evolved as man developed or while he migrated outwards from a central point of human creation, hence subjected to various environmental conditions. Europeans have not presented facts, but they have conquered lands of other races, plundered natural resources of other races, subjugated other races, brainwashed other races, enslaved other races, and done numerous ugliness that defies the tenets of humanity to other races. What we are saying is that there are no reasons that all of these should happen. South Africans are suffering in their land, economically marginalised and oppressed by those whose ancestors invaded the land. Until now, the issue of racial discrimination has not been resolved, and this has given birth to xenophobia which is actually economic related. The world must find a lasting solution to racial discrimination otherwise this planet will know no peace. China is growing stronger every day, and if the issue of racial discrimination is not dealt with in time, this planet will face a third world war, a war of nuclear, biological, and chemical weapons, which will put an end to the human race.

On the 20 May 2008, during the heat of xenophobic hostility and violence in the Republic of South Africa, I wrote several articles which were published in the *Citizen*, *Tribune*, and *Sowetan* newspapers, encouraging Africans to see the need to destroy negative stigmas like tribalism, racism, and xenophobic violence in South Africa, which are prominent amongst the ill-informed and uneducated class. I made them understand that all of those stigmas are reflections of mental slavery.

I stated and I quote:

> Fear is an emotion just like any other emotion, but sometimes the extent to which one reacts to an emotion is what counts, as there may be damaging effects of one's reactions to an emotion; hence the emotion may no longer count but the damaging effects. Africans have to collectively fight the major worms eating up the African continent – worms like HIV and Aids, poverty, false religion and God abuse, and most of all mental slavery – and not to be distracted by tribal hate, racial prejudice, and self-inflicted fears like xenophobia. Xenophobia in particular is a diversion from the real struggle.

Africans migrating to other African countries should do so within the confines of the immigration laws of that country. African refugees should also follow the legal processes of establishing their status anywhere they go, and Africans must be constructively productive to the system where they are welcome, for a man who welcomes you into his land truly appreciates you; hence, African immigrants must not be threats to their fellow African brothers who welcome them into their lands.

Xenophobia is fear based, and I advise South Africans to destroy fear completely and start living. We must start thinking collectively as one people. Africa is a great continent, and as children of Africa, we must start learning to live with the reality that we are one, no matter how separated by nationalities and tribes we might be and no matter how we try to run away from that reality.

Fellow Africans from other nationalities living in South Africa, let us not forget the fact that South Africans have been through a rigorous struggle in life and need time to get rid of the psychological effects of the struggle; hence, we must pardon all acts of xenophobia against us and in as much as we must not necessarily get upset at this point in time when they call us foreigners. We have to let them understand that an Africans cannot be a foreigner in Africa. Africa is one. We must look into the brighter side of life, but cry unto the government of South Africa to ensure that South Africans are empowered both economically and in the mind to face the bigger challenges ahead. Our South African brothers who also lived in the rest of the continent during the struggle should not forget all of a sudden the collective labours of Africans all over the world and the collective labours of African heroes in the liberation struggle that gave birth to the 'new' South Africa which they enjoy today. We must learn to love and respect one another, and we must not abuse one another. We must not burn one another.

Leaders of African nations should start thinking and acting properly if they are actually working in the best interest of the people they lead. The humiliations suffered by children of Africa all over the world are becoming unbearable. Africans have suffered a lot on this planet, be it physical slavery, mental slavery, brain drain, HIV, poverty, hunger and starvation, and now becoming refugees and illegal immigrants in African countries. The government of South

Africa should also play a vital role in empowering South Africans economically and encouraging education in South Africa and at the same time give 'foreigners' opportunities to demonstrate their positive creativity so as to contribute to nation building and be a part of this great system.

The South African government should reduce alcohol consumption amongst the poor and uneducated class as they are vulnerable and prone to violence. Also African brothers who migrated to South Africa must start being part of the nation-building process by making constructive contributions to the nation. In that case, their presence would be consolidated and not be seen as a threat. Xenophobia is a reflection of mental slavery, no matter how you look at it both from the affected victim's angle and from the angle of the xenophobes themselves; hence, all of them need mental healing. I also believe that it is not wise for all Africans to converge only in South Africa in the name of African unity; if that aspect of African unity must make sense, then all Africans must then spread across the continent. Native South Africans must also migrate to other African countries and make such countries their home and not only Europe and America. African immigrants should not live in South Africa as oppressors, bearing in mind what South Africans have been through in the past and also numerous other struggles they are going through at the moment.

Those were my words and contributions in the days of xenophobic hostility in South Africa. I have embarked on the same struggle in Nigeria for political sanity and reform together with abolition of tribal hatred, religious intolerance, and violence in that country. I think it is time Africans realised that the world is beginning to think twice about our humanity by the way and manner we carry on with our life's affairs in and outside our continent. It is time that the entire human race fought racism. It is time that the entire human race understands the ultimate plot of the new world government.

Though I may not agree with President Robert Mugabe of Zimbabwe, but if the British people are one of the founding fathers of democracy, how come the queen of England is still ruling the country one way or the other? They are supposed to be role models of democracy, yet they still maintain a monarchy. How come Tony Blair wanted to run for the third term, yet they find such trends ugly if they happen in other countries most especially the third world country? I used to worry with the prolonged stay of Gadhafi,

Musaveni of Uganda, Robert Mugabe, Mubarak of Egypt and more, but I came to realise that my worries were based on opinions I formed from the democratic force that was sweeping across the world. But when I began to study democracy I found out that in reality there was no true democracy. I wondered how democracy can work for uncivilised people. Africans will always copy without proper understanding of what they are copying. Granted that democracy is a great political philosophy, but the question is whether such a political philosophy will work for uncivilised and undeveloped minds. The fundamental issue would have been to help underdeveloped and poor civilised people who suffer from hunger, diseases, and poor infrastructures to rise from that state at least to prepare a ground for true democracy. It is all about control and power.

I still believe that other qualified individuals including the younger generations should be given a chance to participate in politics, hence abolishing the 'sit tight' form of government. I also advocate for abolition of double standards and hypocrisy when it comes to international politics. But the most important issue is development of the African continent. I am not sure that America as a democratic force does not see that the queen of England commands more power than the prime minister of Britain, yet that office of the queen is a monarchy and totally undemocratic. Hence, how come the advanced nations go about other less advanced nations instilling democratic values when Britain still practices monarchy? Africans must be able to feed themselves. They must copy technology and science in its true and original context and take charge of their lives. They must embrace their heritage and appreciate their roots. They must begin to question everything that is happening around them, which is transforming them into guinea pigs of this New World Order. It is unfortunate that due to hunger, ignorance, and laziness, most Africans will choose not to agree with me that if the pharaohs did build the pyramid, if Imhotep was the first scientist, if the best plastic surgeon in the world is an African, if Philip Emeagwalli did play a major part amidst all odds in the invention of the Internet, and if Dr Ave Kludze is a top NASA scientist, then we can develop.

Sorry to say that Europeans love our natural resources and our lands, but it is evident that they are racist towards us. I will not use the word 'hate', but I will say they discriminate from us even when they forcefully occupied our lands without equitable arrangements, siphoning our natural resources against our will, sometimes with a slave tool that blindfolds us not to ever know what is happening. I have fought for racial harmony, but I have found out that it seems it will not happen since God himself created us to possess different skin colours and physiognomy and also God may have allowed some race to invade and occupy the lands and resources of other race. What I am fighting for is the cause of a human being who is rejected so as to stop seeking for acceptance and love but stand out and reclaim his dignity and identity by beginning to forge a future that will benefit him and his generations. Africans have tried to be accepted everywhere they are. They have tried to be loved, but it seems that their skin colour and their physiognomy will never be accepted; hence I say, a man who is rejected never rejects himself. Unite, reorganise, and begin to reshape your future.

In this book, I have dealt with the Zimbabwean situation carefully, separating the facts from all sorts of prejudiced notions, and I have asked the question as to why Europeans want Africans to be their servants, even in African lands if not for racial discrimination. I asked how a man could invade your house through the window with guns and slave uniforms, take all your belongings by force, and make you serve him in your own land if not for racial discrimination. I asked whether that person thinks you are a human being at all. I needed the answer to that question from the reader. You see, I have asked whether the pharaohs of Egypt did really enslave the Israelites in the past, accounting for why slavery of all forms seems to be a form of revenge or a form of human nature. Neo-colonialism, colonialism, slavery, forceful dominance, mental slavery, and economic slavery are all happening in Africa today, and they are mostly affecting those in the part of Africa that did not enslave anyone in the past; hence, I ask whether the story of pharaohs enslaving the Israelites was created to perpetrate a game of fraudulent possession of people from west, east, and south Africa, possessing their lands and natural resources, a conspiracy plot to achieve dominance. It is unfortunate that Africans, mostly the hungry souls and traitors in our midst, do not see these things. Most African leaders are conniving with the New World Order to perpetrate control of the African continent still by those who colonise us wrongly and forcefully. Most African leaders are puppets of the New World Order, and they have sold us and sold the struggle for African renaissance.

Who says that without the coming of European colonisers we would not have developed? How could numerous languages and culture develop in the past if we did not have natural intelligence? How can Europeans use racial discrimination to justify their atrocities and deal with their guilt asserting that some humans are better evolved than the others? This led to the destruction of African cultures, values, and economic evolution in the past. You see, we were created in Africa to adapt with the forces and natural condition in Africa. It is time that Africans begin to think of how to reshape their future and flea from a problem that will not end and also a problem that has almost transformed them into guinea pigs of the New World Order – a breed that will become extinct in time to come, an endangered breed.

Look at the African union for instance; look at NEPAD for instance. Sometimes you ask yourself what these organisations are doing in terms of unity, structural and economic development of the African continent that they speak about. Is the AU uniting to submit to the New World Order for control purposes or uniting as a force to fight for African renaissance? We need to restore the dignity and pride of the African child or else we stop breeding a generation of slaves and guinea pigs. Today we have Common Wealth of Nations, headed by the queen of England, but can you visit those countries that are members of this organisation and see how impoverished they are? I am not saying that the queen should develop those nations; rather, what is the essence of an organisation that members pay allegiance to an authority that will not care much about the welfare of members of those countries? Is it not just control, and control of what? The leadership of those countries, the land and natural resources, including the human beings in those countries. It is time that Africans woke up. Today, a disease that man created is ravaging the African continent, killing its children, and drugs that are more dangerous than the diseases itself are sold to Africans. Africans cannot even make any drug to cure any disease. We are full-blown guinea pigs of the New World Order. We have mosquitoes hovering around. We can neither kill them nor invent drugs that cure malaria; rather everything comes from outside. I must state that in as much as I agree that without the colonialists destroying our cultural development, we would have developed, I have a problem with most Africans who are exhibiting features seemingly close to those of animals, not able to think and effect changes in their environment.

History has always shown that a few dedicated people are enough to effect changes and affect the course of a generation. We see examples as far as the biblical times such as Jesus Christ, Joshua, Nehemiah, Paul, David. We also see examples in our generation such as the great Nelson Mandela, Kwame Nkrumah, Julius Nyerere, Jerry Rawlins, Bob Marley, Haile Sllasie, Marcus Garvey, Martin Luther King, Malcolm X, just to name a few. Most African countries today are suffering and lacking in the midst of abundance. Our problem is certainly not lack of resources but rather poor management of the available resources, which arises from corruption and tribal and religious sentiments amongst other things, including mental slavery. Actually, there is hope for the African continent.

I am of the opinion and do strongly believe that Africa can arise from its current predicament, if only we can lay a solid foundation for development in African nations. I believe that we have all it takes to turn the ship called Africa around. But that is only achievable if we begin to genuinely invest in our youth, because they are the hope of any nation. Today, we like to run to countries that are doing well, but these countries started from somewhere. America's forefathers (George Washington, Abraham Lincoln) built their nations trusting in God, but beyond that, they gave their all and united selfless services to the growth of America. Another good example is Japan, whose forefathers might not have 'trusted in God', but they believed in themselves and sincerely worked hard for the success of their nation, and today it is counted as one of the wealthiest nations. With a determined mind, a persevering spirit, a united front, a culture of selfless service, and with trust in the universal God, we would lift this continent to where it truly belongs. It is quite funny to hear people speak of the better days, when everything (education, health care services, etc.) worked. This dates back to the 1960s and 1970s. The early years of our nationhood, our time of plentiful, should not be in our past but in our today; after all, even the Bible says, 'The glory of the latter, shall be greater than the former'. Why should ours as a continent be different? How can we then move our continent forward?

The future of any nation is in its youth, and it is time the youth rise up to the challenges of their time. They must take responsibilities now! Africa is our continent, and we can only move forward in truth and unity. We must shun the tribal, xenophobic, religious, and political sentiments we see around us! We are the hope and the future of the continent. It is true that our continent glorifies wealth, rather than patriotism, achievements, and commitments, and hence it is seen as an unforgivable sin to retire from public service without looting millions. Our continent truly lacks role models for our youth. Please do not get me wrong; they actually do exist, but because they do not have millions of dollars in Swiss bank accounts, no one acknowledges them. Yet we must live beyond these constraints. We must find ways to make the system work for us, and we must start doing those things now, instead of waiting till we get older. All of us cannot be the presidents of our countries someday, but we all can contribute from wherever we find ourselves by simply being faithful in the little things we are given to do. Our individual little contributions would one day result in a great change. We must be ready to do the right things, and we must be ready to stamp out the menace of corruption in our continent. However, it is a task that we must begin now. There's a saying that goes, 'The morning shows the day'. We can't live our lives the way we like and hope to be upright as leaders when the time comes. We have all it takes to move this continent forward. It is high time that we become patriotic and do our best to contribute to the growth of our continent. What we really need is for us all to re-orientate ourselves and change to a patriotic 'we can do it' attitude. My fellow youths, what is your dream for Africa in the next forty to fifty years to come? Have you started actualising these dreams or do you think you are too young or doesn't it concern you? Don't forget history would place our generation somewhere. What would the unborn generations coming after us think of us all? Yes, we can have good roads, constant power supply, good infrastructures, portable water, sound education; all we need to do is for each and every one of us to stand up and be counted in the new generation of patriotic youths of Africa.

I am an African, and that can never change, no matter how I try to be like others who do not want to be like me. Since it has been proven with facts that Europeans copied and improved civilisation from ancient Egypt during the beginning of modern civilisation, nothing stops me from copying creativity from them.

It is time that the youth of Africa run away from scarcity mentality, a mentality of lack in the midst of abundance. It is time that the youth of Africa run away from crime, for it is a negative application of creative energy, and the results thereof subsequently attract negative consequences, for life is cyclical; whatever you sow, you reap. It is time that the youth develop entrepreneurial spirit, acquire skills, and develop talents to conquer the harsh economic realities of the day. It is time that the youth adopt health caution as AIDs is no respecter of anybody, whether it is a natural disease, a curse from 'God', or a capitalist manipulation to extort money from the blood of poor innocent Africans and regulate their population.

HIV virus has come to kill, and it seems as if it is killing more of Africans, making it look like a tool of dominance. HIV is a dehumanising virus, a tool of the so-called 'Antichrist', a virus which destroys the immune system, a direct enemy of life. Today we must wage war against HIV, at least for our children and generations to come; we must stand up on our feet today and face the challenges we meet, for posterity will place judgment on our heads, having brought them into this world when they did not ask or beg to come with no provisions or plans for their future and well-being. We are economic slaves in this New World Order, and we know it; yet we still want our children and children's children to inherit the same stigma by not doing anything about it.

It is time that we say enough is enough to poverty, alcohol, drug and sex abuse, and mental slavery.

Brain Drain of African Intellectuals.

It is shameful that up till this present time in human history, Africans still import God, food, religion, culture, lifestyle, education, languages, and identity. We have nothing to call our own. Is it not time that someone starts thinking, or must we all remain mental slaves and guinea pigs in this only world we know? The world is trying to prove a theory that some people are more human than the others, yet Africans do not notice this. This is the time for Africans to begin to produce what they consume and also to consume what they produce to be free from economic slavery. This is the time for Africans to begin to invest in their youth to secure the future just like the other continents are doing. This is also the time for Africans to develop mental curiosity to be free from mental slavery. This is the time for Africans to know that God is either for all or for none. Africans must know today that no matter how long they cry over the treatment they receive from the world, nothing will change unless they start finding themselves 'in' the system and not just 'with' the system, for the fittest survives this New World Order.

Many great African leaders are well known around the world, including Nelson Mandela, Kwame Nkrumah, Steve Biko, Menelik (II), Haile Selassie of Ethiopia, and Julius Nyerere, just to name a few. Africa's contribution to leadership philosophy has also been remarkable, starting from the days of Zoser, the best pharaoh who built the first pyramid in Egypt, one of the greatest wonders of science and civilisation. Today, a new wave of leadership in the African continent amongst other factors is responsible for the underdevelopment of the African continent. They are underperforming, amassing power unto themselves, siphoning the resources of the continent to Swiss banks, corrupting their people, and virtually having no developmental goals to achieve in their respective countries. In most cases, they are puppets of colonial and neo-colonial arrangements.

Militocracy, a transformation of ex-military servicemen into democrats possessing 'military mentality' in most African countries, has achieved nothing, but renders the countries impoverished, favouring only those who engineered it. An example can be taken from the case of Nigeria, which they say is the giant of Africa, yet the only visible proof of this giant status is abundance of poor people and natural resources, which does not benefit the overpopulated ordinary citizens of that country. Apart from that, the transformation of politics into a moneymaking scheme, spearheaded by a group of inexperienced, unqualified political cabals and Mafioso, secret cult members, has drastically impaired development in the African continent in general. They create a cloud of political prostitutes, sycophants, praise singers, propagandists, and 'nepots' who assist them in perpetuating their agenda. This group of people has virtually nothing to offer to the people. They are there for selfish motives, perpetuating their stay in power, ensuring that senior members of their cabals or puppets succeed them when they 'step aside' after amassing sufficient loot so as to not expose their loot and atrocities while in power. This group of people undermines the yearnings for infrastructural development, economic development, and improvement of the standard of living of the people in their country. They engineer the proliferation of false religions and weak reverse education, which achieve nothing but mental slavery, enabling them to slow down the ability of their subjects to think rationally and question incompetent leadership and atrocities in the country. They are ever ready to destroy and deal ruthlessly with any individual, organisation, or a group of people who oppose or question their activities while in power.

Another breed of African politicians is the puppets and indirect appointees of past colonial regimes that existed in the continent. This group has nothing to offer to the people also; rather, they enhance the exploitative agenda of the past colonial regimes in the continent, favouring themselves also. They are there to protect the investments and wealth of the colonial regimes that left the continent and also amass wealth for themselves. Neo-colonialism still exists in the African continent. Up until this present moment, the past colonial regimes are facilitating the appointment of African leaders, whom they use to indirectly administer the affairs of African countries, enslaving the people mentally, economically, and politically and deploying false religions and weak reverse education that impair creativity and development. In the process, they plunder the resources of the countries in a manner not obviously visible to the ordinary eyes. Unfortunately, colonialists who invaded the African continent in the past came along with their military might, which they used to subjugate the tribes in the continent. At the end of their exploitations, they left and handed over power to an indigenous military force which they developed in the continent, and this force, instead of protecting the people and the continent, looted the resources of continent and also oppressed the people.

The military in the Western world protects the people, their leaders, and their countries. They take orders from their leaders, but the reverse is totally the case in the African countries where colonialism took place, and from all indications, it seems as if it was a calculated attempt for the colonialists to use those forces to keep the continent in check, having claimed that we are the conquered people. These colonialists and imperialists will not stop at any length to destroy any power or regime in the African continent which opposes their indirect exploitative tendencies in the continent but will gladly support any regime that favours their activities and their interests. A lot of instigated wars have taken place in the continent. Civil wars especially have resulted in genocides, and while the wars are going on, our rich natural resources make their ways to the Western world. Who does not know that the wars going on in DRC have something to do with their rich natural resources since DRC has been found to be the richest country in the continent due to their rich natural resources? Look at the entire African continent generally, and you will get a clear picture of what is being stated here. If African people embrace their heritage and take charge of their lives today and begin to produce what they consume and also consume what they produce, there will be no market for foreign goods; hence Europeans, Asians, and Americans are making every effort to see that we do not achieve political and economic freedom while at the same time they blame us for not doing so. Who will save our continent? I am glad that Barrack Hussein Obama acknowledged in his trip to Ghana that only Africans can save the continent and no one else.

In the past, we suffered from slavery and human trafficking which took place in West Africa, resulting in the development of America and Europe that we know today. Granted that colonialism returned civilisation back to the African continent where it originally began, it also enslaved the African people further. Colonialism is another form of slavery, in which case the continent was divided into colonies belonging to France, Britain, Portugal, Spain, and Italy for the sole intention of acquiring their lands and natural resources. When a wave of resistance sprang up in the continent, another form of colonialism, neo-colonialism, surfaced.

Today, another form of slavery is happening in the African continent, which is far more dangerous than the others. This type happens in the minds of the people, and the weapon used is information. Mental slavery is gradually reducing Africans to a level of lower human species and also transforming the continent into a guinea pig and a slave continent. This is the time of awakening in the African continent. This is the time for Africans to be free from the clutches of mental slavery fuelled by false religion, reverse education, weird traditions, and superstitions. This is also the time that the Western world liberates Africans from political and economic slavery. This is the time if Africans cannot concoct their own ideas or innovations, then they begin to copy science and technology in their true and original context just like Asians did, so as to develop the continent. This is the time for Africans to begin to invest in their youths so as to secure the future. This is the time for Africans to embrace their heritage and take charge of their lives.

Human capital flight, more commonly referred to as 'brain drain', is the large-scale emigration of a large group of individuals with technical skills or knowledge. The reasons usually include two aspects which, respectively, come from countries and individuals. In terms of countries, the reasons may be social environment (in source countries: lack of opportunities, political instability, economic depression, health risks; in host countries: rich opportunities, political stability and freedom, developed economy, better living conditions). In terms of individual reasons, there are family influences (overseas relatives and personal preference: preference for exploring, ambition for an improved career, etc.). Although the term originally referred to technology workers leaving a nation, the meaning has broadened into 'the departure of educated or professional people from one country, economic sector, or field for another, usually for better pay or living conditions'.

Brain drain is usually regarded as an economic cost, since emigrants usually take with them the fraction of value of their training sponsored by the government or other organisations. It is a parallel of capital flight, which refers to the same movement of financial capital. Brain drain is often associated with de-skilling of emigrants in their country of destination, while their country of emigration experiences the draining of skilled individuals.

The term 'brain drain' was coined by the Royal Society to describe the emigration of 'scientists and technologists' to North America from post-war Europe. Another source indicates that this term was first used in the United Kingdom to describe the influx of Indian scientists and engineers. The converse phenomenon is 'brain gain', which occurs when there is a large-scale immigration of technically qualified persons. There are also relevant phrases called 'brain circulation' and 'brain waste'.

Brain drain is common amongst developing nations, such as the former colonies of Africa, the island nations of the Caribbean, and particularly in centralised economies such as former East Germany and the Soviet Union, where marketable skills were not financially rewarded.

The absence of opportunities at home and growing demand for skills abroad has turned the African 'brain drain' into a flood. Lack of development in African countries caused by poor leadership and poor management of African resources resulting in poor capacity building has drained the African continent of its vibrant intellectuals, and this calls for serious concern.

During the build-up to the G8 Summit in July 2005, perhaps no group of Africans felt (or should have felt) more humiliated and distressed than 'brain drain'/diaspora Africans (BDDAs) residing in rich countries, as Africans were sometimes depicted in the international media, usually with disturbing and depressing video images, as unfortunate, helpless, incompetent, starving, wretched, and pitiable people who cannot do much for themselves. And, of course, many African leaders have continued to engage in the destructive behaviours that perpetuate Africa's dismal image as a continent that is pathologically prone to obscene violence and serial eruptions of conflict and wars in one country after another. There is also increasing scepticism that more aid from rich countries will have a substantial impact on African progress, in light of the unique nature of the so-called 'African predicament'. Obviously, whether or not the G8 and other rich countries choose to provide more assistance to African countries, it is ultimately incumbent on Africans themselves to ensure that their leaders judiciously utilise whatever resources their countries have, however meagre, to alleviate poverty as much as possible.

As often noted, such judicious management would prevent the need for aid in many countries, especially resource-rich ones that should never have needed to beg for aid handouts in the first place. It would also prevent much of the (often man-made) strife and humanitarian crises and the associated gruesome, haunting, and humiliating images of the continent, which are broadcast on TV screens worldwide.

Surely, if accomplished BDDAs (Brain Drain Diaspora Africans) previously lacked strong motivation, the global humiliation of the continent in 2005, which clearly did not seem to bother many African leaders, whose priorities continued to be to consolidate power and amass wealth at the expense of the poor, should now galvanise them to become more proactive and do something about the continent's problems, especially with respect to leadership and governance.

As we have previously argued, Africans themselves have the ultimate responsibility for building leadership and governance capacity in their countries, with or without help from the international community. This is one area where Africans can take charge of their countries and destinies, and BDDAs are well placed to take the lead in this regard. To be sure, many diaspora African groups and individuals have successfully implemented several useful projects at local, community, sub-national, national, and continental levels. And of course, remittances of funds from diaspora Africans have had major economic impacts in their homelands.

However, while most diaspora Africans want to contribute to African progress, for a variety of reasons (limited resources and capacity, etc.), only a small fraction of them are actively involved in high-impact initiatives, which therefore remain largely small scale and of limited scope. Thus BDDAs' collective impact on African development has remained far short of what is potentially achievable if their resources were to be more effectively harnessed and leveraged.

In light of the limited accomplishments, the challenge for diaspora Africans is therefore to develop much more innovative and effective strategies for pulling their immense, but largely untapped, intellectual, technical, financial, and other resources and implement initiatives on much more substantive scales, in order to have much greater impact on African progress.

Diaspora Africans in Western countries are particularly well positioned to make substantial contributions in areas such as research, analysis, information dissemination, networking and partnerships, capacity building, training, mentoring, counselling, technical assistance, advocacy, etc. in their respective areas of expertise and interest. Examples of initiatives are provided at the end of this document.

With the numerous options made possible by modern information and communications technologies, implementing initiatives would require only short visits by BDDAs to their home countries, and this may not even be necessary in some cases. In other cases, especially where governments are oppressive, high-impact initiatives outside the countries would be more effective.

Furthermore, substantial financial resources may not be required—innovative use of technology at a modest cost can be highly effective for establishing strong global networks and for pulling intellectual and technical resources, which BDDAs possess in abundance. Of course, help from the international community, rich countries, foundations, and wealthy organisations and individuals would make a big difference by greatly boosting such efforts. For example, as we argue in another brief, a fund that provides substantial financing, through a highly competitive, purely merit-based process, for establishing top-quality, independent initiatives that focus sharply on transparency and accountability could become a powerful force for addressing the much-discussed governance problems in Africa. Most highly competent BDDAs, who have the requisite expertise but spend much of their time lamenting the failures of leaderships in the continent, would obviously jump at the chance to be actively involved in such initiatives with strong motivation and dedication.

In recognition of the substantial contributions BDDAs can make, African and rich-country governments, pan-African and international institutions such as the African Union/NEPAD, World Bank, and others have made numerous pronouncements about their desire to facilitate more effective utilisation of diaspora Africans' resources for African development. It remains to be seen, however, whether the African Union, the World Bank, the G8, and others will soon match their statements with substantive, large-scale, and high-impact initiatives that can have powerful transformational effects. Clearly, given the non-conducive political and economic climates and poor professional working conditions that persist in most African countries, and the resultant high economic and professional risks (and in some cases personal danger) involved, it is unrealistic to expect that most accomplished BDDAs will choose to relocate permanently to their countries any time soon, even when offered what may appear to be generous incentives. As in the case of the investment climate and capital flight problem, even in countries where governance is improving significantly, it will be several years before conditions are conducive enough for permanent return of BDDAs on a substantial scale.

Hence, permanent relocation efforts have had very limited success, and the need to think beyond the unrealistic approach of simply 'reversing the brain drain' in this way is obvious. NEPAD's Mboya, for example, acknowledges that most of these people cannot be brought back, but NEPAD is encouraging them to consider how they can make an investment back into the continent. We would like to see them participating in institutions in Africa for development or investing in business activities in the continent.

Efforts must therefore be largely focused on the 'diaspora option', i.e. more realistic approaches that do not involve permanent return. Examples of 'brain gain' or 'brain circulation' approaches are short-term education, training, research, capacity building, technical assistance, and other programmes (in science and technology, business, medicine, education, law, etc.), where projects might require short or extended visits to home countries. Many projects would typically involve active collaborations with counterpart professionals residing in African countries. 'Knowledge networks', 'virtual networks', 'virtual linkages', publishing, etc., which facilitate exchange of ideas, information dissemination, discussion groups, knowledge and technology transfer, capacity building, collaborations, advocacy, etc., all of these will continue to be made easier by advancements in Internet and other modern information and communications technologies.

Eventually, African governments and the African Union/NEPAD will, hopefully, come up with programmes that will enable them to effectively utilise diaspora Africans using these and other approaches. However, BDDAs do not have to (and should not) wait around for African governments or pan-African/ international organisations before they implement worthwhile initiatives, as many have done already using their own resources. In fact, independent, non-governmental initiatives are more desirable in many areas such as fostering transparency and accountability, developing exceptional young people with leadership talent into visionary and transformational leaders, private investment, etc.

Success in these areas where many initiatives do not even require BDDAs to be physically present in their native or other African countries will in turn help to foster better governance and efficient management of resources in critical areas such as education, health, infrastructure, etc. Ultimately, such contributions will lead to the creation of conducive political, economic, and professional work environments that will make many BDDAs decide to return permanently to their native (or other African) countries. In effect, BDDAs, most of whom would like to relocate permanently to Africa as quickly as possible, would be working to hasten their return if they pull their resources and utilise them to make their countries better.

In several areas, diaspora Africans are best positioned and best equipped to lead efforts in their areas of interest and expertise by virtue of their unique attributes—their geographic location: access, connections, and proximity to global political, policy, and financial power centres, for example, in Washington, DC, New York, and European capitals, advocacy on the Africa-related policies of the United States, European Union, G8, World Bank, IMF, etc.; facilitation of private investments, networks, partnerships, etc.; their demonstrated capabilities and expertise as highly accomplished professionals in very competitive professional fields and environments; their access to resources and knowledge networks that are not easily available to counterparts in their home countries; their multi-faceted knowledge and understanding of (a) their home countries' political, economic, social, and cultural environments and (b) issues and trends in their countries of residence and the global geopolitical and economic environment; their abilities to bridge differences; their ability to develop strong and effective professional relationships and collaborations with individuals, organisations, or teams of professionals in their native countries, based on connections and long-term relationships with former schoolmates, friends, relatives, etc., many of whom occupy top and influential positions in the public, private, academic, and civil society sectors; their strong personal, patriotic, economic, emotional, and psychological connections with their native societies, as well as their distress about slow progress in their countries and Africa's dismal image, which translate into a strong sense of responsibility, passion, and motivation to help alleviate poverty in the continent; their better knowledge of their countries compared to the foreign experts who are usually sent there at great cost. Most diaspora Africans with comparable professional qualifications would be willing to accept much less financial compensation for providing the same services, in light of the additional 'social return' they will get by contributing to their countries' progress and helping to create the conducive climate that will enable their permanent return.

While there are extensive analyses and documentation of the activities, performance, and impact of other (older, larger, or more developed) diaspora Asian, Latin American, etc., helping to foster progress in their countries, there is very little of such information on diaspora Africans beyond anecdotal reports.

Africa is the second largest continent in the world (only Asia is bigger). The continent Africa is divided into East Africa, West Africa, North Africa, Southern Africa, and Central Africa. Although Africa has an area three times that of Europe, its population of more than 400 million is only two-thirds of Europe's. Africa is divided into more than 1000 different ethnic groups. In all these groups, some of them have less than 100 members, and each has different languages, social customs, religions, and ways of life. In the past, the vast size of the continent and the geographical barriers, such as mountains, deserts, forests, and lakes, have tended to isolate groups of people from one another. Because of the isolation of one group from all the others, the people saw no need for a common language, and each group's language developed separately. Each group regarded the languages spoken by other groups as 'wrong'. Even today, some bushmen in the Kalahari refuse to believe that anyone whom they do not personally know can speak their language.

The total isolation of groups from one another began to end when the Arabs first crossed the Sahara with their caravans. The arrival of the Europeans, with their roads, railways, telegraph wires, and stem boats, further reduced the importance of natural barriers and distances. Despite the improvement in communications, the number of ethnic groups and dialects is not decreasing. Ethnicity, one of the major problems faced by modern national governments, has not disappeared with independence. The reasons for this can be traced back to the way of life of the people before the coming of the Europeans. The Tuaregs of the Sahara, the Masai of Kenya, the Steppes of Tanzania, and the pygmies of Zaire were all adapted to surviving in the harsh surroundings in which they lived. They accepted the hyenas, jackals, leopards, and lions as natural hazards which they had to live with, in much the same way that the people in the Western society accept the dangers of the motor car.

In the same way, they were either afraid of other people or they despised them. For example, the Bedouins of the desert still despise men who do not follow the austere life that they lead herding camels, hunting gazelles, and eating locusts. The Somali are feared as raiders by their neighbours in Kenya and Ethiopia. The Bantu-speaking people of Southern Africa once feared the Bushmen, who poisoned their wells and killed their cattle. Until the 1870s, the Kikuyu of Kenya sought safety from raiding Masai in the sanctuary of the forests. Even if they did not fear each other, each group regarded the others with suspicion. Even today, villagers are known to flee with their goods into the forests at the approach of government tax collectors.

Africa is still under-populated. In the past, any group of people who were oppressed, afraid, or merely overcrowded could leave one area and start a new life in another less densely inhabited region. This process has produced more than 1,000 languages in Africa over the years. As the process continues, languages split up into different dialects. When one group splits into two, it may only take two generations before the two new groups are speaking different dialects. As with languages, each group believes that its dialect is the correct way of speaking. Occasionally, a large ethnic group may absorb a smaller weaker group mostly by conquest. When this happens, the smaller groups will become bilingual (speaking two languages equally well). Most modern African states south of the Sahara enclose a large number of different languages within their borders. Many people would object to seeing any language other than their own becoming the sole national language of their country. For this and other reasons, many independent African nations are continuing to use the language of the former colonial power as their official language. More importantly, no African language, except Swahili, Hausa, and Malagasy, has an adequate vocabulary for technical and administrative purposes. Africa presents a considerable problem to students of social, cultural, and environmental behaviour, physical characteristics, and distribution of man. To study the people of Africa, scholars want to first classify them. The main factor which distinguishes the different ethnic groups from each other is the different languages. Distinctions of religion, economic life, and social behaviour are not precise enough for the purpose of accurate classification. Often people speaking one language show different racial features, while elsewhere people belonging to one racial group speak different languages.

While the people of Africa south of the Sahara are basically Negroid in racial character, many of them are of mixed ancestry. Some types, such as the pygmies of Zaire, have retained their racial but not their linguistic characteristics. The invasions of the Arabs in North Africa and, to a lesser extent, the Europeans in the South of Africa, have brought about a mixed racial heritage. For example, people in Ethiopia and Somalia show evidence of Arab ancestors, as do the Swahili in East Africa and the Fulani of West Africa. Few 'pure' Bushmen or Hottentots now remain. Most of them have mixed with the Bantu-speaking people. Madagascar, in spite of its isolation, is inhabited by people who have roots in Africa, Arabia, India, and predominantly, Indonesia. The coloured of South Africa are the result of inter-marriage between European colonists, Malays (from Asia who were brought into the country as slaves to work on farms), and Africans.

Africans practice many different religions. A few are monotheists, worshipping one high God as in Christianity or Islam. Others are polytheists, worshipping many gods. Some ethnic groups are spirit worshippers, some worshipping the spirits of their ancestors and make sacrifices to them. The sun, the moon, and the natural elements of thunder, wind, and rain are appeased with prayers and sacrifices. Some people claim to have mystical relationship with their totem animals—that is, they believe they descend from an animal ancestor. Animists believe that inanimate objects such as stones and trees are alive, and they worship the spirits which they believe live in them. Many people do not conform to any rigid religion or they practice a mixture of several. For example, some who call themselves Muslim will also worship spirits.

Africa is made up of many different environments—Savannah, woodland, forests, and so on. The people who live in the various conditions lead a way of life adapted to their surroundings. The Somali are nomadic herdsmen, wandering over the sparse vegetation of Somalia, southern Ethiopia, and northern Kenya with their cattle in search of grass. Where the land is more fertile, people live in villages and cultivate staple food crops, such as maize or cassava. The Nkundo of central Zaire live by hunting the animals of the forest, catching them with cunningly devised traps. People who live in the coastal regions often live by fishing, as do those who live near the great lakes and rivers. The fellahin (peasants) of Egypt carry on the same traditional farming methods along the banks of the River Nile, which are shown on the beautiful wall paintings in the ancient Egyptian pyramid.

As with race and religion, the economic ways of life of Africa cannot be divided into neat and tidy compartments. While some people do follow one occupation, such as cattle herding, to the exclusion of all others, most people combine different means of livelihood. Nearly all Africans keep goats in addition to whatever other animals or crops they may raise. Many people who grow crops also hunt. The economic way of life of a people is not only determined by their tradition but also dictated by the environment in which they live. Because the natural surroundings influence the economic way of life, it also influences the cultural habits of the people.

Our continent is the second largest continent on the planet with a population of almost half a billion. Our ethnic groups number more than 1,000; hence, we have more than 1,000 languages. Africa is rich in culture, but today we must understand it and try to create a balance between culture and civilisation. We must remain Africans but civilised people. Also strange and unhealthy culture and traditions in Africa must be abolished whether they are indigenous or imported.

Africans never felt any need for a common language because of the separation of the people from each other. In Africa, each group language developed separately and each group that saw others speaking different languages referred to them as different, but today Africans must realise that we are the same and also that united we stand divided we fall. Unity is strength. Let no one confuse this with the struggle to destroy political barriers and create one united Africa. Africans must develop a common African language today as a token of unity. Africans must rise up today, appreciate their heritage, and take charge of their lives.

Unfortunately, the African continent faces serious leadership problems. Mental slavery agreeably is the strongest worm feasting on the soul of the continent, but I must state that African leaders are in a way helping this worm to achieve its destructive goals. Most of them, in their selfish political ambitions, stir up violence in African countries, sometimes sacrificing the lives of poor innocent Africans while their own children are always abroad, living in large houses, driving luxury cars, and signing 'diplomatic business' documents.

It is time that Africans rise against bad leadership and ensure that they appoint for themselves visionary and creative leaders who will look after them and their interests and not puppets imposed upon them by the military and ex-colonial masters. Most African leaders are powerless puppets who only take orders from the West and have nothing to offer to their own people.

An African leader thought that AIDs was a result of hunger and poverty. I also thought that the strong anti-retroviral drugs are the real killers. Some say that fear and stress instilled in a victim's minds are the killers. Others say that immune-related diseases do the killing. Another told me that the needle that penetrates your body during the test period as well as the nurses, doctors, and the hospitals are that which transmit the disease because you have no way to know whether what they told you was made up or true. Some say a lot of things, but is it not better for African leaders to find out the truth about this monster virus called HIV and deal with it once and for all than assuming things? Is it not better for us to stop saying this and rather engage the right mercenaries to find out the truth about this worm? Is the world making so much money from the sale of HIV and malaria drugs rather than finding an everlasting cure for them? And why is it that our leaders are not doing anything about it, not even challenging the assertion that HIV originated from green monkeys in Africa? This and many more are what African leaders should find out. If Scientists have been able to visit the moon and landed their probe gadgets in mars, then with the level of scientific sophistication, man definitely is capable of finding a solution to HIV and AIDs. Africans both at home and abroad are major victims of AIDs all over the world and must rise and start a revolution against HIV or this king virus will slowly exterminate all of them from the face of this earth. It is beginning to look like a biochemical warfare, an instrument of dominance.

AFRICA AND SECRET CULTS

A secret society is a club or organisation whose activities and inner functioning are concealed from non-members, having a ritual of demanding a pledge of commitment and secrecy, prescribing ceremonies of a sacred character. Secret societies are institutions which absolutely hide their rules, activities, names of their adherents, signs, symbol, and codes from the rest of the public who are not initiated or who are not part of the organisation.

As a rule, the members of these societies are bound to the strictest secrecy concerning all the businesses of the association by oath or promise or word of honour, often under the threat of severe punishment in case of its violation. If such secret society has higher and lower degrees, the members of the higher degree must be equally careful to conceal their secrets from their brethren of a lower degree. In certain secret societies, the members are not allowed to know even the names of their highest officers. In those days and in most advanced nations, Secret societies were founded to promote certain ideal aims, to be obtained not by violence but by moral measures. By this, they are distinguished from conspiracies and secret plots which are formed to attain a particular object through violent means. Secret societies may be religious, scientific, political, or social.

A cult could be seen as a set of practices and beliefs of a group in relation to a local god. A secret cult could be seen as an organisation whose activities are kept away from the knowledge of others, or a group of people whose activities are carried out in exclusive locations and unusual times without being exposed to the uninitiated. These activities are essentially covert, disguised, and are usually carried out behind closed doors. I ask again as to what these cults and secret cults in Some African countries have done so far to promote African growth, development, and civilisation.

Some African countries are homes to numerous secret societies, cults, secret cults, and strange religious activities. InAfrica, most secret societies and cults have transformed into malicious institutions conniving and concocting atrocities against the people, the nation and also non-initiates who may be part of the society at large. Their activities range from witchcraft, voodoos, ritual killings and ritual sacrifices and occult practices. Secret cults now exist in institutions of higher learning in some African countries. During conflicts they kill fellow students and maim anyone who opposes them; they threaten and rape innocent women, steal from non-initiates, intimidate and extort money from non-initiates, catalyse rampage in schools, indulge in exam malpractices, and commit carnage in institutions of higher learning. It is time institutions of higher learning and the government of African countries did something about this ugly situation.

In America, you find numerous gangs amongst African Americans fighting over women and superiority. Of all that America has to offer, most African Americans have chosen to become gangsters instead of acquiring skills as a tool of capacity building and empowerment. I have decided to deal with these issues because from all I have observed, we Africans tend to exhibit narrow-mindedness and lack of great visions, and this reveals why we chase rats when our houses are on fire. To make matters worse, the world idolises gangsters. The world even makes idols out of gangsters, making an average African American crave to be one. At schools, most of them are involved in clandestine activities that involve killing, abuse of guns and violence. Nigerian institutions of higher learning house the worst-case scenario, where most of these cultists idle away their times by not attending lectures and wasting their parents' hard-earned money, and causing so much mayhem in schools.

We have numerous religious organisations, secret societies, and cults whose activities are similar in some ways and differ in some of their practices. I am concerned that something should be done about the proliferation of secret societies, cults, and false religious activities as they have no contributions to the growth and development of Africa. In fact, Africans should constitute structures which will be dealing with the realities of today, which is advancement in science and technology. It should be the one promoting creativity and human development in Africa as we are far behind considering the millennium development goals already set up by the world system. Most religious institutions in Africa are gradually transforming into cults with fear-based teachings that defy rational thinking. Superstitions, pseudoscience, Religious intolerance and the lack of religious freedom in some parts of the African continent have ended up diverting the attention of Africans from the reality of science and technology. I wonder how up until now Africans till import God and religions. Instead of fashioning how we can join the cue of scientific and technological innovations, Pentecostal churches are busy splitting into untold numbers and Islamic suicide bombers are bombers are busy keeling God seekers in churches and at the same times, taking their own lives.

Africa has close to fifty-two independent countries today and numerous independent tribes. Each of these tribes has its own way to practise religion. In tropical Africa alone, some 1,000 different languages are spoken, and in each language, there are many tribes and patterns of worship. Arabic, Swahili, Berber, Bantu languages, Zulu, Sudanic, Hausa, Xhosa are spoken, just to name a few. Many African countries, after their independence, kept as official also a European language, Christianity and Islam. A few others still held to the African ways of worship.

So many traditional religions are practised in Africa, and as there are many tribes and many languages, so also are there many religions. The Muslims and Christians changed most of African religion. But it is estimated that a lot of Africans still practise 'animism', often in syncretism with their new Christian or Muslim religions. My worry is how we can channel our beliefs to the growth and development of Africa. Other continents are developing and advancing fast in science and technology while we are advancing in religion, cults, and secret societies, yet we make more use of products of science and technology, even more than those who actually developed them.

Cultism has become a major social problem both within and outside Nigerian universities. The emergence of secret cultism has been characterised by some bizarre and violent activities which include physical torture as a means of initiating new members, maiming and killing of rival cult members, and elimination of real and perceived enemies. To effectively combat secret cultism, the universities must enjoy improved funding, recreational academic facilities must be improved, and virile student union activities must be encouraged. For the general Nigerian society, the present culture of violence in the society must be curtailed. All over the world, universities have often been regarded and referred to as 'centres of learning'. This also applied to the Nigerian universities until recently, when as a result of incessant secret cult activities, the centres of learning have become 'centres of violence and bloodshed'. From the universities to the polytechnics, colleges of education and other tertiary institutions and some secondary schools, come stories of violence, torture, and unwarranted intimidation executed by members of secret cults. Common observation reveals that many Nigerian newspapers and magazines have become 'bulletin boards' for reporting the daily exploits of members of secret cults. Unfortunately, despite all efforts to tackle the problem, secret cult activities in the African institutions of learning have defied all solutions.

The secret cult phenomenon is not new in Nigeria. Membership of these secret cults provides sources of status, economic, social, and political security only to their adherents. Hence there seem to be a relationship between the ones in the school and the ones outside school. The ones in the schools graduate to join the ones outside school. Today in Nigeria, tertiary institutions suffer the adverse effects of the activities of secret cults which have been characterised by violence and bloodshed.

Outside the school, people are attracted to secret cults by status, economic, social and political security, but on the scale of students in institutions of higher learning, they are attracted to cultist groups for a variety of reasons. Generally the social atmosphere prevailing in the Nigerian universities provides an inspiring environment for secret cults to thrive. These may include lack of virile student unionism, erosion of the traditional academic culture, absence of intellectual debates, and all other activities that are components of traditional campus culture.

Those who eventually enlist in secret cult groups might have been compelled to do so because of 'sagging egos' that needed to be boosted. Others join in order to have a sense of belonging and the need to be well 'connected'. Still others may join because of the need for financial assistance, to secure girlfriends or for self-protection. Some students are also attracted to cultist groups because they are seeking meaning, direction, comfort, and love. Secret cultism seems to have special attraction for youths who are emotionally disturbed and distressed. The youths, especially those from broken homes, destitute, and youngsters who have flexible minds easily fall prey to the entreaties from cult members. Youngsters who are lonely, depressed, dejected, disorientated, and frightened sometimes drift into the waiting arms of secret cultists. Apart from the categories mentioned above, there are some youngsters who join secret cults out of sheer curiosity.

A very important element in the mode of operation of secret cults is recruitment. Like any other social organisation, recruitment must occur so that membership which might be lost through graduation, rustication, or even death must be replenished. The recruitment exercise is closely tied to the willingness of students to become members of secret cults. Apart from some physical and emotional attributes, which have been referred to earlier, prospective cult members must—demonstrate the ability to use weapons, while ability to consume alcohol and use of drugs are added advantages. New recruits must also demonstrate some stoic abilities, especially the ability to bear pain. The initiation process commences immediately after new recruits have been thoroughly screened. The first step in the initiation process is swearing an oath of allegiance and secrecy. During an initiation ceremony, the eyes of the initiate are expected to be closed while some incantations are recited. New entrants are subjected to thorough beating as a means of toughening them and testing their endurance for pain. On the initiation day, the new entrants are made to drink some concoctions, sometimes mixed with their own blood. Sometimes they are given some tough assignments like raping a very popular female student or a female member of the university staff or even attacking a member of an opposition, sometimes killing him.

In Nigeria, the family influence has greatly receded; thus the average family has failed in its function to provide a solid moral foundation for children. Consequently, children are weakly prepared to resist negative peer group influences which they daily encounter in their interaction with others. Secret cult activities in higher institutions of learning in Nigeria today have become a major social problem. This problem, however, is a symptomatic of a society in a state of anomie. It is also an indication of other security problems simmering in the inner core of the society. As mentioned earlier, the problem of cultism is a symptom of society which has undergone total moral decadence and where institutionalised and personal violence has become a way of life, where brute force has supplanted vigorous intellectual debate and with a conspicuous absence of dialogue as a veritable element of conflict resolution.

Nigeria is a society where more money is yearly allocated to 'defence', to the detriment of social welfare for citizens and education. To successfully combat the problem of secret cults, some changes must occur both in the general society and within educational institutions. General education of the citizens on the corrosive effects of secret cultism must occur. Consequently, the society at large must fuse efforts to combat cultism. It is very necessary and urgent for the Committee of Vice Chancellors of the Nigerian universities to adopt a common and uniform approach to solving the problem of cultism. This approach would involve thoroughly investigating and finding root causes of the problem. It would also involve strengthening administrative powers to eliminate the scourge from the campus. It is necessary to reactivate, strengthen, and reinvigorate different student unions which would accommodate the interests of all students. Cultists are usually found among non-union members. Also, the issue of former cultists who sometimes return to universities as staff must be thoroughly investigated.

More emphasis must be placed on character building, responsible leadership, and citizenship. Incidentally, Nigeria, after wandering in a political wilderness for that long, seems to have finally found its bearing. Under the democratic dispensations, efforts must be made to strengthen the police and law enforcement agents to assure citizens of total security of life and property.

It is also hoped that the government would improve the funding of the education sector so that the universities again would return to their former glory where they would remain centres for debate of excellence. For all this to occur, the African governments need to have a moratorium on education. This would include a very thorough and objective examination of funding, admission policy, and the general welfare of students and staff.

Secret cults in general have not yielded positive results in the African continent considering all evidences on ground and the situation of the African continent at the moment. May be Europeans, the Jews and Americans did establish secret cults and secret societies to foster their interest but those found in Africa work against the people and must be checked. Today religion seems like a cult and we encourage the government of African nations to regulate religious activities and also encourage religious freedom and tolerance. It is time that Africans wage war against mental slavery.

AFRICA AND GOD

If a place called Garden of Eden does exist in reality and physically as most Africans from the Christian community believe and someone wrote about it, it means that the person may have seen the place. Such a place should be the highest tourist attraction in the world as of today, a place where the first man and first woman were created. How come modern man cannot identify such a place with exact precision? How could someone write about the creation of Adam and Eve who were created when he was not yet born since Adam and Eve were the first human creations? If this information was passed through him via inspiration then how do we know that he is truly inspired and also how do we know that such information is not either exaggerated or facts removed from it. Every information in the Bible as we were told are by God's inspiration.

Sometimes they do not allow us to ask questions when information is not clearly understood. In extreme cases, it becomes blasphemy if you ask critical questions or if you become skeptical about matters that are unclear or matters that seem untrue. For instance, they claim that through inspiration, God revealed to the writers of the book of Genesis of the Bible, the name of the place where Adam and Eve, the first man and woman was created as Garden of Eden. Hence I ask, how such a person is inspired to have such serious information about where God created the first man and woman yet that person was not inspired to know where it is located.

That place should be the greatest tourist center in the world. That same inspired man happens to be born before Adam and Even for him to write about them or was he born after them. We want to know the true meaning and process of inspiration as anybody could claim to be inspired.

I have chosen to believe that since man has the capability to create, then we may not have emerged from nowhere. There must have been a highly advanced intelligent design that brought man to manifestation. The English people call him 'God'. I call him the infinite intelligence or the universal God. I choose this trouble-free definition so as not to confuse anyone, because if you go further, someone would ask me that if someone created man, then who would have created that someone. I do not want to think though that there is a particular God in charge of the planet Earth who chooses some people and abandons others to live under the mercy of those he chooses; a God that permits some people to enslave others; a God that tolerates wars and racism; a God that is partial; a God that forgives sins all the time, promoting crime and injustice. The world is suffering today because of racial discrimination and religious intolerance. These two elements, religion and race, have caused innumerable problems on earth, and they are turning the world into a jungle where no rules apply. Some religions claim superiority over others, and some race claims superiority over others, hence the fundamental question is how we can directly hear the truth from God and not from men who concoct their own truth to gain control.

Evidence and facts rule the strong and wise, illusions and beliefs rule the weak and ignorant; God is a universal God, supreme above all, designer of the universe and all in it. God has exalted man above all creations on earth, yet man has decided to reduce himself below the level of all God's creations, behaving like lower animals.

In the past, Africans, apart from the Arabs who were mostly Muslims, were known to worship numerous gods; they were always concerned about the unknown but not in a manner as to unravel the mysteries within the unknown but to worship them. Some believed in trees, some believed in spirits of the ancestors, some believed in mermaids that I have never seen before since I have been hearing about them, some believed in spirits in the air, thunder, lightning, rain, forests, and some worship fire, boas, anthills, and pythons until the visit of the arabs and colonial masters who introduced Islam and Christianity respectively.

Christianity on its own has too many denominations: the Roman Catholic Church established by Italians, the Anglican Church established by the British people, and numerous 'living churches' established by Americans. Lately, the new evolution in the Christian community called living churches is spreading like a virus. These living churches have so many branches that count up to thousands and thrive on stage-managed miracles, prosperity teachings, salvation, heaven and more. Unfortunately, Africa has more churches than factories.

Some preach against wealth acquisition, some preach in favour of wealth acquisition, some preach about life after death, some say that every soul that lived righteously will come back to inherit the earth, some say that you shall resurrect to face judgement, and some preach exactly what the audience crave to hear so long as they are ready to pay since most churches have become trading places, party grounds, and banks.

Some religions claim that when you die, you get born into another country by other parents, while others believe that when you die, you either evolve in another planet or descend to a level of a lower animal, depending on what you did on earth. The point is that many doctrines are being preached in these present times and they are beginning to contradict one another. Most religious sects have beliefs that totally differ from those of others. The major frustration I have with the whole arrangement is that the teachings thrive on fear, myth, superstitions and illusions and you are not allowed to ask questions where you do not understand the teachings. Whenever a doctrine has been labelled spiritual, whether it makes sense or not, you are not allowed to ask questions. There is always some form of punishment for those who ask questions. Is it not mental slavery not to ask questions about teachings you do not understand completely?

I told someone to explain to me how sin came into human existence since most religions claim that God created everything and also that God is perfect. I know the existence of a perfect universal God, but the way religions position their own God(s) and the attributes they assign to those God(s) seem not to hold substance but when debate gets intense, if they lack the ingredients to back up their God(s), they label you ugly names to dissuade others from taking similar stands. They could say you are blaspheming.

For true liberation to take place, we must ask questions about everything, especially when it concerns doctrines that impair rational thinking, thus hampering human development. Doctrines which promise hopes only when we are dead. Religious organisations deal with our spiritual lives (the unknown), but it baffles me that we are not paying attention to the 'known' that we are faced with today, or at least we should pay attention to both. Africans are mostly concerned with the unknown when we live in a physical earth and a scientific world.

Africans must begin to discuss solutions to HIV, Malaria, TB, and other diseases ravaging the continent in these present times. The discussions should take place in the same way they gather together in religious institutions to discuss how to go to heaven when they die while not desiring to die; they should have institutions that assemble people to discuss African problems and possible solutions.

In my own humble personal opinion, I think that the journey of a human being on earth is to positively contribute to the works of the universal God in areas relevant to the needs of humanity for continuity sake, for the generations to come and not to make a muddle of everything, including values that will allow the future generations to live safely and healthily. Our purpose on earth is not to destroy the ozone layer causing global warming that we may all perish from diseases like cancer due to too much radiation. We must desist from creating diseases and creating their cures just for wealth acquisition; we must stop abusing capitalism and individualism. We must refrain from brainwashing others with doctrines that cannot be proven in any practical ways—doctrines that the creators do not believe in.

The forces of nature are constantly achieving balance; life is cyclical, hence we must reap what we sow whether we know how or not. Our generations will reap the fruit of our labours whether good or bad. For those who believe that the business of God or nature is to sit and listen to pleas for forgiveness of 'sins' when they have no plans to quit, this is the time for the entire humanity to think again.

The divinity and powers which shape a man's destiny dwell in his hands. The wheel of fate is never stationary. Man is the architect of his own destiny, and also man is the architect of his own greatness or destruction. Africans must realise today that man is also god on earth. Man can create in his own little scientific ways the same way the universal God created man, the universe, and all in it. If we are created in God's image, does that not mean that we are created to create? If God is creative and we are created in his image, then what is preventing Africans from creating like others?

I am embacking on this struggle to enlighten Africans on the need to protect our land from dominance as I see it happening with time, considering the way Africans are behaving in these present times as if their brains are different from those of others. With the New World Order in force, those human breeds that are incapable of outliving their lower nature and embrace higher scientific nature of man will face a lot of troubles. It is important that Africans know that the world is beginning to conclude, that this great continent gave birth to human apes who cannot reason like fully functional human beings. They even assert that we are still evolving, considering the ways we think and act. How could people gather in churches every Sunday, their lives yet remaining the same? How could a drug dealer come into the same church with his 'business' cell phone and when his client calls, he goes out, answers the call, proceeds to deliver the hard drug, and afterwards comes back to the same church to worship God. Which God is he worshipping? How could a prostitute comes to church every Sunday and go back to her profession without any plans to quit? How could an assassin go to church every Sunday and still continue in his murderous ways without any intentions to quit? I used to tell my friends that no evil perpetrated by a man is ever forgiven unless atoned for. They did not believe me because they have been indoctrinated over time to believe and accept the erroneous doctrine that you can commit atrocities, then pray, and God would forgive you just like that. I asked, what about those who knew what they were about to do, and after doing it, they still ask God for forgiveness, but they could give me no logical answers. One of my friends said that God forgives all sins no matter the gravity and ugliness of the sin and that as soon as one is forgiven, the past is obliterated. I tried to convince them that in this life, the universal God endowed in every man a conscience, and if a person's conscience is no longer functioning, then God would understand as in the case of mentally disabled people and morons. But as long as it is functioning, every man knows when he is deviating from the right course unless it is by accident, and God also knows that it is by accident. God's job is not to sit and wait for us to commit all sorts of atrocities and then revert to him for forgiveness even when we know what we are doing. Man must wake up today and understand the workings of the universal God when it comes to actions and reactions. Man must stop treating God like a person even though it is said that we are created in his image.

Sometimes I ask whether a soul reincarnates after death; whether a man goes to 'heaven' or 'hell' after death; whether a man dies, gets buried, and merely gets eaten up by ants and worms in the grave; whether a man in death gets born into another plane of existence like other planets which may be trillions of light years away from ours' or even in other stars or galaxies; whether our spirits after death become the ancestral spirits Africans worship; whether a man in death assumes other forms of life depending on his previous actions; whether a man reaps all that he sows while alive; whether the punishments to the sins of a man are transmitted unto his generations. After I have asked myself all these questions, I discover that I have no definite answers and also that most religious institutions and schools of thoughts have tried to answer these questions but ended up confusing their followers. Those are secrets of nature, and they are revealed to no one; all we know is that when we sow a grain of maize, we end up reaping maize. What we sow, we reap.

Finally, I decided to put it that the business of God with the dead is known to no man; that the unknown still remains unknown, but since in all forms of existence the forces of nature are balanced, I do not see how man would escape the justice of life. The moon is hanging up there without falling to crash against the earth; the human body is so complex yet in biochemical harmony unless we choose to destabilise it ourselves. I even prefer when people talk about Karma, cause and effects, or retributive justice. God forgives no sins at all, and let it be known to Africans today for mental freedom to take place that there is no certain place called 'heaven' or 'hell', and if at all there are such places, maybe they are here on earth and within us and in our lives, creating balance, for every man reaps what he sows.

The flow of the rivers and oceans, gravitational forces, and many more natural features point towards the fact that there is balance in life. Also the fact that the Universal God has positioned man above all life creations on earth proves the fact that human beings may not be mere mortals, hence a man could not just be born on earth only to die and get planted in the graves to end up only as food to ants and worms. There is a possibility of a different form of consciousness which the inner being of man will assume, but we do not know.

There could be more to life than we could possibly imagine, but in the simplest form of it, everyone should contribute his own quota to the betterment of this earth at least for the unborn and the generations to come. Everyone should strive to live right, for when you live right, then there would be no need for the fear of death. A fear of death is for those who have committed so many atrocities that they are now uncertain of what happens next. But those who live right usually do not fear death. The universal God, however, achieves natural balance though we do not know. He always puts the 'good guy' in his rightful place and the 'bad guy' too in his own place, here or thereafter, as the case may be, and whatever he does would always be to achieve the same balance which has always been in all his creations. It would be wise for men to pay attention to the words of wisdom as the current state of things on earth calls for living in reality.

Africans have failed to participate in the active process which brought about the advancement of civilisation they say started in Africa, and this also calls for a deep concern. Africans have chosen to abandon the real cause of building a sustainable future for the generations to come and decided to cling on to beliefs of a place which has been decorated by God for a lazy and idle man—a better place built with gold and diamonds, meant only for poor, idle, and lazy ones who do not think creatively like others yet make more use of the products of other people's creative thinking, more than those who created them. History has it that the Egyptians built the pyramids which remain one of the greatest wonders of this earth, how then did they harness the intellectual resources to commence the civilisation of that time? The science which was available then, how did it commence? Three things answer these questions; man was born with the intelligence and he developed it by creative thinking; man made contact with extraterrestrial intelligence; the universal God revealed this knowledge to man one way or the other. Whichever way we look at it, every man is capable of being part of this cause. I question why Africans have decided to abandon this cause of advancing civilisation, continuing their economic and cultural development, a process which originally began in their continent as history says; even to copy the existing form of science and technology at the moment at least to be self-sustaining economically. Granted that sometime in the past, they had these processes in motion but stopped by the interference of slavery and colonialism but how come that up until now, since the colonialists have left Africa, we are still not making frantic efforts to continue from where the colonialists abandoned? Are our problems external or internal? After all these questions, I discovered one thing which is mental slavery. Today, I implore African leaders to initiate an aggressive move towards restructuring our academic institutions, establishing research institutions, making universities truly institutions of learning and academic escellence, for it seems we go to school to become better slaves. Considering all that is happening in Africa today, the youth should acquire education, skills and also develop talents as tools of capacity building, since the system is not creating sufficient jobs to accommodate the volume of graduates being harvested in African institutions every year; rather the African system is creating more churches and bars.

One who is ahead of you in knowledge will not teach you if you are considered a slave hence it is wise you strive to copy if you are unable to invent your own base ideas. Only with genuine intent can a slave master teach a slave what he knows otherwise the slave is acquiring more enslaving information to perpetuate slavery. This is also one of the causes of mental slavery in Africa. Africans are acquiring information designed for slaves or better say, information that perpetuate slavery. This is the time to copy knowledge and technology from anywhere available for the future of Africa. We can do better if we start rediscovering our real mission in life; the youths could help focusing on their studies and avoiding distractions. Africans should realise that schools are not only meant to pass exams and come out with flashy certificates only to remain unemployed; if only we could know that education is meant to refine and empower an individual and ignite creative potentials.

Africans seek God but in reality what they seek is peace and happiness. They seek but they never find due to the fact that they seek wrongly. It starts by thoughts and well directed actions. If one is true to himself, he would realise that genuine peace and happiness could only be achieved when one's energy field is positive and not the opposite. If one's energy field is positive, surely the person would radiate the same to others and in return he will attract people of like energy fields and would be peaceful and happy. One cannot exploit the happiness of another and be happy; he would end up in emptiness. Peace of mind comes by living in peace with others and not the opposite. When you live in harmony with others and nature, surely you will have peace in your life and you will be happy also. What you give is what you get, happiness and peace are like kisses, we only get them when we give same to others.

Genuine peace and happiness do not come via material acquisitions, though they could bring comfort if properly acquired and utilised. We live in a physical world and must strive to acquire material wealth, but we must also understand that material wealth also have their own energy fields, and those energy fields interact with man's complex energy fields bringing peace, harmony, love, hate, happiness, pain, disharmony, problems, or sadness depending on how they are acquired. I must say this today that criminally acquired wealth cannot bring happiness rather the opposite. Ill-gotten wealth is surrounded by complex negative energy fields, and this in turn attracts negative people, negative emotions, negative habits, and negative energies. Those who pursue wealth with aggressive animal instincts, undermining the peace, lives and security of others, would not be guaranteed peace and happiness in their lives.

When you are making negative efforts, you will find out that most of your close friends, without positive influences in your life would most likely be negative as well. If you are making negative efforts and you are married to a woman with no positive influence in your life, watch out that woman she will also be negative in her nature.

Your relatives who know you well and still be with you without any intentions of instilling positive values in your life will most likely be negative also. You will always attract negative habits and negative people. This is the law of attraction and homogeneity and also the order of life. What goes around comes around. Life is cyclical. The universe is balanced in all its ramifications. When you are making negative efforts in life, you are most likely going to be surrounded by negative people, events, and habits, and all of these would create problems and fears in life; but when you are making positive efforts in life, the reverse happens, and of course you will be happy and at peace with humanity and nature.

Ill-gotten wealth breeds unhappiness because it has negative fields around it and your body also has fields hence the fields interact, bringing you unhappiness. Watch most people who abuse alcohol, women, drugs, and many other substances, when you ask them why they do those things, they will tell you that it is a habit, but when you dig deep, it is either there is something wrong in the person's life, a problem the person is facing that affects his emotions that he tries to fight with, or in most cases the person is making negative survival efforts and uses those elements to suppress the reactions of the energy fields generated by his negative actions. Those substances only create illusions of happiness and peace, feelings that fade away as soon as the substance dilutes in the body and the individual rewinds back to reality ready to face his self-created demons.

I have demonstrated my anger and dissatisfaction over the humiliation of Christianity by those who perform prearranged miracles in churches. When I make references to biblical miracles, such references are not intended to incite rebellion. Rather, I am asking that since false and prearranged miracles are being made in churches in these present times and people sheepishly believe them without asking questions, then how would the perpetrators of those false miracles expect curious-minded people not to doubt biblical miracles? Because if what they are doing is what Christ did, then automatically they are making some critics doubt the whole miracles of Christ. The primary reason for this part of the book is to alert the government and religious bodies to see the need to address abuse of religion, mostly falsification of miracles in churches and suicide bomb attacks of rival religious groups in the name of God as perpetrated by the Boko Haram group in Nigeria.

We must be wary of false prophets who perform illusions and magic tricks in the glorified name of miracles; con men who pose as prophets, and fake voodoo priests who deceive people with illusions just for material gains instead of herb treatments. We must be careful of teachings that focus one's mind on the sky to search for a heaven made of gold and diamonds, while the wise ones are focusing on the ground exploring and exploiting our natural resources, refining them and selling back to us. We must watch out carefully as we are systematically being transformed into inferior human beings and enemies of ourselves.

Most especially, we must watch out for Neocolonialism, a progression of colonialism. A policy where major powers use economic and political means to extend its influence over past colonies. A geopolitical practice of using capitalism, business globalization, and cultural imperialism to control a country, in lieu of either direct military control or indirect political control, i.e. imperialism and hegemony. The term neo-colonialism was coined by the Ghanaian politician Kwame Nkrumah, to describe the socio-economic and political control that can be exercised economically, linguistically, and culturally, whereby promotion of the culture of the neo-colonist country, facilitates the cultural assimilation of the colonised people, and thus opens the national economy to the multinational corporations of the neo-colonial country.

Christians believe that Jonah was swallowed by a fish and he came out alive after four days. This is designated in the Christian fold as a miracle, but a non-Christian should be allowed to ask as to why the enzymes in the belly of that animal could not digest Jonah when natural laws were in operation in the belly of that animal, and when he asks this question, he needs a convincing answer; he must be sure deep in his heart that he has received a scientific, practical, and convincing answer in order to avoid being a victim of mental slavery. Since the beginning of time, there has been logic, and if God becomes illogical sometimes, there must be explanations. There are many non-Christians in the world today, and the need to have trained Christian theology experts explaining to them how miracles happened in the Bible is vital or else they will continue to have doubts.

According to a scientologist that I know, God created Adam first and took ribs from him and made Eve. From the story that Adam and Eve were God's first human creations, it would mean that whoever recounted the creation story or wrote about it was not created or born after Adam and Eve were created. Hence my question is: How could such a person recount an event that happened when he was not yet born or was he created before Adam and Eve? Did Adam and Eve recount these stories to those born after them? If the person was inspired to know such information, how sure are we of the person considering a lot deceits being perpetrated by religious institutions in this present times. If the person was inspired how come he was not inspired to know the exact location of this garden of Eden. These matters have to be clarified to those who are non-Christians to avoid continuous doubts regarding the teachings of the Bible.

A Buddhist said, 'If Daniel was offered to the lions as a meal and the lions refused to feast on him, I would like to have a clear explanation as regards to how the miracle took place because most people who are non-Christians do not believe in miracles. If Christ resurrected from the dead and also did raise Lazarus from the dead, then let me be convinced as to how it happened for me to believe as I am open to beliefs that make complete sense to me. Also let some of those pastors who claim they are healing the deaf, dumb and cripple also walk on the sea publicly for all to see'.

An atheist said, 'I have no problems in believing that Christ healed the blind, deaf, dumb, and even walked on water, but such stories need to be clarified scientifically because many con men and impostors are simulating what Christ did by arranging seemingly stage-managed healings. Let no man get upset, but evidence around us nowadays proves these points. Just accompany your blind, deaf, dumb, or crippled relative to a church and see if he would be healed, but in the same churches, many blind, deaf, dumb, and crippled people are healed in front of the eyes of unsuspecting audiences'.

According to the Bible, in many instances, Christ is referred to as God, son of God, and son of Man, hence doubtful minds should be made to understand the differences with all the instances used to designate Christ. The difference between him being son of God, son of Man, and God himself should be made clear to avoid confusion.

Africans need to be free from the crunches of mental slavery so as to develop like other human beings on this planet as some improperly explained religious teachings are gradually reducing us to the status of inferior human beings who can neither think nor question anything.

Many fake houses of God and fake men of God (religious banks and their bank managers) loot billions of dollars from Africa every year in the name of 'God', yet they do not contribute anything to African development; rather, we are being brainwashed and enslaved mentally so as not to recognise the tricks going on. When you have encounters with genuine men of God, you would know because they are not fanatic about wealth acquisition. They practise what they preach, and they do not practise religion of convenience; they do not tell the people what the people want to hear in order to gain a congregation. They rather say the truth and are driven by the will of God and not the will of man. Such people could be found amongst both Muslims, Christians, and many other religions, and their activities speak for them.

Impostors who claim to be men of God could be spotted easily by their flamboyant lifestyles, ostentatious behaviours, consistent display of pre-arranged miracles, and a fanatic hunger for attention that they are now taking the glory of Christ. They amass wealth and convey to their imaginary God and their founding fathers while children of Africa wallow in penury, hunger, and starvation. These days due to ignorance, poverty, unemployment, and narrow-mindedness, hungry souls have converted themselves into men of God, and if you see what they do to their congregations, you will surely know that such men are crooks.

A so-called man of God took so much from the poor to build universities and schools so expensive that the same poor people he took from can neither afford the school fees nor ever think of attending the schools, yet no one speaks about it. Some call themselves prophets, and whenever they fly their white handkerchiefs, people fall and if you visit their prophetic churches (banks and magic houses), you will see their photos or family photos hanging on the walls instead of that of Christ, Isaiah, Elijah, Moses, and others as if it has become a family thing. They have hijacked the glory of their God. I think the photo of Christ or Christian prophets should be mounted on the walls in churches and not that of pastors and their wives. These days some of these strange pastors even contest for the presidency of African nations. What a joke! I shall not hesitate to speak against all the evil, atrocities, and injustice against the African continent; when we speak the truth, they tag it blasphemy. I tell whichever God who receives the hard-earned money of poor and wretched Africans to start giving it back—the sooner, the better. I am not sure false prophets are serving the true God of justice and humanity.

Mercenaries of mental slavery, those false prophets who claim that they could cure HIV and AIDS merely by placing their hands on a victim's head and praying, I ask them to visit hospitals where HIV victims are concentrated and administer the cure and get paid in return rather than asking them to have faith and build castles in the air when of course everyone knows that no one with such a deadly disease would ever have faith to be cured magically. In fact, we must demand those 'imaginary gods' whom Africans pay so much money through their false prophets to send a cure for HIV, malaria, and tuberculosis in the continent. We should be insisting that those 'gods' provide a solution to poverty, hunger, and starvation in Africa, also a solution to faulty leadership in Africa. Africans must begin to live practical lives before people conclude that we are all unfit to exist in this New World Order. I had a chat with an African traditional healer who told me that he uses bones and 'charms' during divination to see (not even predict) people's future.

I was so stunned because I know that this 'bone man' can only see the figments of his own imaginations. Africans are not telling themselves the truth these days, and it does not help us at all—traditional healers in Africa should concentrate on herbs and not on non-existent voodoo. I must say today that without the white man coming here, God revealed to our ancestors through our scientific ways the trees, herbs, and roots where cures to most of our diseases could be found. In these present times, however, African herbalists forget these herbs and concentrate on illusions and magical acts. Someone, a voodoo priest in Malawi told me about his power of divination, then I asked him to tell me where my car that was stolen was situated, and, to my amazement, he started to chant and throw bones. I dropped him 100 Malawian Kwacha and walked away because I knew he was just wasting my time.

Being born in a Christian community and adopting Christianity at an early age, I use to pray a lot, but I also compliment it with hardwork. Both prayers and hard work must go together. This is a wake-up time for Africans. Today science and technology has changed the world and Africans are making greater use of the fruits of science and technology, but most teachings fed to African minds do not give room to scientific explanations. Most religious teachings contradict science, and most scientific principles contradict religion, yet most religious 'warlords' make use of scientific gadgets in carrying out their 'mental wars', hence the relationship between God and the scientific realities of today must be explained to the people by religious institutions for mental freedom to take place.

Apart from the king worm devouring our continent, which is mental slavery, HIV/AIDS and faulty leadership are other 'worms' feasting on our great continent. I have embarked on this expedition to address all of these issues without fear or prejudice.

Misinterpretation of religious doctrines is the greatest source of mental slavery in Africa. The twisted education prevalent in Africa makes someone a polished slave, one which after being acquired removes from a person, the ability to invent ideas, innovate, or discover. A type of education that disempowers an individual. Not to say that Education is not worthwhile rather we should reform our education pattern and system to suit our developmental needs and our current situation in the continent., one with which the abundant natural and human resources we have, allows Africans to still suffer and make the continent stagnant and paralysed. Africans must conduct a thorough research on the kind of education we are acquiring today to know why it is not yielding the desired result and also to know whether it is the same as those in the developed world. We have to seek solutions to our problems, and this is the time.

The creation of this work is born out of the unflinching love I have for our great continent Africa; for the unquenchable craving for improvement and positive changes in Africa; the need to immortalize and exalt the living and fallen heroes of Africa; for the need to heal Africans oppressed all over the globe; and most especially because of the need to exalt the spirit of our great continent Africa.

I wrote this book because of the spirit of self-sacrifice and the desire to lead by example as we live in times when Africans have lost touch with realities and do not understand the true meaning of self-sacrifice and service to humanity.

I also wrote this book essentially for the need to confuse the greatest enemies of our time for true liberation and mental freedom to take place; for the need to destroy the 'worms' feasting on Africa; the need to arrest mental slavery through constructive creative thinking and sceptical criticism and above all, the need to bring to the minds of Africans the fact that mind has total power and control over matter.

For Africans to know that true empowerment exists in the mind and nowhere else, mind over matter, all powers lie within; for the need to propagate a new force, a new movement, the culture of creativity and rational thinking in Africa; I wrote this book essentially for those reasons.

For the need to destroy fear completely, destroy aggressive pursuit of materialism with animal instincts undermining the peace, life and happiness of others; and also to destroy purposeless living as this earth is a shrine and no one departs here with anything not even a single hair on his body, Essentially for these reasons I wrote this book.

For our concern is not what happens to us when we die, but the good we do for the society and mankind when we are alive, for the good we do for ourselves dies with us but the good we do for the society and mankind lives forever. For the need to encourage Africans to copy only the positive values of others and not the negative ones; for the need to encourage Africans all over the globe to reduce their pleasure levels and channel their energy towards confronting the fears and challenges of today, tomorrow, and the future. Most especially, the need to enforce spiritual unity amongst native Africans and diaspora Africans. Essentially for these reasons I wrote this book.

Who says the spirits of great achievers and scientists like Albert Einstein, Isaac Newton, Michael Faraday, Alexander Graham Bell, Martin Luther King,

Malcolm X, Dr Nnamdi Azikiwe, Marcus Garvey, Julius Nyerere, Walter Sisulu, Oliver Tambo, Tai Solarin, Miriam Makeba, and many other great achievers are not living forever even though they have passed on? Who says that if I spend all my life doing good works for humanity and making positive contributions towards African liberation, my spirit would not live forever even when I depart from this plane of existence? For I believe in this concept of eternity whereby your energy remains useful to the world when you are no more on this plane. Who says that the spirits of Bill Gates of America, the great Nelson Mandela, Philip Emeagwali, Chinua Achebe, Chike Obi, Wole Soyinka, and those of the living heroes of Africa would not live forever even when they depart from this plane? This is my concept of eternity.

I am of the opinion and do strongly believe that Africa is still the greatest continent on our planet. Africa is beautiful and blessed abundantly both in human and natural resources. Look at the shape of our great continent Africa, like a heart. Africa is the heart of the earth. It is said that Africa is where everything began; it is also said that civilisation, which is one of the greatest wonders of our time, began in great Africa. Hence I ask: why is it that the continent where everything began is the least developed? I also ask why and when civilisation which started in Africa stopped. The pyramid of Egypt, also one of the greatest wonders of our times and one of the most prominent and obvious symbols of ancient civilisation, is in Africa. Hence my question is: what is happening to our great continent and its people? Why have we chosen to abandon the process that began in our land which the entire world copied?

Today children of Africa all over the globe must be proud of who they are, for they are blessed abundantly. They must also begin to harness those blessings, for if something was done by someone, then we can also do it as we are not less human than anyone, neither is anyone more human than us; rather mental slavery, religious diversions, and HIV are systematically doing their jobs of reducing us to the status of inferior human beings.

This is a book that has come to introduce the concept of spiritual unity in Africa and amongst children of African all over the globe. We are not here to preach a gospel of the creation of the United States of Africa but to enlighten and pave way for Africans to develop team spirit and also confront issues facing the African continent. We are here to sensitise Africans on various issues that affect our day-to-day lives. We believe that Africans need to start thinking collectively as one people; start pursuing common goals like poverty alleviation, technological revolution, capacity building, eradication of HIV, good governance; figure out the real enemy (mental slavery), and embark on

148

the real struggle which is the eradication of mental slavery and development of productive capacity so as to be free from economic slavery. Africans must begin to abolish mind arrest and religious diversions from our lives.

This is a book written to inform African leaders that the only way we can move forward is by genuine concern for the people and also the nations we lead; leaders must stop being oppressors and killers of those they lead just because they have power over them; leaders must not be plunderers of the resources of the nations they lead just because they have control over those resources.

This is a book written to reveal to African leaders the need to face serious business of good governance and not an aggressive pursuit of power and wealth that would definitely dissolve to zero someday abandoning the welfare of the people they lead and the growth of the nations they represent. This is a book that has come to bring to the minds of Africans the need to live in reality and also the need for Africans to be broad-minded.

This book is also written to destroy the negative stigmas as a result of racial, tribal, and national barriers. This is an empowerment, practical and positive philosophy and a message intended to heal the minds of every African against errors of the past either by commission or omission. This is a philosophy that has come to reveal to Africans the need to love and respect one another and to know that a visitor must not oppress or dominate the true owner of the land. This is a messsge that has come to enforce creativity in the minds of Africans, for the only way we can fit into this new world is to join the creative force or else the dominant principle which is impersonal, the principle of 'survival of the fittest' will displace us just as it has happened in the past to the indigenous inhabitants of America, Australia, and New Zealand. The new world system is impersonal, running like the operating system of a computer, and once set in motion, it starts running until it achieves a result, and if you do not fit into the system, you are definitely bound to be displaced, so it is no longer a personal thing but just a system in motion. We Africans do not see these things and indulge in so much pleasure that our mind's eyes are blinded from seeing realities; from seeing the invincible war and the unseen enemy: mental slavery.

Africans must become broad-minded in these current times or stop breeding children whose future may not be determined with the advancement in science and technology which is giving birth to all sorts of strange ideas, biological weapons, chemical weapons and weapons of human destruction. If it means to copy or clone, then let us copy or clone. Let us copy or clone science and technology in its true contexts; let us sit back and think about future and destiny now before it is too late; let us examine our education system and find out why it is not yielding the desired results; let us examine our minds and find out why we are not functioning exactly like others and in the right direction; let us find out why we are only concerned with what happens to us when we die, abandoning what is happening to us when we are alive in the only world we know.

African leaders must wake up today and be more mature in their thinking and behaviour and know that a leader is truly a servant and not a shrine or a deity to be worshipped. Also, African leaders struggling to cling to power at the expense of national security, safety, and lives of the people (not their own children and family members as they are always overseas driving limousines, living in spacious houses and signing diplomatic documents), for the sake of the people should relinquish power to a more qualified and acceptable person to usher in development, peace, and harmony so that there would be no more bloodshed, for it seems their immediate family members and children do not die in this blood-soaked quest for power. We do not have collective love and genuine love for one another, and this is a big problem. Without true love, there may not be team spirit and self-sacrifice, and without self-sacrifice and team spirit, there would not be progress, and let no one think that I am preaching communism for showing true love to one another and demonstrating the spirit of self-sacrifice, for our great continent has nothing to do with communism but humanism.

Europeans, Americans, and Asians have demonstrated true love for their continents and their own people, and from their levels of advancement today, we can understand the power that exists in true love, team spirit, and self-sacrifice. With self-sacrifice, team spirit, and dedicated duty to their nations, born out of genuine concern, they have advanced beyond our imaginations such that their works now look like magic to us. We are still struggling for power; we are still struggling to survive amidst abundance; we are still importing more 'gods' and religions; we are still raising more fake preachers and hypocrites; we are still searching for a place to go when we die; we are still purchasing food when we have vast lands; we are still purchasing languages; we are still experimenting with democracy that some African leaders now practise their own type that the late Fela Kuti called demo-crazy. Is it not time that someone starts thinking? Or are we all to be collectively fooled at the same time? Hatred, insensitivity, illiteracy, selfishness, greed, mental slavery, false religious doctrines, wickedness, false beliefs, and aggressive quest for power and wealth are plunging Africa into total collapse, so this is the time to address all these issues.

God does not choose people, rather people choose themselves. Today Africans must begin to choose themselves in this new dispensation and destroy the erroneous impression that greatness visits only those that God chooses. Africans must open their eyes widely and recognise mental slavery wherever it is and wherever it interplays in their daily lives as I have just unravelled that our problems are mostly mind related, fuelled with euro-judo-exopolitical religion, illiteracy, poverty, HIV, and faulty governance. Today we must crush mental slavery, for we are mentally arrested in these current times, and any man who is mentally arrested has also been physically incapacitated, for mind rules over the body. Mind above matter, all powers dwell within.

Children of Africa were taken into slavery, and from the labours of African slaves, the great nations were built, yet those nations do not find any need to appreciate such labours of Africans who were enslaved and they have changed into another form of slavery—a more dangerous form of slavery, one that may be happening under our noses, yet we do not notice it. This I call the invisible enemy. The world has transformed physical slavery into mental slavery. Behold, the chains of slavery have changed positions from hands to minds. Watch out for false prophets who sell 'God' and dreams to blindfolded Africans due to hunger for money and power.

The resources found in Africa are nourishing most world technologies today, yet the world has seen no need to put an end to the worms devouring African children every day. The world has seen no need to put a final stop to poverty, HIV/AIDS, and malaria in the African continent because of their capitalist greed and quest for material wealth. The world has not seen a need to put a stop to false religions spreading in Africa, as it is helping them to transform us into mental slaves. I believe that if the world could visit the moon, land a robot in Mars, break the atoms, develop machines that are exploring the stars, planets, and other worlds, then the world could also easily destroy HIV/AIDS, Malaria and TB, including all other worms devouring the African continent.

Same-sex marriage was never an African problem, and I see no reason why the world decided to bring Africa into the matter thereby abandoning our major problems. Global warming and the ozone layer crisis are problems created by the advanced nations, and now Africa inherits part of this problem, yet all other major problems that plague the African continent are ignored by the advanced nations. Since the world has nothing to offer to African people, and it is obvious that all we get in return is brainwashing, foreign debts, mind diversion and new diseases, Africans must commence deep creative thinking, copying/cloning technology, producing what they consume and consuming what we produce to extricate themselves from economic slavery; the first step is to attack mental slavery by purging our minds of all doctrines, beliefs, and superstitions that cannot be proven in any manner and by also correcting our faulty education system.

The most serious case is the rumour that HIV was discovered in green monkeys in DRC in Africa. I ask whoever discovered the virus what he was searching for in the first place. Was he actually searching for a virus? Was there an epidemic at that particular time that provoked a research or was he looking for something that they were sure they would definitely find in a particular place and at a particular point in time in African history? Did they export the virus to DRC only to announce its existence there on arrival ? These and many more are my questions, and I implore Africans to learn to resist these ugly trends just as Europeans would quickly do if confronted with similar circumstances.

Africans must start asking questions regarding some stories and doctrines in religious books today for mental freedom to take place since they are unable to separate allegories from literal statements. For instance, King Solomon of the Bible married 300 wives and had 700 concubines; Jesus Christ came and said 'one man one wife', hence where is King Solomon now, in heaven or in hell? And what is the fate of the 999 women abused by King Solomon if Christ was right in his 'one man one wife' rule? Or were they both right? And was that not women abuse, considering the fact that the same God was in control both when Solomon was in charge and when Jesus Christ emerged by divine conception?

I do not want to be told that because Solomon existed in the Old Testament, his mistakes are pardoned or ignored. Rather, I need a clear and convincing answer as regards to the condition of Solomon now whether in 'hell' or in 'heaven' after all he did to those women. I also need to know why God decided to send 'his only begotten son' Jesus Christ to establish that a man should marry one wife only making Solomon a chronic polygamist and an abusive character. What about African polygamists who still attend churches with their numerous wives defiling the teachings of Jesus Christ? Are they going to hell or heaven? I also want to know as to why God had to send Jesus Christ to die for us at the 'cross of Calvary' and he had to usher in the New Testament. At what point did God decide to introduce the New Testament and why did he do so since he is a perfect God and would have predicted a faulty old testament. Are we going to have another testament that will legalise same-sex marriage?

It may surprise you to know that 90 per cent of African Christians do not understand the full meaning of the first Bible verse regarding the creation of the heavens and the earth, and none can give a clear interpretation of the book of John 1: 1 (John chapter 1 verse 1) where the Bible says that in the beginning was the Word and the Word was with God and the Word was God. You find out today that everyone that preaches this part of the Bible preaches with confidence as if he understands this part fully. This is part of what I call mental slavery, when you transmit unto others information which you do not understand fully.

Why would the testaments change in the first place from old to new? Does God change sometimes? The same Bible that says in the book of Revelation, 'let no man add or remove' is being revised from one version to another. So what is being added or removed that we do not know as they are being revised.

God created Adam and Eve and also created a serpent which induced Eve into deceiving Adam. They discovered their nudity, gave birth to a set of twins (Cain and Abel), and Cain ran away after killing Abel. Where did he run to and whom did he marry? What happened to him after he ran away? Who was there when God took the rib of Adam and made Eve? And how did such a person record this information as it seems there were no writing instruments then? Was the prophet that recorded this scene of God creating Adam and Eve born before Adam and Eve since Adam and Eve were the first of God's human creation? Here we are told that God revealed all these happenings to his prophets through inspiration, hence we demand that the people question how such pieces of information are received by inspiration and how the receiver manages such information without adding or removing any information since there is no vividly clear way of replicating a dream or a vision without addition or subtraction of minute information which is in line with human nature. We just need deeper explanation of how the receiver or the inspired person could vividly picture God removing the rib of Adam to make Eve and other happenings when he was not there in person. If these are all allegories, the question is, do African Christians understand them as allegories or real happenings? During the time of creation, there were no writing instruments even some milleniums after hence how was the information documented. Did God reveal this to someone after some milleniums.

Africans must become mature and strong in their reasoning and stop acting like little children who enjoy fables. Of course, God created man, and even those who believe in the scientific evolutionary process still own up that creation or evolution was engineered by a complex process via an infinite intelligence which we all call God and which I call the universal God or the supreme Godhead, but all I am saying is that Africans must learn to distinguish from allegorical illustrations meant to give deeper understanding and transmit deeper meanings from real happenings. Africans must start asking these questions and not just accept the 'ask no questions as God would strike you' attitude. We must ask questions all the times when teachings fail to make clear sense to us, and we must also ensure that we properly understand the answers we get and that they make true sense to us. False prophets and untrained minds are making religious books look like self-created human prophesies of events which are happening in our presence today. These days we hear that some scientific inventions bear '666' marks as called 'mark of the beast', and I wonder who this beast is and what the person who created this '666' story wanted to achieve.

Are they going to forecast the coming of a new disease worse than HIV and then later on create one? What else is the world going to tell Africans? Is it that a disease would invade Africa? And when we believe the story, they would go ahead and create one and also create the cure and then revert to their human mercenaries in our midst, to deceive us again. Few people in the world today have been able to explain the book of Revelation in the Bible, and I must tell you that 90 per cent of the Bible preachers who try to do so are either ill-informed, ill-trained, or do not even understand what they are telling others.

I do not mean to be rude or disrespectful, but I must say today that our minds crave for stories that would only intoxicate the minds of little children, and sometimes when I have conversations with a sixty-year-old African friend and he persistently tells me ridiculous stories which he has been told since childhood about the end of the world and the end of time in a manner as if he is absolutely sure that the world would come to an end, then I begin to question our minds.

Of course everything in life is cyclical, and anything that has a beginning will also have an end for a cycle to complete, but no one knows exactly how the earth will be destroyed, whether a huge asteroid will hit the earth like it did in California or whether the sun will burn out its own gasses and consume all the planets around it or whether the earth will be flooded by global warming which is rising the oceans or whether any of the planets that make up our solar system, as we were scientifically told, will disintegrate causing a problem in the entire sun's magnetic field affecting other planets. Nobody knows whether the human race will be consumed by the faults in their own creations like nuclear facilities, ozone layer depletion, and HIV.

You must be careful of some old and unproductive people who have failed in life as they will plant fear-based stories in young minds, destroying their zeal to face the world just as they failed after being mentally incapacitated with stories that cannot be proven absolutely and scientifically, yet they have no stories to tell the world out there. I have not seen a ghost before, and I will never see one. I have not seen a spirit that lives in water or trees before, and I will never see one. I have not seen a witch turn into a snake or a snail, or a flying bird turn into a human and I will never see one. I have not seen a man shot with a gun and the bullet could not penetrate his body, and I will never see one. Anyone who has seen any of these things should come forward so that we can clearly prove what he saw.

How does heaven and the afterlife beyond look like because whoever is telling me about heaven with so much certainty must have been there or have relatives who communicate with him from there? The worst scenario is that those who speak about the afterlife are those who are alive. Is there any way apart from prayers that I could communicate with God? Is there any way I could communicate with dead people apart from illusions from voodoo priests who claim to consult mediums? (I am asking these questions to help you also be free to ask the same questions. Yes, there could be heaven and hell, but how much efforts have we made to find out if they are here on earth or somewhere else? What efforts have we also made to find out where our ancestors are and what they are doing whereever they are? What efforts have we made to find out if truly someone reincarnates or gets born in another planet after death and what determines which planets one finds himself in?) Those who do not live by evidence are the greatest victims of mental slavery.

In the only world we know, the world has refused to provide us a real cure for Malaria, TB, HIV and AIDS, but it marvels me at the speed and pace with which misinterpreted and twisted religious doctrines are spreading in Africa; promising a place where the poor, idle, lazy, and weak would go and enjoy 'when they die' instead of enforcing hard work and creativity to consolidate our economic existence and future when we are alive. Numerous false teachings in Africa provide solutions to our problems only when we die, but they ignore the fact that we have children who may not die alongside with us when we die. They ignore the fact that we have generations that would not die when we die. They provide no solutions to problems of the living in Africa. Why is it that Africans have failed to broaden their minds and see realities? Or do we prefer illusions to realities or are we afraid to face realities? What are we afraid of when at the end of the day we would still die and we all know it? Mercenaries of mental slavery are raised under our noses every day, yet no one speaks; men who sell false dreams and false hopes Africans; men who have mortgaged their consciences just for the sake of money and material gains and no one speaks against it because 'God' would punish us or kill us when we speak. I think it is time when these issues are addressed for African liberation to take place.

The essence of this work is to commence a new era in Africa, an era of mind revolution. Today we fight mental slavery. Today we invoke creativity in Africa, which is the only way to face the challenges of today, tomorrow, and the future. Today we fight the invisible enemy, mental slavery. Behold the voice of mother Africa; the revelation of truth liberates men from bondage. The wheel of destiny is never static. The destiny of a man exists in his hands, the destiny of a nation exists in the hands of the people, and the destiny of Africa exists in our hands.

Evidence and facts rule the strong and wise, while illusions and beliefs rule the weak and ignorant. If God be God, he is one God for all human races. This is a wake-up time for Africa.

To all stories fed to African minds that are not helping them deal with the problems they face in their lives rather create mental and economic slaves; to religious stories that offer Africans hopes only 'when they die'; to institutions that are exploiting the African continent both in human and natural resources yet Africa owes so much debt that they may not repay until eternity; to conspiracy propagandists and imperialist institutions that destroyed the African cultural and economic evolution yet condemn Africans as incapable of self-actualization, I ask for clemency as I have decided to start this journey again from the known to the unknown unleashing a fierce battle against the greatest enemy of Africa which is mental slavery. I shall also absolve you for allowing theories that conflict one another to rule the lives of human beings and most especially Africans, for allowing religious theories and scientific theories to conflict one another, yet men must believe both and not strive hard enough to find out which of them should they follow.

Today, let it be known to Africans all over the globe that God is universal and operates on strict principles, God is logical, scientific, and practical. God does not encourage mental slavery. God is loving, peaceful, and harmonious in his ways. God is of no religion, race, nationality, or tribe. *God is either for all or for none and also God created everything including the forces of good and evil and gave man free will*

African Achievers and Freedom Fighters

The labours of our heroes shall never be in vain neither shall they be forgotten in history. Men who sacrificed their lives to liberate the African continent shall be remembered today up until the end of time—men who never feared the fierce weapons of our colonial masters, men who were ready to die for the sake of others, men who have defended our cause on this planet, men who have made us proud, men who have proven that every human being is fundamentally the same irrespective of the differences in physical appearance. Africans who have marvellously advanced human intelligence beyond the ordinary, Africans who have proven the world wrong, today they shall be remembered. Those who had the impudence to challenge the oppressions against African people, men who adopted the creative intelligence of our colonial masters and not just their strange lifestyles to serve the African continent, visionary men, the light of Africa, men who love the people and sacrificed all for the people, today you are remembered. May God bless you all, for Africa loves you all.

There are many African heroes, achievers, revolutionaries, and freedom fighters, men who opposed the injustice against the African continent. I am using this medium to mention just a few. In my subsequent book titled *Labors of African heroes*, I shall reveal detailed biographies of all of these extraordinary individuals. African heroes in this context are Africans who stood up against all odds to fight for the liberation of African people and also those who fought against the oppression of African people both by external and internal forces.

We live in a world filled with racial prejudice and with people who live biased lives. If issues like the Zimbabwe crisis are presented at a discussion table, an average European will waste all the time demonising Robert Mugabe, and also an average African will also waste all the time demonising the Europeans. I have taken a rational stand on this matter as one who thinks 'out of the box'. People should learn to rationalise issues and not think or act based on prejudice. I analysed the Zimbabwe situation during the period of developing this work, and during that period, I involved three Zimbabweans, namely, Tafirenyika, Ncube, and Pascal, who were seeking political asylum in the Republic of South Africa.

On interrogating them, Tafirenyika told me that Mugabe is a tyrant who brought untold hardship to the country and to the people of Zimbabwe, which is why most of them ran away amidst growing fears of cholera and hunger and settled in their sister country, South Africa, where xenophobes (those who fear and hate African immigrants—Afrophobians) chased them around like rats. Unfortunately for Tafirenyika, Ncube who was also a refugee in South Africa did not buy that story completely. Ncube saw Mugabe as the solution to the sustainable survival of the African continent. Ncube said that Mugabe should be seen as the messiah in Africa. In fact, Ncube claimed that he was a 'Mugabite', and I wanted to know what that meant. He said that Mugabites were disciples of Mugabe scattered all over the world, believers in his philosophy. He claimed that Mugabe was one who had come to bring revolution and sustainable changes in the continent, which of course came with a big price tag. He claimed that Mugabe was currently the strongest and most courageous man in Africa. He said that if African leaders could emulate the footsteps of Mugabe that the African continent and its people though will suffer temporarily, will see the light of the day afterwards and that such light will shine until the end of time.

He said that Africans were afraid to suffer temporary pain and they were also afraid to make sacrifices. He also said that the continent was filled with hypocrites and puppets of the imperialists who were willing to sell their own people like Judas of the Bible did—those who beg for food and comfort from 'Babylonians' and are ready to kiss their feet any time, mortgaging their conscience and the future of the African continent and its children in general. Ncube got very angry and said that the Bible that Europeans brought to us with guns proclaimed that we should do unto others as we will have them do unto us; hence, which part of this Bible command are Europeans obeying? Why the double standards? Why the racism in dealing with Africans? Why make Africans believe in their religious doctrines while at the same time treating Africans like animals? He told Tafirenyika that Zimbabweans had been infested with cholera and sanctions because Mugabe had refused to dance to the tune of the imperialists who wanted to take total dominion and full control of the lives and lands of Zimbabweans. Ncube said that these imperialists would always be waving their economic wands in the faces of Zimbabweans and Africans in general with threats of withdrawing them if Africans did not dance to their demands. According to him, Mugabe did not want to be a puppet leader dancing to the tunes of colonial invaders who did nothing but milk the African continent of its natural resources and who also had the impudence to enslave Africans in their own lands, making biased laws that exonerated them from all crime and blames.

Ncube got more and more furious and told Tafirenyika that the sufferings and pains they faced then was temporary and that it was a sacrifice that had to be made to change the face of events and the course of history in Zimbabwe and in the African continent in general. He continued to say that even if it meant dying he would because he supported Mugabe. He quoted Thomas Jefferson who had said that 'from time to time, the tree of liberty is refreshed and watered with the blood of patriots and tyrants', and he also said that as an individual he was ready to pay the ultimate prize if called to the struggle. He asked if there was any European country in the world where Africans had gone to with their soldiers and religious books, violated the already established order within their lives, abused them and taken over their lands, and enslaved them in the same lands that they took over. On asking this question, there was immediate silence. He demanded to know whether that was not racial injustice. He demanded to know whether that was not a crime.

Tafirenyika stood and said, 'But Zimbabwe was the food basket of Africa before Mugabe started his crazy one-man campaign.' Ncube said to Tafirenyika that she should realise that Mugabe had an agreement with the Europeans that in time to come the land will be given back to Zimbabweans, that Mugabe was just waiting for that time to come, and when it did come, Europeans neglected the agreement and all dialogue and diplomacy applied by Mugabe failed, which was why he reacted. Ncube said that the whites had even planned to overthrow him so that the agreement they had would be invalidated and forgotten in history.

Pascal who had been silent all along said, 'I do not take sides, but I have a problem with Mugabe and I also have a problem with white people. Mugabe wants to stay in office until the end of time as if he is the only intelligent person capable of ruling the country. Can you not see that he is making himself a God?' He said, 'I also want to sit my ass on that Zimbabwean royal throne.' Everyone laughed.

Ncube snapped and said, 'What about the queen of England who has been sitting on that royal throne as if God brought the seat from heaven and gave to her ancestors?' He also exclaimed, 'Who are the people that created democracy? Is it not the same "white people"? Is the queen a democrat? Is her position democratic? What about Tony Blair, who acts as if he is the most righteous democrat, yet he wanted to run for the third term in the UK prime minister race? Is he not a European? Are they not the ones who created democracy? Is it because Mugabe refused to give in to their demands that they now want to demonise him and destroy the economy of a great country like Zimbabwe, even invading us with hunger and cholera, using their stage-managed media to blacklist Mugabe and paint Zimbabwe black?'

Pascal said, 'Please, Ncube, calm down. We are not fighting. My primary problem is because Mugabe has so many university degrees and he is a highly placed politician by European standards, so how come he is not leading by examples?'

Ncube snapped again, 'What about Tony Blair?'

And Pascal said, 'But Mugabe is a more mature, more intelligent, more educated, and a more enlightened person politically than Tony Blair.' Ncube said that he believed that Mugabe was a man on a mission who wished to accomplish that mission no matter the sacrifices he made. He went on to say that Mugabe wanted to see to it that the agreement they established to hand over the land at a certain period was kept as rules had to be kept and agreements had to be kept. Ncube went on further to say that if they could not honour such an agreement, why then should Mugabe maintain any political arrangements with them?

Pascal became funny and said, 'I told you that I have not finished. I have a problem with white people also. Before they came to our lands, our parents used to give us names in our traditional languages. Africans speak languages which progressively evolved amidst our forefathers because they were intelligent, so how come the "white man" thinks that we are no longer intelligent human beings and that our languages are no longer good enough, and now they call me Pascal. Can you imagine "Pascal"? What is the meaning of my name "Pascal"? This is a slave name, putting the chains on my neck forever. They even replaced our traditional toilets, and now you have a toilet in the same house you live.' I interrupted them before a world war could erupt in that room. He asked a question that touched me. 'How can a man come into your house with a slave uniform, take away your house from you with brute force, then give you the slave uniform to wear and serve him in your own house? What happens to your self-esteem, your pride, and dignity as a human being whenever you watch that person sit in your house while you wear the slave uniform calling him a master? Does that not prove that you are not human enough? And if that is the case, does that not prove that the person came in the first place to degrade your humanity?

'Let it be known today, all Africans, that humanity is the same whether you are from Europe or from Africa or from Asia. Nature has placed us in different geographical regions and given us adaptive features suitable to those regions. Let no man hate his fellow neighbour. I must admit that I have had encounters with good Europeans who harbour no racial prejudice and who also share my views that all humans are fundamentally the same irrespective of physical differences. All that I am saying is that our colonial masters and some European leaders did create the problems that are affecting the image of most good Europeans today. Let us also look around amidst our anger and see that some Europeans have done marvellously well on this planet and deserve a lot of credits despite a few flaws and their presumed insensitive and racist tendencies.'

Let us all admit that there was no formal invitation by Africans for European colonisers to invade the Africa continent (I use the word 'invade' because they came forcefully and also deceitfully using military and religious books). They designed the programme, knowing what they wanted to achieve despite what some of the hypocrites amongst them patronisingly claim—to please a few narrow-minded hungry souls in the African continent. Evidence on the table shows that they were actually gathering slave colonies, taking over the lands, and also plundering the African rich natural resources to develop their own lands, and some of them wanted to displace Africans from their natural habitat having presumed that Africans are a dark and inferior race (it was all about land, power, control, and natural resources).

Who wants to tell me that they don't know that American and European economies were originally built by African slaves whose lives were sacrificed to establish capitalist economic empires centring only on profit making. Colonisation was an aftermath of slavery. Slavery of the Africans was a dehumanising effort of leaders of the Western world, and they have not seen anything wrong about it, which is where I have a huge problem with them when they hypocritically make laws specifying rewards for right and punishments for wrong. They have not admitted any wrong, and this means a lot to real hard rational thinkers. Let it be known to all Europeans that I am only upset with their leaders who created this capitalist worm that infested the African continent. I hold no grudges against an ordinary European, for the evil of some of their leaders and past colonisers indirectly affects them individually today.

I quoted a part of the Bible where it was said that the pharaohs enslaved the Israelites, and I wanted to know if that biblical aphorism was used to forge a theological conclusion that slavery is a normal thing; hence, Africans must not worry about the past ugliness of slavery since it also happened in Africa during the days of the pharaohs. I do not want to say that the Bible story was concocted to keep Africans as perpetual slaves, hence accepting slavery in any manner that it came, but what I am saying is that if the Bible story is true, then it means that Africans did enslave others in the past; hence, slavery and colonialism (which is also another form of slavery) could be seen as human nature but a nature that one must fight against. If that Bible story is a fabricated fairy tale, then European leaders have a lot of questions to answer. As a free thinker, I want everyone reading this part of the book to think out of the box, leave unhealthy prejudice and emotions aside, and examine this matter critically.

European colonisers invaded the African continent with military might; they did not send any notices that they were coming so that indigenous Africans could prepare to counter the invasion, but they just came without warnings. First of all, they enslaved our people whom they shipped to their lands in ships and chains, whereby millions of Africans perished during the cold Atlantic crossing. After that, they saw a need to divide the continent into colonies which they did and then gathered colonial slaves. As if that was not enough for them, they invaded parts of the African continent with the sole intention of dominance as it happened in North America in the case of the Red Indians, Australia in the case of the Aborigines, and New Zealand in the case of the Maoris.

They came with their own religious books, proclaiming and introducing their own God which made ours look like demigods, demons, evil, savage, etc. They also came with guns; hence, we had no choice other than to accept their religion or die. A lot of evil was perpetrated against Africans at that in time in history, which I cannot mention here to avoid development of ugly emotions, but the problem still lingers between the descendants of Europeans that came to the southern region of Africa and the natives of Africa in those regions. It seems as if colonialism and slavery are still going on in those lands but this time in a different dimension. Racism is so high in that part of Africa that I begin to wonder if God whom they say created all of us beginning with Adam and Eve in the Garden of Eden has vacated those lands.

In the west, east, and north of Africa, I believe that the colonialists left after those countries fought hard and regained their freedom, but they settled in some parts of Southern Africa, or did they originally come there to settle? They saw the countries in those regions as habitable, extremely rich in natural resources with good weather, full of cattle, diamonds, and gold; then they settled there, assuming the name 'white settlers'. I must say in all sincerity without fear or prejudice that in South Africa I have a problem with the extension of the name of euro-South Africans to Afrikaans. Those born in South Africa by European settlers are children of South Africa and must bear the same identity and name as South Africans and they must also respect indigenous South Africans. I also have a problem with the level of poverty and AIDs amongst indigenous South Africans when Europeans were there, and I believe they have solutions to those two major problems; hence, I begin to wonder what appreciation they have shown to those who welcomed them in their land. I am not sure Mugabe is completely wrong. The argument that he seized commercial lands and handed over to subsistence farmers invoking hunger and poverty does not hold water; after all, people developed commercial farming in Zimbabwe, so why couldn't the natives do the same with the land given to them? The argument that Mugabe took lands without knowing what to do with them does not also hold water as Mugabe is just one individual. It is time that Zimbabweans come together and fashion out a new future for their country's economy and leave Mugabe alone.

Let us go back to the story of the Bible where we were told that Saul was told by the prophet of God to go to the Amalekites, destroy them, and take their wives and children as slaves. I also wanted to know if it is the same kind of prophesy that made the British to go to America and destroy the natives of Indians (the Red Indians since they were presumed as idol worshippers) and take over their lands. Is it the same prophesy that made the British and Dutch people invade the southern region of Africa and take over their land? Is it the same instruction that was given for the land of Australia to be taken over by the British, displacing the Aborigines? Is it the same instruction that was given to the Europeans to displace the Maoris of New Zealand?

Should I now have a problem with Robert Gabriel Mugabe, who decided that this is unjust and must stop by acting in a military way? I know that most African leaders especially the puppets of the Western leaders have decided to blame Mugabe completely, and they have also forgotten all his struggles in the past for African liberation, but I must say that if it had been Europeans that were affected in the same manner that Africans were affected in the land of Zimbabwe, they would have fought for what they believed to be 'just', for they love 'justice'. Are Europeans making laws that make them immune over the atrocities against Africans or do they think we are not human enough? What is happening that we do not know?

Sometimes I also wonder and ask myself what the native Zimbabweans who were given the reclaimed land are doing with it as one doesn't eat land.

Can they not develop the capacity to carry out large-scale farming like in the past when white farmers were in control of those lands? Are they making such efforts or just possessing the land, allowing it to waste while the people starve only to turn around to blame Mugabe? Perhaps they expect Mugabe to till the land for them.

Most African leaders cannot take decisions on their own, even when their houses are on fire. I always tell them to clean up their diapers because Europeans cannot do it for them. Take for instance malaria disease in Africa, I asked someone in the Ministry of Health in Nigeria why it was more important to advertise the sale of malaria drugs than to campaign for the destruction of the mosquito breed which caused the disease. The gentleman told me that until those mosquitoes started biting the leaders and their children who were living in America and London, inflicting them with malaria, they would never give it a thought. He also told me that Africa was a continent where leaders sent their children out of the country to attend the best schools in the world while schools in the continent rotted and received less attention. He also said that when there was war, their children did not come home to fight those wars; rather they unleashed their subjects and children of poor people to go and perish.

I never said that Mugabe did the right thing or the wrong thing, but I want anyone reading this book to use his rational sense of judgment and conscience devoid of prejudice to analyse this matter critically. If you want to understand this matter, be the other person. If you are an African, be a European and think freely to feel how the other person feels, and if you are a European in this analysis, be the African to see also how the other person feels.

> Until we take how we see ourselves and how we see others into account, we will be unable to understand how others see and feel about themselves and their world. Unaware, we will project our intentions on their behaviour and call ourselves objective.

I want to ask any rational thinker or any sane person if what Mugabe did was totally wrong, I mean 'completely wrong', even if some of his approaches were presumed wrong. The Bible which they gave us says that you should do unto others as you will have them do unto you. According to the Bible also, Christ did say love one another' ; hence, I ask if European leaders could give us Christianity, it means that they believed in our humanity (because if not, we cannot share the same religion). Hence where is the love for one another? Where is the love for Africans or was the religion a scam tool? How come when it comes to those they call 'black people' that rule does not apply any more? Does that not tell any rational thinker that this is another technique to strip the African continent away from its original inhabitants just like it happened in America, Australia, and New Zealand using religious books and other tricks?

How do you measure the strength of a man? Is it in his wickedness or in his unceasing expression of humanity? In these present times, the wicked is considered strong. It matters not how we twist things around to favour our points of views. I always say to people that the pure justice of life has nothing to do with our biased self-sense of judgment; it is inescapable. Good attracts good and evil attracts evil, and what a man plants that shall he reap.

Let us go back to analyse a European kid born in Zimbabwe. Let us not doubt the fact that Zimbabwe is his natural birthplace; hence, he's a full citizen of Zimbabwe. If this hypothetical European kid is not prejudiced and is following this journey, he will admit that his forebears took this land by force. He should also acknowledge that taking a land of people by force is a crime.

I want the African kid who is a native of Zimbabwe to examine this matter critically to see that if the European kid is asked to completely surrender all of the land which he inherited from his forebears though forcefully, it will mean that he will have nowhere to live. We must also remember that this kid did not originally steal this land but his ancestors did, and he subsequently inherited such stolen land. Now on the part of this kid, I would like to know if he was asked to surrender any part of this land, would he honour such a request. Has he been reminded in the past that this land was stolen from the natives, hence there should be a discussion about it? Does he really see forceful possession of people's lands as a crime? Has he ever accepted that his forefathers made mistakes in stealing the land of the African natives in the name of colonialism? Has there been any time that an agreement was reached that in time to come the stolen land will be given back to the natives with or without compensations? Was that agreement later upheld or ignored or better say trashed? Was violence applied because dialogue and diplomacy failed? If the violent approach resulted in the sufferings of the masses of Zimbabwe including economic sanctions and cholera, does that not imply retaliation or counter attack from the Western leaders? If this hypothetical European kid was an African, how would he look at this matter?

Let there be progress in great Zimbabwe, the home of one of the greatest wonders of the earth, the home of an African heritage, the home of the great

Victoria Falls. As I said, I am a free thinker and I do not want to drive you into the depth of my own base thoughts; hence, you have to finish the thoughts' journey yourself, but while doing that, learn to tell yourself the truth and learn not to take sides. Where Mugabe is wrong, say that he is wrong, and where Europeans are wrong, say that they are wrong.

Heroes by my ratings are activists who brought sustainable positive changes in their society and in the lives of their people, sometimes paying the ultimate price (death or incarceration) for what they stood for in their times, most particularly when what they stood for was justified and for the service of humanity devoid of selfish motives, also when what they believed strongly in was meant to usher in positive transformations within the society at large and in the lives of their people in general. They are reformists who fought various struggles in their times as a token of sacrifice to humanity. Also, I consider Africans who have made extraordinary achievements in their various fields globally for the benefit of mankind in general as heroes. Leaders who look in the mirror and see the people and not themselves are also my true heroes. God bless our heroes.

This part of the book is very necessary so as to remind Africans all over the globe that Africans are great people except that they have chosen to let their creative thinking, their creative abilities, and their greatness go to sleep. This is also to inform African leaders about the need to make agriculture, youth empowerment, human and social development, creativity, technology copying and cloning, development of productive capacities, and education ultimate priorities in Africa. Africans must know today that the world has no more respect for children of Africa; the world has ignored the works of people like Prof. Phillip Emeagwalli in one of the greatest science mysteries of our times—the Internet. The world has ignored the first scientist in the world, Imhotep, who built the pyramid. We wonder about the kind of a world we live in; hence, Africans must rise up today and embrace creativity and copy and clone technology. Africans must begin to delay gratifications and face the harsh realities of our times for posterity sake. Africans must stop drinking a lot of alcohol, stop abusing sex and drug, and become strong for our children and generations to come.

Africans must become warlords in this war against mental slavery and economic slavery by producing what they consume and also consuming what they produce. Africans must wage this war as they are gradually reducing children of Africa to guinea pigs and making them the endangered human species in the only world they know, while also making the African continent a perpetually slave continent. African leaders and successful African businessmen in the continent and diaspora must come together and pull resources together to engineer the 'copy-clone technology' initiative. Chinese, Indians, and Japanese did the same, and today they have won the battle against survival. We must do this today for our children and generations to come.

African leaders must wake up today and stop amassing wealth that ends up in Swiss banks, instead of investing in education and the people. I have briefly profiled Africans who have made eternal marks on the stones of history, those who have made the African continent proud. We must follow their positive footpaths; they have justified our humanity on this planet and they have also proven the world wrong. May the universal God bless them and guide them on their journey in this universe. Today we remember them. The youths must acquire their strong and positive virtues.

Hannibal Barca

Hannibal Barca is the most famous of the three Carthaginian military leaders, known as Hannibal. Hannibal Barca is the one who famously led his forces including elephants into Rome, where he terrorised Roman forces during the Second Punic War. The son of a general, Hannibal became the commander of the army and waged victorious campaigns across north-western Iberia (modern Spain). He was determined to have revenge on Rome for its victory in the First Punic War.

Stephen Bantu Biko

Stephen Bantu Biko was a noted anti-apartheid activist in South Africa in the 1960s and early 1970s. A student leader, he later founded the Black Consciousness Movement, which could empower and mobilise much of the urban black population. Since his death in police custody, he has been called a martyr of the anti-apartheid movement. While living, his writings and activism attempted to empower black people, and he was famous for his slogan 'black is beautiful', which he described as meaning: 'Man, you are okay as you are. Begin to look upon yourself as a human being'.

Chris Hani

Chris Hani was the leader of the South African Communist Party (SACP) and chief of staff of the armed wing of the African National Congress (ANC). He was a fierce opponent of the apartheid government. He was assassinated in 1993. He took over from Joe Slovo, a Jewish anti-apartheid activist.

Nelson Rolihlahla Mandela

Nelson Rolihlahla Mandela is a former president of South Africa, the first to be elected in fully representative democratic elections. Before his presidency, Mandela was an anti-apartheid activist and leader of the African National Congress and its armed wing. He spent twenty-seven years in prison, much of it on Robben Island. Mandela has received more than one hundred awards over four decades, most notably the Nobel Peace Prize in 1993. He is currently a celebrated elder statesman who continues to voice his opinion on topical issues. In South Africa, he is often known as Madiba, an honorary title adopted by elders of Mandela's clan. The title has come to be synonymous with Nelson Mandela.

Albert John Luthuli

Chief of his tribe and president general of the African National Congress, Albert John Luthuli was the leader of ten million black Africans in their non-violent campaign for civil rights in South Africa. A man of noble bearing, charitable, intolerant of hatred, and adamant in his demands for equality and peace amongst all men, Luthuli forged a philosophical compatibility between two cultures—the Zulu culture of his native Africa and the Christian-democratic culture of Europe. He was awarded the 1960 Nobel Peace Prize for his role in the non-violent struggle against apartheid. He was the first African and the first person from outside Europe and the Americas to be awarded the Nobel Peace Prize.

Benjamin Nnamdi Azikiwe

Benjamin Nnamdi Azikiwe usually referred to as Nnamdi Azikiwe or, informally and popularly, as 'Zik', was the founder of modern Nigerian nationalism and the first president of Nigeria, holding the position throughout the Nigerian First Republic. As a result of publishing an article entitled 'Has the African a God?' written by I. T. A. Wallace-Johnson, he was brought to trial on charges of sedition. Although he was found guilty of the charges and sentenced to six months in prison, he was acquitted on appeal. The writings of Azikiwe spawned a philosophy of African liberation, Zikism, which identifies five concepts for Africa's movement towards freedom: spiritual balance, social regeneration, economic determination, mental emancipation, and political revival.

Chief Obafemi Awolowo

Chief Obafemi Awolowo was a Nigerian nationalist, a political leader, and a principal participant in the struggle for Nigerian independence. He wrote his first book, *Path to Nigerian Freedom*, in which he was highly critical of British policies of indirect administration and called for rapid moves towards self-government and Africanisation of administrative posts in Nigeria. He also expressed his belief that federalism was the form of government best suited to the diverse populations of Nigeria, a position to which he consistently adhered. Also in 1945 in London, he helped found the Egbe Omo Oduduwa (Society of the Descendants of Oduduwa, the mythical ancestor of the Yoruba-speaking peoples), an organisation devoted to the study and preservation of Yoruba culture.

Dedan Kimathi

Dedan Kimathi Waciuri (truly, Kimathi wa Waciuri) was a Kenyan rebel leader who fought against the British colonial government in Kenya in the 1950s.

He was convicted and executed in 1957 for murder and terrorism.

Kofi Atta Annan

Kofi Atta Annan is a Ghanaian diplomat who served as the seventh secretary general of the United Nations from 1 January 1997 to 1 January 2007, serving two five-year terms. Annan was the co-recipient of the Nobel Peace Prize in 2001. Annan served as Undersecretary General until October 1995, when he was made a Special Representative of the Secretary General to the former Yugoslavia, serving for five months in that capacity before returning to his duties as Undersecretary General in April 1996. On 13 December 1996, Annan was recommended by the United Nations Security Council to be Secretary General, and was confirmed four days later by vote of the General Assembly. Annan took the oath of office without delay, starting his first term as Secretary General on 1 January 1997. Annan replaced outgoing Secretary General Boutros Boutros-Ghali of Egypt, becoming the first person from a black African nation to serve as Secretary General.

Oliver Reginald Tambo

Oliver Reginald Tambo was a South African anti-apartheid politician and a central figure in the African National Congress (ANC). In 1940, he along with several others, including Nelson Mandela, was expelled from Fort Hare

University for participating in a student strike. Tambo, along with Mandela and Walter Sisulu, was a founding member of the ANC Youth League in 1943, becoming its first national secretary and later a member of the National Executive in 1948. In 1955, Tambo became Secretary General of the ANC. In 1958, he became Deputy President of the ANC and in 1959 was served with a five-year ban order by the government. He was involved in the formation of the South African United Front, which some believe helped bring about South Africa's expulsion from the Commonwealth in 1961. In reality, South Africa became a republic in 1961 and voluntarily left the Commonwealth. In 1967, Tambo became Acting President of the ANC, following the death of Chief Albert Luthuli. In 1985 he was re-elected President of the ANC. He returned to South Africa in 1991 after over thirty years in exile and was elected National Chairperson of the ANC in July of the same year.

Julius Kambarage Nyerere

Julius Kambarage Nyerere served as the first president of Tanzania, previously Tanganyika, from the country's founding until his retirement in 1985. He was also referred to as Baba wa Taifa (Father of the Nation). On his return to Tanganyika, Nyerere took a position teaching history, English, and Kiswahili, at St. Francis' College, near Dar es Salaam. In 1953, he was elected president of Tanganyika African Association (TAA), a civic organisation dominated by civil servants, which he had helped found while as a student at Makerere University. In 1954, he transformed TAA into the politically oriented Tanganyika African National Union (TANU). TANU's main objective was to achieve national sovereignty for Tanganyika. A campaign to register new members was launched, and within a year, TANU had become the leading political organisation in the country. He also spoke on behalf of TANU to the Trusteeship Council and Fourth Committee of the United Nations in New York. His oratory skills and integrity helped Nyerere achieve TANU's goal for an independent country without war or blood.

Herbert Samuel Heelas Macaulay

Herbert Samuel Heelas Macaulay was a Nigerian nationalist, politician, engineer, journalist, and musician and was considered by many Nigerians as the founder of Nigerian nationalism. Macaulay was one of the first Nigerian nationalists and for most of his life a strong opponent of British rule in Nigeria. As a reaction to claims by the British that they were governing with 'the true interests of the natives at heart', Macaulay wrote: 'The dimensions of "the true interests of the natives at heart" are algebraically equal to the length, breadth and depth of the white man's pocket.' In 1908, he exposed European corruption in the handling of railway finances, and in 1919, he argued successfully for the chiefs whose land had been taken by the British in front of the Privy Council in London. As a result, the colonial government was forced to pay compensation to the chiefs. In retaliation for this and other activities of his, Macauley got jailed twice by the British. Macaulay became very popular, and on 24 June 1923, he founded the Nigerian National Democratic Party (NNDP), the first Nigerian political party.

Queen Anna Nzinga

One of the great women rulers of Africa, Queen Anna Nzinga of Angola fought against the slave trade and European influence in the seventeenth century. Known for being an astute diplomat and visionary military leader, she resisted Portuguese invasion and slave raids for thirty years. A skilled negotiator, she allied herself with the Dutch and pitted them against the Portuguese in an effort to wrest free of Portuguese domination. She fought for a free Angola until her death at age eighty-two, after which weak rulers left the country open for the Portuguese to regain control.

Herbert Chitepo

He was the first African in Southern Rhodesia to qualify as a barrister. On returning to Rhodesia in 1954, he practiced as a lawyer and defended many African nationalists in court. In 1961, he served as legal adviser to Joshua Nkomo, founder of the Zimbabwe African Peoples Union (ZAPU), at the Southern Rhodesia Constitutional Conference in London.

Muhammad Ali

Muhammad Ali is a retired American boxer, former three-time World Heavyweight champion, and winner of an Olympic light-heavyweight gold medal. In 1999, Ali was crowned 'Sportsman of the Century' by *Sports Illustrated* and the BBC. Ali was best known for his fighting style which he described as 'float like a butterfly, sting like a bee'. His movement is often described as a dance; some go so far as to call it beautiful. Throughout his career, Ali made a name for himself with great hand speed, as well as fast feet and taunting tactics. While Ali was renowned for his fast, sharp out-fighting style, he also had a great chin and displayed a great heart and ability to take a punch in his 1974 fight against George Foreman in Zaire, called the Rumble in the Jungle.

Marcus Mosiah Garvey, Jr

Marcus Mosiah Garvey, Jr, was a national hero, a publisher, journalist, entrepreneur, black nationalist, orator, and founder of the Universal Negro Improvement Association and African Communities League (UNIA-ACL). Garvey was unique in advancing a Pan-African philosophy to inspire a global mass movement focusing on Africa known as Garveyism. Promoted by the UNIA as a movement of African redemption, Garveyism would eventually inspire others, ranging from the nation of Islam to the Rastafarian movement (which proclaims Garvey to be a prophet). The intention of the movement was for those of African ancestry to 'redeem' Africa and for the European colonial powers to leave it. His essential ideas about Africa were stated in an editorial in the *Negro World* entitled 'African Fundamentalism', where he wrote: 'Our union must know no clime boundary or nationality.' Let us hold together under all climes and in every country.

Desmond Mpilo Tutu

Desmond Mpilo Tutu is a South African cleric and activist who rose to worldwide fame during the 1980s as an opponent of apartheid. Tutu was elected and ordained the first black South African Anglican Archbishop of Cape Town, South Africa, and primate of the Church of the Province of Southern Africa (now the Anglican Church of Southern Africa). He received the Nobel Peace Prize in 1984, the Albert Schweitzer Prize for Humanitarianism, and the Magubela Prize for liberty in 1986. He is committed to stopping global AIDS and has served as the honorary chairman for the Global AIDS Alliance. In February 2007, he was awarded the Gandhi Peace Prize by Dr A. P. J. Abdul Kalam, President of India. He was generally credited with coining the term 'Rainbow Nation' as a metaphor for post-apartheid South Africa after 1994 under African National Congress rule. The expression has since entered mainstream consciousness to describe South Africa's ethnic diversity. Tutu is widely regarded as 'South Africa's moral conscience'.

Walter Max Ulyate Sisulu

Walter Max Ulyate Sisulu was a South African anti-apartheid activist and member of the African National Congress (ANC). He joined the ANC in 1940. In 1943, together with Nelson Mandela and Oliver Tambo, he joined the ANC Youth League, founded by Anton Lembede, of which he was initially the treasurer. He later distanced himself from Lembede after Lembede (died

1947) had ridiculed his parentage (Sisulu was the son of a white foreman). Sisulu was a brilliant political networker and had a prominent planning role in the militant Umkhonto we Sizwe (Spear of the Nation). He was made secretary general of the ANC in 1949. He was sentenced to life imprisonment on 12 June 1964. With other senior ANC figures, he served the majority of his sentence on Robben Island. In October 1989, he was released after twenty-six years in prison, and in July 1991, he was elected ANC deputy president. He remained in the position until after South Africa's first democratic election in 1994. In 1992, Walter Sisulu was awarded Isitwalandwe Seaparankoe, the highest honour granted by the ANC, for his contribution to the liberation struggle in South Africa. He married Albertina in 1944. The couple had five children and adopted four more. Sisulu's wife and children were also active in the struggle against apartheid. The government of India awarded him Padma Vibhushan in 1998. Walter Sisulu was given a 'special official funeral' on 17 May 2003.

Mzee Jomo Kenyatta

Mzee Jomo Kenyatta founded the Pan-African Federation with Kwame Nkrumah. His reputation with the British government was marred by his assumed involvement with the Mau Mau Rebellion. Kenyatta became prime minister of the autonomous Kenyan government and was known as *Mzee* (a Swahili word meaning old man or elder). At this stage, he asked the white settlers not to leave Kenya and supported reconciliation. He retained the role of prime minister after independence was declared on 12 December 1963. On 12 December 1964, Kenya became a republic, with Kenyatta as executive president.

Samora Machel

Samora Machel protested against the fact that black nurses were paid less than whites doing the same job. He later told a reporter how bad medical treatment was for Mozambique's poor: 'The rich man's dog gets more in the way of vaccination, medicine and medical care than do the workers upon whom the rich man's wealth is built.' In 1962, Machel joined the Front for the Liberation of Mozambique (FRELIMO), which was dedicated to creating an independent Mozambique. He received military training in 1963 elsewhere in Africa and returned in 1964 to lead FRELIMO's first guerrilla attack against the Portuguese in northern Mozambique. By 1970, Machel had become commander-in-chief of the FRELIMO army, which had already established itself amongst Mozambique's peasantry. His most important goal, he said, was to get the people 'to understand how to turn the armed struggle into a revolution' and to realise how essential it was 'to create a new mentality to build a new society'. That goal would soon be realised. The FRELIMO army had weakened the colonial power, and after Portugal's coup in 1974, the Portuguese left Mozambique. Machel's revolutionary government then took over, and he became independent Mozambique's first president on 25 June 1975.

Kenneth Kaunda

Kenneth Kaunda was the youngest of eight children. He was born at the Lubwa Mission in Chinsali, Northern Province of Northern Rhodesia, now Zambia. In 1951, he became Organising Secretary of the Northern Rhodesia African Congress for Northern Province, which included at that time Luapula Province. On 11 November 1953, he moved to Lusaka to take up the post of Secretary General of the ANC. He broke from the ANC and formed the Zambia African National Congress (ZANC) in 1958. ZANC was banned in March 1959. In June, Kaunda was sentenced to nine months' imprisonment, which he spent first in Lusaka and then in Salisbury (Harare). On his release in January 1960, he was elected president of the newly formed United National Independence Party (UNIP), which replaced ZANC. In July 1961, he organised a civil disobedience campaign in Northern Province, the so-called Cha-cha-cha campaign, burning schools and blocking roads. Kaunda ran as a UNIP candidate during the 1962 elections. This resulted in a UNIP-ANC Coalition Government, with Kaunda as Minister of Local Government and Social Welfare. In January 1964, UNIP won the General Election under the new constitution. Kaunda was appointed Prime Minister. On 24 October 1964, he became the first president of independent Zambia.

Kamuzu Banda

Kamuzu Banda was the leader of Malawi and its predecessor state, Nyasaland, from 1961 to 1994. After receiving much of his education overseas, Banda returned to his home country (then British Nyasaland) to speak against colonialism and help lead the movement towards independence. In 1963, he was formally appointed Nyasaland's prime minister and led the country to independence as Malawi a year later. Two years later, he declared Malawi a republic with himself as president. Nyasaland became the independent Commonwealth of Malawi. It was Banda himself who chose the name 'Malawi' for the former Nyasaland; he had seen it on an old French map as the name of a 'Lake Maravi' in the land of the Bororos and liked the sound and appearance of the word as 'Malawi'.

Kwame Nkrumah

He was an influential twentieth-century advocate of Pan-Africanism and the leader of Ghana and its predecessor state, the Gold Coast from 1952 to 1966. Kwame Nkrumah as a leader of his government faced three serious challenges. First, he needed to learn the art of government. Second, he needed to create a unified nation of Ghana from the four territories of the Gold Coast. Third, he needed to win his nation's independence. Nkrumah was successful in all three goals. Within six years of his release from prison, he was the leader of an independent nation. At 12 a.m. on 6 March 1957, Nkrumah declared Ghana independent. Nkrumah was now hailed as 'Osagyefo'—which means 'the victorious one' in the African language. On 6 March 1960, Nkrumah announced plans for a new constitution which would make Ghana a republic. The draft included plans for an eventual surrender of Ghanaian sovereignty to a union of African states. On 19, 23, and 27 April 1960, a presidential election and plebiscite on the constitution were held. The constitution was ratified and Nkrumah elected president, beating J. B. Danquah, the UP candidate, 1,016,076 to 124,623. In 1963, Nkrumah was awarded the Lenin Peace Prize by the Soviet Union. Ghana became a charter member of the Organisation of African Unity in 1963.

Haile Sellassie

In the 1950s, Haile Selassie worked to absorb into Ethiopia the important Red Sea province of Eritrea (this was accomplished in 1962). Later he founded the University College of Addis Ababa and welcomed home many Ethiopian college graduates from abroad. In the 1960s, the emperor was clearly recognised as a major force in the pan-African movement (a movement dedicated to a united Africa), demonstrating his remarkable capacity for adapting to changing circumstances. It was a great personal triumph for him when, in 1963, the newly founded Organisation of African Unity established its headquarters in Addis Ababa. Unlike other African leaders, Haile Selassie, of course, had not had to struggle once in office to prove his legitimate authority to his people. Rather, his control of government for more than forty years had given him enough time to demonstrate his strength.

Laurent Kabila

Laurent Kabila was a saviour when he and his supporters fought their way across what was then the devastated nation called Zaire in 1996 and 1997. Adoring crowds saluted him everywhere he went—they believed the little known Laurent Kabila would set them free from the poverty and corruption of the decades of dictatorship under former President Mobutu Sese Seko. After the death of Leurent Kabila, his son Joseph Kabila became the president of Democratic Republic of Congo, most likely the richest country in the African continent.

Patrice Emery Lumumba

He helped to find the non-tribal Movement National Congolais (MNC) in 1958, later becoming the organisation's president. He attended the Brussels conference which culminated on 27 January with the declaration of Congolese independence and the establishment of 30 June 1960 as the independence date with national elections from 11 to 25 May 1960. On 31 May, it was confirmed that Lumumba and the MNC had won electoral victory and the right to form a government. Lumumba and the MNC formed the first government on 23 June 1960, with thirty-five-year-old Lumumba as Congo's first prime minister and Joseph Kasa-Vubu as its president. In accordance with the constitution, on 24 June, the new government passed a vote of confidence and was ratified by the Congolese Chamber and Senate. Congolese independence from Belgium was finally gained on 30 June 1960. On Independence Day, in a ceremony attended by dignitaries, the foreign press, and the Belgian elite including King Baudouin, Patrice Lumumba delivered his famous independence speech after being officially excluded from the event programme, despite being the elected Congolese Prime Minister. In direct contrast to the paternalistic glorification of colonialism in the speech of King Baudouin, as well as the relatively harmless speech of President Kasa-Vubu, Lumumba's outspoken anti-colonial speech resonated with the Congolese for its inspired honesty while simultaneously humiliating and alienating the King and his entourage.

Josiah Tongogara

Josiah Tongogara, Josiah Magamba Tongogara was a commander of the ZANLA guerrilla army in Rhodesia. He attended the Lancaster House Conference that led to Zimbabwe's independence and the end of white minority rule.

Robert Gabriel Mugabe

Robert Gabriel Mugabe is the second president of Zimbabwe. Mugabe rose to prominence in the 1960s as the Secretary General of the Zimbabwe African National Union (ZANU) during the conflict against the white-minority rule regime of Ian Smith. Mugabe was a political prisoner in Rhodesia for more than ten years between 1964 and 1974. Upon release, Mugabe left Rhodesia in 1975 to rejoin the Zimbabwe Liberation Struggle from bases in Mozambique. Mugabe acquired numerous degrees while he was in prison. At the end of the war in 1979, Mugabe emerged as a hero and a freedom fighter in the minds of all Africans.

Dr Joshua Nkomo

He was the founder of the Zimbabwe African Peoples Union (ZAPU). He rose to the leadership of the Railway Workers Union and then to the leadership of the African National Congress in 1952. In 1960, he became president of the National Democratic Party, which was later banned by the Rhodesian government. He also became one of Rhodesia's wealthiest self-made entrepreneurs. Nkomo was detained by Ian Smith's government in 1964, with fellow revolutionaries Ndabaningi Sithole, Edgar Tekere, Maurice Nyagumbo, and Robert Mugabe, until 1974 when they were released due to pressure from South African President B. J. Vorster. Following Nkomo's release, he went to Zambia to continue the liberation struggle through the dual process of armed conflict and negotiation.

Shamba Bolongongo

Shamba Bolongongo was hailed as one of the greatest monarchs of the Congo. King Shamba had no greater desire than to preserve the peace, which is reflected in a common quote of his: 'Kill neither man, woman nor child. Are they not the children of Chembe (God), and have they not the right to live?' Shamba was also noted for promoting arts and crafts and for designing a complex and extremely democratic form of government, featuring a system of checks and balances. Shamba likewise brought to his people some of the agreeable pastimes that alleviated the tediousness of life. The reign of Shamba Bolongongo was really the 'Golden Age' of the Bushongo people of the Southern Congo. After abolishing the cruder aspects of African warfare, Shamba Bolongongo introduced raffia weaving and other art of peace. According to the legends of the Bushongo people, their history as a state goes back fifteen centuries.

Menelic II

Menelic the second, in 1889, while claiming the throne against Mengesha, signed at Wuchale in Wollo province (Uccialli in Italian) a treaty with Italy acknowledging the establishment of the new Italian Colony of Eritrea with its seat at Asmara. This colony had previously been part of the northern Tigrayan territories from which Ras Mangasha and his allies such as Ras Alula generated support, and the establishment of the Italian colony weakened the northern Rases. However, it was soon found that the Italian version of one of the articles of the treaty placed the Ethiopian Empire under an Italian protectorate, while the Amharic version did not. Emperor Menelik denounced it and demanded that the Italian version be changed. Negotiations failed, so Menelik renounced the treaty, leading to Italy declaring war and invading from Eritrea. After defeating the Italians at Amba Alagi and Mekele, Menelik inflicted an even greater defeat on them, at the Battle of Adowa on 1 March 1896, forcing them to capitulate. A treaty was signed at Addis Ababa recognising the absolute sovereign independence of Ethiopia.

Great King Moshoeshoe

Great King Moshoeshoe was given the name Lepoqo (Lepoqo means disasters) at his birth, due to the deprived conditions in which he was born and raised. Moshoeshoe's parents had a large influence on the child as he grew up, teaching him about virtues and discipline in a politically inclined way. Moshoeshoe gained his place as a leader after a punitive raid on a cattle thief, returning with hundreds of heads of cattle, earning him his name 'Moshoeshoe (the shaver)' as he was said to have shaved off the beard of his adversary (Ramonaheng). Moshoeshoe's reign coincided with the growth in power of the well-known Zulu chief, Shaka. Although he had ceded much territory, Moshoeshoe never suffered a major military defeat and retained most of his kingdom and all of his culture. His death in 1870 marked the end of the traditional era and the beginning of the modern colonial period. Moshoeshoe Day is a national holiday in Lesotho, celebrated every year on 11 March to commemorate the day of Moshoeshoe's death.

Osei Kofi Tutu

Osei Kofi Tutu I was one of the co-founders of the Empire of Ashanti, him and his chief priest, Okomfo Anokye. The Ashanti were a powerful, warlike, and highly disciplined people of West Africa, whose history goes back more than 2,000 years. The Ashanti are said to be the descendants of those Ethiopians mentioned by Diodorus Siculus and Herodotus, who were driven southward by a conquering Egyptian army. Osei Tutu led an alliance of Ashanti states against the regional hegemony, the Denkyira, completely defeating them. Then, through force of arms and diplomacy, he induced the rulers of the other Ashanti city states to declare allegiance to Kumasi, his capital. Throughout his career he was closely advised by Okomfo Anokye, his chief priest. The

Empire of Ashanti was officially formed in 1701, and Osei Tutu was crowned Asantehene (King of all Ashanti). He would hold that position until his death in 1717 in a battle against the Akyem. Osei Tutu was the fourth ruler in Asante royal history, succeeding his uncle Obiri Yeboa.

Shaka Zulu

At the time of his death, Shaka ruled over 250,000 people and could muster more than 50,000 warriors. Shaka was probably the first son of the chieftain Senzangakhona and Nandi, a daughter of Bhebhe, the past chief of the Elangeni tribe, born near present-day Melmoth, KwaZulu-Natal Province. He revolutionised war tactics in his time.

Philip Emeagwali

Philip Emeagwali won the Gordon Bell Supercomputing Prize in 1989 for applying the power of networked computers to analyse the oil field reserves. In the 1980s, he worked on advanced formulas in networked computers, leading to the Gordon Bell Prize. Emeagwali has won several other awards, including a 1998 Distinguished Scientist Award from the World Bank. Philip Emeagwali conducts research on Internet and supercomputing technologies, targeting applications that benefit petroleum engineering, weather forecasting, and global warming. His knowledge of massively parallel programming (using thousands of processors) was mostly self-taught, and in 1989, he performed the world's fastest computation of 3.1 billion calculations per second. Emeagwali used previously unaccepted technology that became the standard for supercomputers. Emeagwali also invented a method utilising supercomputers, which enabled oil companies to extract more petroleum from oil fields.

Dr Ave Kludze

Dr Ave Kludze was a Ghanaian American astronautical engineer and strategist for NASA. Growing up in Accra, Kludze was fascinated by science and how things worked. He was not able to fulfil his childhood dream of being a pilot, but Ghanaian scientist Dr Ave Kludze has arguably gone one step better: developing and flying spacecrafts for NASA to go to Moon, Mars, and beyond. When he realised he could not become a pilot because of his eyesight, he channelled his energies into studying engineering, moving to the United States to complete a course in electrical engineering at Rutgers University. On graduating, Kludze initially planned to return to Ghana to develop solar technologies, but then NASA came calling in 1995.

Tai Solarin

As a columnist, Tai was a relentless critic of Nigerian military rule as well as of corruption in the government and church, and this got him into lots of trouble, often being jailed for his public remarks. As an atheist and vehement critic of irrationality and hypocrisy, Tai Solarin has few kind words for religion in his country. 'Nigeria is dying today of religion,' Tai proclaims, 'outrageous religious beliefs.' Africans, says Tai, are taught by religion and superstition to fear too many things. 'Witches, angels, the Devil or Satan, thunder, lightning, nocturnal birds are all objects that generate fear.' He tells the tale of a magistrate in Lagos who refused to decide a case because he believed 'juju' men were casting spells on him. 'The worst bane of African non-development', Tai insists, 'is chronic dependence on the deity to solve all earthly problems.' Dr Solarin says that 'blacks hold on to their God just as the drunken man holds on to the street lamp post—for physical support only.'

Oprah Winfrey

Beautiful Oprah Winfrey is the world's most powerful African-American woman. She is world's richest woman, the queen of 'talk shows', and one of the most famous celebrities, not to mention the third richest black person.

Mohammed Al Amoudi

Mohammed Al Amoudi from Ethiopia is the world's richest black person and the richest businessman in the entire African continent. (Why does he inspire you besides being the richest person? You have to remember that at the end of the day, it's not always about money, but about the creative efforts which bring about the wealth and recognition.)

Alhaji Aliko Dangote

Alhaji Aliko Dangote (born 10 April 1957) is a businessman based in Nigeria. He is the owner of the Dangote Group, which has operations in Nigeria and several other countries in Africa, including Benin, Cameroon, Ghana, South Africa, and Zambia. A wealthy supporter of former President Olusegun Obasanjo and the ruling People's Democratic Party (PDP), Dangote controls much of Nigeria's commodities trade through his corporate and political connections. With an estimated current net worth of around US$ 2.5 billion, as at 2008, he was ranked by Forbes as one of the richest black African citizens and the third richest person of African descent in the world behind Mohammed Al Amoudi ($9.0 billion) and Oprah Winfrey ($2.7 billion.)

Patrice Tlhopane Motsepe

Patrice Tlhopane Motsepe is Executive Chairman of African Rainbow Minerals Limited, the non-executive Chairman of Harmony, the Deputy Chairman of Sanlam, and the President of Business Unity South Africa (BUSA), which is the voice of organised business in South Africa. He is also president of Mamelodi Sundowns Football Club. Mr Motsepe began his business career as a child when he would wake early to help his entrepreneurial father sell liquor to mine workers at his father's shop. He went on to earn a BA from Swaziland University and a LLB from Wits University. Today he's the biggest single shareholder of the world's fifth largest gold mining company. His firm, African Rainbow Minerals, controls 19.8 per cent of Harmony. His family trust owns 43.1 per cent of ARM.

Chike Obi

Chike Obi, with Akpan Ezeilo and Adegoke Olubummo, was one of a trio of black mathematicians who pioneered modern mathematics research in Nigeria. By plain brainwork and without the use of modern technological aid such as computers, world-acclaimed Nigerian mathematician, Prof. Chike Obi, gave scientific proof to a 361-year-old mathematical puzzle known as Fermat's Last Theorem. The theorem, well known amongst mathematicians and other allied professions, was enunciated by one of the two leading mathematicians of the first half of the seventeenth century, Pierre de Fermat and French. By far, the best known of Fermat's many theorems, it states that the equation $xn+yn=Zn$, where x, y, z, and n are positive integers, has no solution if n is greater than two.

Cyprian Ekwensi

Ekwensi began his writing career as a pamphleteer, and this perhaps explains the episodic nature of his novels. One of his well-illustrated piece of works is called the *People of the City* (1954), in which Ekwensi gave a vibrant portrait of life in a West African city. It was the first major novel to be published by a Nigerian. Ekwensi's most widely read novel, *Jagua Nana*, appeared in 1961. *Burning Grass* (1961) is basically a collection of vignettes concerning a Fulani family. Its major contribution is the insight it presents into the life of this pastoral people. Ekwensi based the novel and the characters on a real family with whom he had previously lived. Between 1961 and 1966, Ekwensi published at least one major work every year. The most important of these were the novels, *Beautiful Feathers* (1963) and *Iska* (1966), and two collections of short stories, *Rainmaker* (1965) and *Lokotown* (1966). Ekwensi continued to publish beyond the 1960s, and amongst his later works are the novel *Divided We Stand* (1980), the novella *Motherless Baby* (1980), *The Restless City and Christmas Gold* (1975), *Behind the Convent Wall* (1987), and *Gone to Mecca* (1991).

Chinua Achebe

He gained worldwide attention for *Things Fall Apart* in the late 1950s; his later novels include *No Longer at Ease* (1960), *Arrow of God* (1964), *A Man of the People* (1966), and *Anthills of the Savannah* (1987). Achebe wrote his novels in English and defended the use of English, a language of colonisers, in African literature. In 1975, his lecture 'An Image of Africa: Racism in Conrad's "Heart of Darkness"' became the focus of controversy, for its criticism of Joseph Conrad as 'a thoroughgoing racist'.

Prof. Wole Soyinka

He was a great political activist. Wole Soyinka won the Nobel Prize in 1986 and continuously criticised corruption in the government of democratically elected President Shehu Shagari and often found himself at odds with his military successor, Mohammadu Buhari. The foremost Nigerian dramatist became the first African laureate of the Nobel Prize, enshrined for good in the history of world literature and the heritage of the human nation. The Nobel lecture which Soyinka proclaimed on this occasion was devoted to the South African freedom-fighter Nelson Mandela. Soyinka's acceptance speech criticised apartheid and the politics of racial segregation imposed on the population by the Nationalist South African government.

Bob Marley

Marley, a world-renowned musician and activist, was born in the small village of Nine Mile in Saint Ann Parish, Jamaica. Marley suffered racial prejudice as a youth, because of his mixed racial origins, and faced questions about his own racial identity throughout his life. He once reflected: 'I don't have prejudice against him. My father was a white and my mother was black. Them call me half-caste or whatever. Me don't dip on nobody's side. Me don't dip on the black man's side nor the white man's side. Me dip on God's side, the one who created me and cause me to come from black and white.'

Mutabaruka

Mutabaruka is a Jamaican dub poet. His name comes from the Rwandan language and translates as 'one who is always victorious'. As a young man employed by Jamaican Telephone Company Ltd, he became interested in the Rastafarian movement and converted from Catholicism. His outspoken statements on theology have generated controversy, even amongst Rastafarians, and he has described Rasta as 'part of a universal quest which may also be pursued by other routes, such as Hinduism or Buddhism or Christianity'.

Jaja of Opobo

Jaja of Opobo was believed to be the first nationalist of modern Nigeria. The circumstances surrounding his life and death could particularly throw more light on that of Ken because they are so similar. I doubt that Ken himself was aware of this. Jaja's happy life was brought to a tragic end when he was about twelve years old. That was when he was captured in his native town of Amigbo, in the heart of Igboland. He was sold into the Anna Pepple House in the bonny kingdom of the Niger River Delta, a house he later came to lead. Jaja was so dynamic that he worked very hard to regain his freedom by paying off the money paid for his head.

Seretse Khama

Seretse Khama was the founding president of Botswana in the period 1966-80. He inherited an impoverished and internationally obscure state from British rule and left an increasingly democratic and prosperous country with a significant role in Southern Africa. Between 1966 and 1980, Botswana had the fastest growing economy in the world. It also came to be seen as a remarkable state with high principles, upholding liberal democracy and non-racialism in the midst of a region embroiled in civil war, racial enmity, and corruption. State mineral revenues were invested in infrastructural development, education and health, and in subsidies to cattle production. The result was a great increase in general prosperity, in rural as well as urban areas, though with inequities that increased after the death of Seretse Khama. Seretses Khama was known for his intelligence, integrity, and a wicked sense of humour—puncturing the pomposity of those who had too high an opinion of themselves.

Boutros Boutros-Ghali

Born 14 November 1922, Boutros was an Egyptian diplomat who was the sixth Secretary-General of the United Nations (UN) from January 1992 to January 1997. Boutros Boutros-Ghali was born in Cairo into a Coptic Christian family (Boutros being the Arabised form of Petros). His grandfather Boutros Ghali was Prime Minister of Egypt from 1908 until he was assassinated in 1910.

Ellen Johnson Sirleaf

Often referred to as the 'Iron Lady', Johnson-Sirleaf is Africa's first elected female head of state. Ellen Johnson-Sirleaf was born in Monrovia, the capital of Liberia, to educated parents. Her ethnic background is half Gola from her father's side and one-fourth Kru and one-fourth German from her mother's side.

Fela Anikulapo Kuti

A world-renowned human rights activist and musician, Felas was born as Olufela Olusegun Oludotun Ransome-Kuti in Abeokuta, Ogun State, Nigeria, to a middle-class family. His mother, Funmilayo Ransome-Kuti, was a feminist activist in the anti-colonial movement, and his father, Reverend Israel Oludotun Ransome-Kuti, a Protestant minister and school principal, was the first president of the Nigerian Union of Teachers. His brothers, Dr Beko Ransome-Kuti and Olikoye Ransome-Kuti both medical doctors, are well known in Nigeria. Fela was sent to London in 1958 to study medicine but decided to study music instead at the Trinity College of Music. He returned to Nigeria to commence his activism using music as a medium.

Ken Sarowiwa

Kenule 'Ken' Beeson Saro-Wiwa was a Nigerian author, television producer, environmental activist, and winner of the Goldman Environmental Prize. Saro-Wiwa was a member of the Ogoni people, an ethnic Nigerian minority whose homeland, Ogoniland, in the Niger Delta has been targeted for crude oil extraction since the 1950s and which has suffered extreme and irreversible environmental damage from decades of reckless oil waste dumping. Initially as spokesperson and then as president of the Movement for the Survival of the Ogoni People (MOSOP), Saro-Wiwa led a non-violent campaign against environmental degradation of the land and natural waters of Ogoniland by the operations of multinational oil companies, especially Shell. He was also an outspoken critic of the Nigerian government, which he viewed as reluctant to enforce proper environmental regulations on the foreign oil companies operating in the area.

At the peak of his non-violent campaign, Saro-Wiwa was arrested, hastily tried by a special military tribunal, and hung by the Nigerian military government of General Sani Abacha, all on charges widely viewed as entirely politically motivated and completely unfounded. His execution provoked international outrage and resulted in Nigeria's suspension from the Commonwealth of Nations.

Winnie Madikizela-Mandela

Winnie Madikizela-Mandela is a South African politician who has held several government positions and headed the African National Congress Women's League. She is currently a member of the ANC's National Executive Committee. As a controversial activist, she is popular amongst her supporters, who refer to her as the 'Mother of the Nation'.

Askia Muhammad Ture

Askia Muhammad Ture founded the Askia dynasty of the West African Songhay Empire. He extended the conquests of Sunni Ali, promoted commerce, and increased the political influence of Islam in his state.

Behanzin Hossu Bowelle

He was an African poet king who defeated France from his throne of gold (1841-1906). Behanzin, known as 'Hossu Bowelle' or 'The King Shark,' was the most powerful of the West African kings in the closing years of the nineteenth century. He was not what so often passes for a 'king' in Africa, but a real monarch. He descended in direct line from Tacodounon, who conquered Dahomey in 1610 and took the throne from the Houenous, whose ancestry, incidentally, went even further back.

Jerry John Rawlings

Born Jeremiah Rawlings in Accra, Gold Coast, he ruled Ghana for nearly nineteen years. He embraced democracy in the later part of his reign. He was twice the head of state of Ghana and was the first president of the Fourth Republic. He led a rare revolution that changed the history of Ghana for the better.

Chief Cetswayo

The Zulu king, Cetswayo, whose nation suffered defeat by Great Britain in the Anglo-Zulu War of 1879 travelled to England in 1882 to meet with Queen Victoria, hoping to have his sovereignty restored. While in London, Cetswayo was treated as a celebrity, with his image appearing repeatedly in a variety of periodicals. Cetswayo challenged perceived notions and stereotypes of African races through his London visit.

Imhotep

Imhotep was a priest and high government official of Egyptian Third Dynasty King Zoser. Imhotep designed Zoser's tomb, a step pyramid in Saqqara that's considered the world's oldest stone building. Imhotep's work predates reliable records, but modern scholars put Zoser's reign around 2640 BC, possibly ending around 2613 BC. Imhotep advised the king and supposedly produced journals (now lost) on medicine and healing, and he's credited with designing Zoser's tomb, a forty-acre complex near ancient Memphis, which required the mobilisation of thousands of labourers. Over the next 2000 years, Imhotep's legend grew. He was deified in Egypt, and the Greeks (who called him Imouthes) associated him with their god of medicine, Asclepius. Considered a semi-mythical figure until archaeological finds of the twentieth century, Imhotep is considered by many to be history's first scientist. (The architect of the first pyramid is Imhotep.)

Thomas Sankara

Sankara saw himself as a revolutionary and was inspired by the examples of Cuba and Ghana's military leader, Flight Lt. Jerry Rawlings. As president, he promoted the 'Democratic and Popular Revolution'. He renamed the country Burkina Faso, meaning 'the land of upright people' in Mossi and Djula, the two major languages of the country. He also gave it a new flag and wrote a new national anthem (Une Seule Nuit). Sankara's government included a large number of women. Improving women's status was one of Sankara's explicit goals, an unprecedented policy priority in West Africa. His government banned female circumcision, condemned polygamy, and promoted contraception. The Burkinabé government was also the first African government to publically recognise AIDS as a major threat to Africa. Sankara had some original initiatives that contributed to his popularity and brought some international media attention to the Burkinabé revolution:

Dr Martin Luther King

King's activities and his arrest ended with a United States District Court ruling that ended racial segregation on all Montgomery public buses in the United States of America. King organised and led marches for blacks' rights to vote, desegregation, labour rights, and other basic civil rights. Most of these rights were successfully enacted into United States law with the passage of the Civil Rights Act of 1964 and the Voting Rights Act of 1965. King's 'I Have a Dream' speech is regarded as one of the finest speeches in the history of American oratory.

Barack Hussein Obama II

Barack Obama was born in Honolulu, Hawaii, to Barack Hussein Obama, Sr, a Luo from Nyang'oma Kogelo, Nyanza Province, Kenya, and Ann Dunham, a white American from Wichita, Kansas. Barack Hussein Obama II was Illinois senator for three terms. Obama is the first African-American to be nominated by a major American political party for president. He became the first black person to serve as president of the Harvard Law Review and became the first African-American president of the United States of America.

Kunta Kinte

Kunta Kinte is an African from Gambia, whose arrival in Annapolis is symbolic of the slave trade era where millions of African men, women, and children were captured and sent to the New World. They endured the horrors of the 'Middle Passage', the Atlantic crossing in which Africans were packed into the holds of ships for months, many dying en route. Kinte survived to tell his story.

Malcolm X

Malcolm X was an American black Muslim minister and a spokesman for the Nation of Islam. He also founded the Muslim Mosque, Inc. and the Organisation of Afro-American Unity. Malcolm first went to Africa in the summer of 1959. Malcolm established an international connection between Africans on the continent and those in the diaspora. Malcolm held the view that African-Americans were right in defending themselves from aggressors. On 28 June 1964, at the founding rally of the OAAU, he said:

The time for you and me to allow ourselves to be brutalized violently has passed. Be nonviolent only with those who are nonviolent to you. And when you can bring me a nonviolent racist, bring me a nonviolent segregationist, and then I'll get nonviolent. But don't teach me to be nonviolent until you teach some of those crackers to be nonviolent.

Dr Ishakamusa Barashango

He was a poet, writer, and activist. He fought hard to awaken the African minds on issues of God and reality. One thing he always stressed and that most impressed me was that we can never free our minds as long as we view God as a white man or as long as we keep worshipping white people's holy days (holidays). He was a pillar of our community. Dr Barashango, affectionately known as Baba, received his Bachelor of Arts degree in religion from Oakwood College in Huntsville, Alabama. He studied for his master's degree at North-eastern Seminary in Takoma Park, Maryland.

He wrote:

> Thanksgiving Day literally is a holiday celebrating the beginnings of the almost total extermination of an entire race of people, commonly called 'Indians' and the enslavement, continued oppression and genocide of the African, by European settlers . . . For over 100 years now Black folks in the United States have joined with the descendants of the same European murderers who enslaved them and systematically all but destroyed the Amer-Indian, in feasting and giving thanks to God for the 'opportunity' to live in one of the most racist, imperialist, and oppressive countries on earth. Black People celebrating Thanksgiving Day is like the Americans celebrating the bombing of Pearl Harbor, or the so-called Jews celebrating the rise of the Third Reich, or the Palestinians celebrating the intrusion of the settler colony of Zionist Israel, or moreover the millions of Zulu descendants who are being murdered by the thousands each day, celebrating the establishment of the Union of South Africa . . .

Wangari Maathai

Wangari Maathai was the first African woman to receive the Nobel Peace Prize. One of Kenya's best-known women, Maathai won her Nobel Peace Prize in 2004 for combining science and social activism. She was the founder of the Green Belt Movement, where for over thirty years she mobilised poor women to plant thirty million trees.

In 2004, Wangari Maathai became an internationally recognised figure by becoming the first black woman and the first environmentalist to receive the Nobel Peace Prize. Her honour, however, did not come without controversy. Maathai was best known as the founder of the Green Belt Movement (GBM), an initiative to plant trees in the forested areas of Kenya, which were being stripped for commercial expansion. Critics wondered whether a 'tree planter' was truly a peace activist. For Maathai, there was an important link between the environment and peace. Most of the people involved with GBM are rural African women who, over the years, have planted nearly thirty million trees. As a result they have reaped the rewards of food, fuel, shelter, and employment. More importantly, they have achieved control over their own lives. In an interview with the *Progressive*, Maathai commented on her Nobel Peace Prize win, 'I wasn't working on the issue of peace specifically. I was contributing towards peace, and that is what the committee recognised: that, indeed, we need to step back and look at a more expanded concept of peace and security.'

Alhaji Sir Ahmadu Bello

The Nigerian political leader Alhaji Sir Ahmadu Bello (1909-66) was the leading northern spokesman during Nigeria's drive to gain independence from the British. Ahmadu Bello was born in Rabah, north-west state, a descendant of Uthman don Fodio, the renowned nineteenth-century Muslim leader of Northern Nigeria.

Miriam Makeba

Born in Johannesburg, South Africa, Miriam Makeba has a long and dramatic career behind her, both as a singer and human rights campaigner. She was the first vocalist to put African music on to the international map in the 1960s. She was the first black musician to leave South Africa on account of apartheid, and over the years, many others would follow her example. In America, Miriam Makeba had several hits in the 1960s, amongst them being 'Pata Pata', 'The Clique Song', and the Tanzanian 'Malaika'. She remained an active opponent of the apartheid regime in her own country. Miriam Makeba was African music's first and foremost world star. She was a pioneer who played her early songs and blended different styles long before anyone even began to talk about 'world music'. Her disk production is spread across many companies all over the world—so far and wide that it's difficult to get a panoramic view of it. But no collection of African music should be without one or more of Miriam Makeba's recordings. Makeba suffered a heart attack in Italy and died.

Joaquim Alberto Chissano

Joaquim Alberto Chissano served as the second president of Mozambique for nineteen years from 6 November 1986 until 2 February 2005. Since stepping down as president, Chissano has become an elder statesman and is called upon by international bodies, such as the United Nations, to be an envoy or negotiator. He currently chairs the Joaquim Chissano Foundation and the Forum of Former African Heads of State and Government. Joaquim Chissano represented FRELIMO, the Mozambique independence movement, in Paris during the 1960s. He was known there as a soft-spoken diplomat who worked to reconcile radical and moderate Marxist factions of the FRELIMO party. He went on to fight in the Mozambican War of Independence against the Portuguese colonial government and the authoritarian regime of the Estado Novo, by then engaged in a multi-front colonial war.

Thabo Mbeki

Mbeki has mediated in difficult and complex issues on the African continent including Burundi, Democratic Republic of Congo (DRC), the Ivory Coast, and some important peace agreements. He oversaw the transition from the Organisation of African Unity (OAU) to the African Union (AU). Thabo Mbeki is a South African politician who served almost two terms as the second post-apartheid president of South Africa from 14 June 1999 to 24 September 2008.

King Zoser of Egypt (Pharaoh)

Zoser is the best-known pharaoh of the Third Dynasty of Egypt. He commissioned his official, Imhotep, to build the first of the pyramids, a step pyramid for him at Saqqara.

Joe Slovo

Joe Slovo was a South African politician, long-term leader of the South African Communist Party (SACP), and leading member of the African National Congress. He played active roles, leading to the end of apartheid regime in South Africa. He was succeeded by Chris Hani.

Muammar Abu Minyar (Gaddafi)

Until Gaddafi began a resistant bloody reprisal against the rebellious efforts to oust him from office, he was a hero in the eyes of African people known as the Libyan strongman. He was the Libyan president. Muammar Abu Minyar is accorded the honorific 'Guide of the First of September Great Revolution of the Socialist People's Libyan Arab Jamahiriya' or 'Brotherly Leader and Guide of the Revolution'. Gaddafi was the youngest child born into a peasant family. He grew up in the desert region of Sirte. On 1 September 1969, a small group of military officers led by Gaddafi staged a bloodless coup d'état against King Idris I, while he was in Kammena Vourla, a Greek resort, for medical treatment. His nephew, the Crown Prince Sayyid Hasan ar-Rida al-Mahdi as-Sanussi, became King. Before the day ended on 1 September, King Sayyid Hasan ar-Rida al-Mahdi as-Sanussi had been formally deposed by the revolutionary army officers and put under house arrest; they abolished the monarchy and proclaimed the new Libyan Arab Republic. Unlike some other military revolutionaries, Gaddafi did not promote himself to the rank of general upon seizing power, but rather accepted a ceremonial promotion from captain to colonel and has remained at this rank.

Empowering Philosophy

The creative mind is restless, and every man is creative in his own ways – discover yours and do something constructive with it. There are no limits to the powers of the human mind, rather human beings limit themselves. The realm of ideas is visa-free and accessible to every man and at any time; every man has the power to think and to create; thoughts give birth to ideas; ideas give birth to physical manifestations, and ideas are infinite in their worlds. God does not choose people, rather people choose themselves. It would amount to utter ludicrousness that Africans suffer and cry amidst abundance yet they cannot do anything to challenge such false destiny when all powers dwell within everyone. Wake up today and command your destiny, all you Africans. Happy is the man who is awake.

Ask for strength equal to your task rather than asking for a task equal to your strength.

Before I go further into the empowering philosophy, I must emphasise on the need for positive thinking and positive living; the final results are always positive. Let me also mention the effects of negative thinking by stating that when you choose to think negatively, the final results are always negative. There is positive power in positive thinking and equally there is an opposite of positive power in negative thinking. Both patterns of thinking generate results respectively but one is constructive while the other is destructive.

I enjoy reading the part of the Bible whereby Christ did say that if one could have faith like the mustard seed, a lot of great things would happen, and in my own understanding, Christ was trying to teach the people the power of thoughts, vision, hope, persistence, will, determination to succeed, perseverance, and focus.

This does not mean that one should not work hard. I hereby interpret faith as the ability to focus your mind on your object of desire and moving towards that object by taking physical (practical) actions without giving up, no matter the circumstances you encounter. From this perspective, there should be a force connecting you and the object which you desire, and that force dwells in your mind, while your body advances towards it (enhance that force with vision, concentration and focus and also enhance your physical efforts through hard work, determination, and perseverance, and I tell you, you will find that object of your desire if you do not give up no matter the impediments you face).

We must abstain from thinking that a mountain can ever come to Mohammed; that manna will ever fall from heaven; that AIDS/HIV can ever be eradicated from a person's body without taking the right actions; that you could move a mountain with prayers and that you could ever turn a dollar into a million dollars. Though there are phenomenal happenings which no one has been able to understand, I think they are also scientific if we understand them, because our universal God, divine in nature, is capable of extraordinary happenings, but if we are able to know how they occur, it will be well understood that they are also logical and scientific. After all, a cellular phone, when dialled, connects you to someone in America in seconds, yet we do not see the movement of the sound, but the sound is moving even through walls and our bodies. It is simply about the things we do not know and how they function. We do not want people to dwell so much on those things because of the activities of hypocrites and con men that are siphoning people's resources, promising them miracles and even staging some of them in churches.

With persistence and definiteness of purpose, one can transform thoughts into physical manifestations. Today, we must learn the power that dwells in thoughts, deep-guided creative and constructive thinking, and how to apply these powers to improve our lives. Also, we must learn today to accept and support the creative efforts of fellow Africans in order to transmit the culture of creativity.

According to one of the greatest mysteries in science which has given birth to almost everything we know today, the good, the bad, and the ugly, when one engages in a journey of thoughts, one is actually visiting a world of infinite ideas, for that which one is seeking is seeking him also and is somewhere waiting for him.

When you think, surely you will arrive at a realm of ideas where that substance you seek dwells subjectively (in non-tangible form). Just go there and get it. This is the empowering philosophy which is the basis of all success and mind empowerment.

All powers dwell within man. Also, when you are on a thought journey, you meet objects on the road just as you meet physical objects on the road if you are embarking on a physical journey. Sometimes the objects that you meet may be more useful than what you are actually seeking, so learn to retain those ideas (non-physical objects) that you find on your thought journey. The telephone was almost discovered by accident by Alexander Graham Bell while working on other matters in an institution for those with impaired hearing; Reynolds discovered the ball bearing by accident while on a mental journey and research for other objects of thoughts. Science by Albert Einstein is only a refinement in human thinking.

We must treat thoughts as objects, and we must also understand that they are not distinguishable from the products of thoughts (ideas), and the ideas themselves are not distinguishable from physical manifestations.

Thoughts lead to ideas, and ideas lead to physical manifestations by practical applications of the right actions. (Always remember this whenever you are confronted with a situation: the word TIP; standing for the journey from Thoughts Ideas Physical.)

TIP: The journey between thoughts, ideas, and the physical by Joachim Onyeakor.

As a person, you are always in charge of what you think, and you think with your brain which houses your mind, and the product of every thought process is ideas. When you apply actions to ideas, the product is physical manifestation. You can see that in this simple analogy, all powers exist in you. Always learn to apply TIP, and it will work for you because it has always worked for me. Remember when Christ said, 'seek and you shall find'? Europeans, Jews, Americans, and Asians are seeking and they are finding. What has happened to Africa, the place where it is said that civilisation began?

When you do not think, you are also under the spell of mental slavery, for you have allowed the most functional part of the human body to sleep. This implies that those who do not think are asleep and at the mercy of those who think, hence they must wake up. The fact that some of us have allowed their thinking faculty to sleep is the reason why others are thinking for us, and the iniquitous ones feed our sleeping minds with futile information, just for their own selfish gains.

Africans must start experimenting with the power of thoughts. Have you ever thought about something so hard that it seemed as if your brain was going to crack? You may not find the objects of your thoughts instantly, but when you relax, the idea comes in like a flash via intuition, and this power dwells in everyone. When you think, you send a signal to the subjective realm, the idea world, and somewhere there, an idea transporter brings the idea to you via intuitive perception.

My fight is to ensure that in as much as most of us have accepted total defeat in life and believe that nothing could ever go right in Africa, let the youth and children born today live with the new philosophy that mind has total power and control over matter and could possibly transform Africa into greatness by being creative, and this comes by being able to tap into the brain power which every human being is endowed with. Let us begin to raise our children without fear; let us raise them to possess universal minds and not narrow-mindedness. Let us raise our children to compete with children of the advanced nations. I do not intend to start a physical revolution in Africa but a non-violent mind revolution which is what we cannot do without at this moment, unless we want the world to conclude their research that we are lesser human beings.

Reynolds who invented the bearing stumbled on such an idea that was also as important as what he was seeking. Most Africans who have high academic proficiency still lack the ability to delve into the thought realm, not knowing that if one combines high degree of academic development and deep-guided creative thinking, he would definitely become a creative warrior like others. This is wake-up time.

Our professors and professionals are troubled with lack of challenges and support from leaders, lack of funding, and worst of all the same inferiority complex every African is battling with which accounts for the reasons why they acquire all the mighty degrees and academic achievements only to develop superiority complex towards their fellow Africans with absolutely nothing to offer to the development and advancement in the continent. Inferiority complex is a serious problem in the minds of Africans, and I do not know why someone should feel inferior of the way he was naturally created.

I met a young man who bought a brand-new Hummer Jeep and I commended him for his achievement. Deep down in my heart, I meant to commend him though I was poised to ask him what he does for a living. This man was not very happy that I was not jealous of the car he had acquired, and

I discovered that he felt better when people felt oppressed and jealous. This is a serious problem in the minds of most of us, especially Nigerians. We amass wealth only to impress and oppress others which accounts for the billionaires having mansions situated in the midst of the poorest people and on streets full of potholes and mud to get to their places of residence.

I spoke to a Jamaican in Montreal-Canada and we discussed deep African issues until a Canadian friend joined us. The tone of this Jamaican guy changed, and his attitude and behaviour changed also. Everything he started doing from that time on was to impress the Canadian guy. I also experienced this same attitude with a South African lady. Whenever we had discussions and a European walked in, her behaviour changed completely just to impress the person. This is chronic inferiority complex, and I really do not know why it happens in some people because I seem to be living above such emotions.

I am asking Africans to wake up, for anyone who wakes up would realise the injustice and mind slavery which false doctrines have done in Africa and to the minds of Africans. Some religious sects claim that meditation is evil and occultism, but how did most of the inventions come about if people do not think and meditate. Most of the great scientists of our time like Albert Einstein, Isaac Newton, and Michael Faraday just to name a few used to meditate deeply and embark on a process of deep-guided creative thinking which most religious sects consider occultism. Their founding fathers didn't want us to think for ourselves so they could think for us but in the end made our continent a dumping ground for the fruits of their own thoughts. This is how we have become victims of economic slavery. Our inability to utilize our mind power has by omission enslaved us as well us direct mental slavery caused by superstitions, wrong education and false religious doctrines. Mental slavery gave birth to economic slavery and today we wage war against them.

I know that someday things would be all right if Africans could start thinking like other human beings on this planet. Any man who does not think at all is not better than an animal. Christ said, 'seek and you shall find'. The Jews, Americans, Europeans, and Asians are finding every day because they are seeking, and they are continuously seeking, and if we do not take time, we would look completely inferior to them in intelligence and almost like animals that if care is not taken, crazy ones amongst them will initiate moves to take over Africa.

It amazes me that Africans fail to see that Australia does not originally belong to the British people; neither does America originally belong to the Jews and the British people. A simple illustration is in South Africa, in the province of Gauteng. Sandton is a stone throw away from Alexander, and you find out that Sandton is so rich while Alexander is incredibly poor, with majority of the poorest people in South Africa living there. The system does not know pity or asking for help; the system is impersonal, and if you do not wake up and stand on your feet, the system will displace you. If you cannot afford a luxury house, you go for a less expensive one. If you cannot afford a less expensive one, you go for a lesser one, and if you cannot afford any at all, then you may have no place to live. Can you not see how the impersonal and self-running system can displace one if he does not fit?

In America, the most advanced nations of the world, you find people who trim their intestines through liposuctions; you will also come across people who experiment with all sorts of pills to lose weight, but in war-ravaged African nations like Somalia you find an entirely different scenario. You find people who are so thin and malnourished that you will not believe that a human being gave birth to them. You would not expect Americans to feed you. Rather, if you all die of starvation, they will take over your continent. This is the dynamics of the New World Order, and Africans must know this today and stand up and stop begging. Our leaders must also stand up and clean their dippers.

Jesus Christ of the Christian Bible knew the laws (the law of seeking and finding and also the law of sowing and reaping), and most of his teachings stated in the Bible, if correctly interpreted to the people and well assimilated, will empower them, but the problem we have is the case of a one eyed-man leading the blind and those who lead others through the nose. They pay attention to paranormal happenings and create a cloud of paranormal hopefuls and in the process, amass wealth for themselves. At the end of the day, no paranormal happens. They have confused and twisted almost every message of Jesus Christ and sceptics are beginning to wonder whether anybody like Jesus Christ ever visited earth

The world of ideas is infinite and limitless. It is like an ocean, and all that it takes is to apply the right thought process and in the right directions and you would surely get there.

I engaged a taxi driver in a conversation regarding self-empowerment. I brought out one of my empowerment DVDs called Mama Africa, and I explained to him that I did not go to anyone to finance the production of the DVD. He asked me how I got the money to execute such a task.

I told him that I had been working for four years abroad, and he said that if he had money, he would do things greater than DVD. I quickly recoiled. Most Africans are creative and highly intelligent, but the problem is that there is no support and the government has no provisions to support such people. Also, the strange nature of this system, which does not encourage most people to fit, limits someone, hence most Africans drink and smoke their creative ideas away. Today African leaders must create forums for Africans to demonstrate and develop their creativity.

Our schools are making us polished slaves; we graduate from universities only to be hanging around the streets in search of non-existent jobs when we should actually create one. This is a vital part where African governments should wake up; we need them in terms of policy making, good leadership, and support; we also need them to restructure our academic system. An engineer should dig deep into engineering and not waste time in non-related courses. Everyone knows that jobs are few out there and the number of graduates harvested from university institutions every year outnumbers available jobs, so what happens to them when they come out of school, since it seems they went there in the first place only to get a certificate that they thought is the job.

Most Africans are undeniably intelligent and creative though. I use an example of my photographer when I was producing the Mama Africa DVD in South Africa; this guy, a genius, said to me that he is competing in a system that cannot bring out the best in him; his African brothers would never support him because he is not white as they see whites and their things as superior. Most foreigners, on the other hand, do not engage in corporate businesses, and whites would prefer to support their fellow whites, so who would support him and what should he do in such a situation?

He said that if he could get government support to develop his outfit to the level whereby he could compete with whites, then he would stand a better chance. Team spirit is something we lack in Africa; this is one great virtue we have to learn from Europeans. We must learn to work as a team.

Another problem we have in thinking is the objects of our thoughts. I would not say completely that most of us do not think at all. They do, but in some cases, they dwell on extraneous things.

This does not imply that you should not think about whatever makes you happy, but obsessive thoughts of those things when you do not make out time to think beyond yourself and think of what you can do for your society and mankind is a serious problem, because if people were not thinking in the past, there will be no jobs in the first place, not to talk of affording a car.

The same problem of lack of creative thinking has resulted in most African leaders failing to see that Africa is being taken over systematically, and some of them are even used as tools to achieve this goal (neo-colonialism and others). Also the same lack of attraction to higher thoughts has caused us to lose our roots as human beings on this planet without even realising it. Apart from few Africans who have demonstrated that we can think like other human beings, people like Philip Emeagwali, Chike Obi, Wole Soyinka, Chinua Achebe, Nelson Mandela, just to name a few, the majority of us are not a force in this current cycle of civilisation and creativity.

The mere fact that we have refused to think has made it easier for mercenaries of mental slavery to pollute our minds more with baseless information and hopeless dreams. False prophets, con men, who have no genuine concern for this continent; men who have no genuine concern for their brothers and sisters in Africa; men who do not care about the future of our continent, selfish men, intellectually malnourished vagabonds, now wear robes and suits as men of God, worsening our already miserable condition, adding more fuel to an already burning fire. These men must be stopped today for Africa to see the light of the day.

Examine the book you are reading now and discover that it was created by someone like you. It was also created by a network of man's creations, for instance, the machines that printed the book; the making of the ink, the timber industry, the paper-making industry, the designers, and numerous design ideas that brought the book to manifestation. This creation came through thoughts, ideas, and actions. You are reading the book which has been written by me and every component of this book made by the creative thinking and creative works of others. Why not create something so that others may have a feel of your mind and intelligence? Have you ever wondered how everything around you was created?

You must learn to believe in yourself, for you are a god also. Stop looking for demigods created by man and saved on masks, trees, crosses, oceans, and fire to worship. Stop asking these demigods to do things which you can do for yourself. Everything is contained in the universe. All powers exist within everyone. Just wake up and tap into the infinite power which is in everyone.

If you are not a god, I am one. If you continue to depend on the creations of others, you become an economic slave, and when you outlive your usefulness, your masters will discard you, not minding what happens to you thereafter. That is the order of the New World.

Know today, Africans, that this system is running on its own and it runs like the operating system of a computer, it knows no mercy, and it is impersonal. If the world develops a technology that would replace fuel energy, we are doomed; we would drink our crude oil. It is time that we start thinking and applying science and technology to harness our available resources. Is it impossible? Can we not learn from anyone?

Can we not copy technology? What is it that is militating against us that we have accepted total defeat and cannot do anything for ourselves? An average African will always tell you the reasons why he failed and the reasons why he will always fail. He does not want to initiate actions, knowing that in life, there is nothing like failure. After all, Mr Wax tried thousands of times before he could invent the electric bulb which we enjoy today.

Replicate technology if you can, since no one will teach you as we live in a competitive world and an enemy teacher will definitely teach you nonsense. Dismember a car and clone all the parts from A to Z. Reassemble them and produce the first African car. There is no crime in copying. At least, learn to reason like your Indian, Japanese, Korean, and Chinese brothers.

Africans have adopted the lazy man's attitude of clinging to the weak side of life, not knowing that without pain, there would never be any gain. We must start thinking today and also start thinking real hard for the future of Africa. My friend told me that his father bluntly told him to stop dreaming big, that he was going nowhere in life, for after all no one in his family had made it big.

Some of these negative energies from our parents and old people around us who failed in life and will not live to see others succeed so as not to make their failures evident is another problem Africa is facing.

I had an interview on SAFM and was telephonically questioned by this old guy, not in a very nice way, and I could tell he was just trying to pull me down, even when there was no need for doing so. I controlled my emotions until he mentioned that I should speak English like an African. I started laughing but held back and told him that in the first place, English was not an African language.

I was called upon again on SAFM to debate on preservation of culture. This time they called alongside with me a traditional medicine man, who also happened to be a culture activist. This man came in an official European outfit, while I came in a traditional African outfit. This man was busy condemning European culture, while I did say that good culture should be preserved whether they are from Europe or from Africa so long as they are fine and the awful ones must be destroyed irrespective of where they originate from.

This man made me believe that there were spirits of our ancestors hovering around, and when I asked him if he had seen one, I got no answer but anger. The problem is that we do not know what we want in life. This same man was wearing a European outfit on a crucial culture debate regarding preservation of African culture, yet he spoke against European culture, not knowing that the language you speak, what you wear, and many others constitute your culture unless you are talking about tradition.

Culture is the totality of socially transmitted behaviour patterns, arts, beliefs, institutions, and all other products of human work and thought. The processes of culture should not create a class of supercilious infidels who believe in nothing. It should not make a man lose himself in countless masses of adjustments and be so shaped with reference to this, that, and the other, that the simply good and healthy and brave parts of him are reduced and clipped away, like the bordering of a box in a garden. Good cultures must be preserved and bad ones discarded.

Today Africans must till the land and feed the people, for a hungry man is an angry man; use the anger to till the land and stop waiting for imported food.

In Nigeria, when you say that you are a farmer, most people laugh at you and look down upon you, not knowing that food is man's most basic need. At a party in Vancouver, Canadian friend got jealous because I was having a wonderful time with some Canadian girls. He made a nasty statement, and I quote: 'Black man is still striving to survive.' I did not forget this statement.

Some of these hard core racial statements are what pushed me to stick to the decision to come back home and be part of this struggle, as it is better for a man to die standing than live on his knees. I am optimistic, having identified the problems of Africa which are totally in the mind, and if this chain is unlocked, we would be great like others.

We must also dedicate few hours every week the same way we go to churches to also dwell on African issues. Our leaders must possess unwavering courage, discipline, and self-control, a keen sense of justice, definiteness of decision, purposeful leadership, vision and definiteness of plans and be action oriented.

Our leaders should learn to respect and care for their subjects, and above all African leaders must ensure that they are properly educated and well groomed in matters of leadership so as to transmit sound leadership culture into the minds of future African leaders.

The subjects on the other hand should learn to appreciate, respect, and support their visionary leaders, for uneasy is the head that wears the crown. They must also know that we are practising a borrowed leadership culture hence it would take a while for us to get everything right.

In all that I have written in this book so far, I crave the understanding of Africans in matters of the mind as Africans are held by mind-related problems. We must heal our minds today.

We must flush from our minds all thoughts and ideas that lead us backwards. We must also purge from our lives all actions that lead us backwards. We must feed our minds with the right information. We must wake up to the new reality of today that no one can love us more than we love ourselves.

We must learn to love, support, respect, and encourage one another, for the greatest gift of life is love and in all we must fight this liberation struggle collectively. The weapons of warfare are not physical but mental, for the weapons of slavery have changed position from hands to minds. Learn to identify mental slavery wherever it is.

A practice to achieve relaxation, test your brain power, and also charge your intuitive faculty and make your creative mind work for you.

Lie down comfortably on a bed and face up, stretch your hands, and position them by your sides. Close your eyes and follow your breath with your mind's eyes and count up to 500 breaths. Remember any interesting and vibrant event that happened to you in the past and trace that event with your mind's eye from the beginning to the end.

Afterwards ensure that you have achieved relaxation. Take control of your mind this time and picture somebody you love most in your family. Try and get the picture of that person vividly clear in your mind's eyes. Hold that picture for some minutes. Communicate with that person in your mind's eye and then visualise that person respond to the communication. Try to say to that person 'I love you so much'. Picture that person reply to you. Record exactly what the person tells you.

Now picture in your mind's eye the problem or any object of thought you intend to dwell on or a problem you are seeking a solution for. This could be an idea you are searching for or a problem you are seeking for the solution.

Picture that situation (problem) and make sure that it is vividly clear in your mind's eye. Begin to analyse that situation (problem) and do a critical analysis of it. Begin gathering homogenous (similar) thoughts relating to that situation (problem). Go deep and go deeper, and afterwards, sleep. Always make sure that at every session, you are dealing with one situation (problem) at the same time.

When you wake up, ensure that you have a pen and paper most times during this seeking period. Within this period, avoid stress and also avoid negative people (psychic terrorists and psychic vampires) who suck your energy. What you did would invoke the intuitive faculty and make it work for you. When you are relaxed or not dwelling on that thought, you would be receiving ideas. Ensure that you note them down. Repeat this same process by dwelling on each and every idea that you get. With time, your mind will become a magnet attracting homogeneous ideas to you. If you apply this technique to a problem, you will conquer that problem or find the idea you are seeking.

ARISE, AFRICA!

(Inspirational Motivational Speech)

Let it be known to Africans all over the globe today that the only choice we have in these present times is that we are left with no other choice than to do what we have to do, having claimed that we are equal humans in this world of humans. This is a vital mission at least if not for us, for the unborn and the generations to come who will again live to inherit the struggle of proving their humanity in the only world they shall know if we fail to do something now.

For Africans who claim that they have lost a battle, let them rise again, for there was no battle announced in the first place. For Africans who claim that the 'black man' has no hopes in life, let them rise again, for even a cripple is never a victim of a battle announced in due course. Fear is human nature just like every other emotion, but even fear of death does not avert soldiers from going to war. How long shall we fear, how long shall we live in fears, how long shall we make others' fear just to justify our own fears? A coward dies many times before his real death. How long shall we live under the absolute control of other human beings like us in the only world we know of? Are we not human enough like others ?

The fact that people are made to ignore their problems on earth simply because they have a better place called heaven where they shall resettle when they die is a matter of concern to me. I am pointing the attention of Africans and the readers to the problems we face here on earth which we could take human actions to overcome at least if not for our sake, for the sake of our children and the generations to come who will also live to inherit such problems if we do nothing but live on hopes of going to heaven. Heaven and hell may all be here on earth, but at least since we suffer today because our forebears did not make frantic efforts to protect our future, it is time that we embark on a struggle to protect the future of our children and those who will come after us.

I was born into a Christian society, but I must also admit that Jesus Christ never had kids, hence all of us who have children, and also who believe in that part of Christ's teaching, should remember that no one goes to heaven without the call of death, and when someone dies, he does not usually take his children along with him to the grave or beyond. They remain here on earth hence we must struggle to protect the future of our children who will live after us.

Arise, Africans, take up the shields as symbols of protection from all attractions to negative existence; take up the helmets as symbols of wisdom; take up the spears as symbols of power. Let us think collectively as one people. Let us advance the cause our heroes started. Let us not be displaced from the only world we know because we have failed to fit and compete favourably with others. Let us become broad-minded in these current times and see the forces around us and the major worm feeding on us which is mental slavery, the major enemy challenging our existence. Arise, Africans, let us learn to love one another. Let us learn to render selfless services.

Arise, Africans, let us wage a war against mental slavery, let us wage a war against false religions, and let us revamp our academic institutions. Arise, Africans, let us wage a war against faulty governance and tyrants in power and let us fight for our rights. Arise, Africans, let us question when and why civilisation which began in Africa ended; let us force the world to erase HIV from our lives.

Let us tell the world that our problem is not same-sex marriage, rather we want to reclaim civilisation. We want to be free from the grip of mental slavery so as to make better use of our minds. We want to develop Africa and improve our lives; we want to feed and clothe ourselves and not to be fed and clothed like children and animals; give a man a fish, you feed him for a day, but teach him how to fish and you feed him for a lifetime. Arise, Africans, let us be brothers again. Let all Africans all over the world, home and abroad, come together in one spirit. Let us choose one African language and transform it into a universal language just as other universal (slave) languages we know today.

During the early era of slave trade, our ancestors played a major role in the trading of fellow Africans to Europeans for money. We completely blame Europeans, asserting that if they did not come into our lands, there would be no slavery, but the question is how a man who professes true love sells his own child (flesh and blood) to strangers, just for money and material gains. Europeans did not do well either by abandoning their land to hunt for poor innocent Africans to buy and kidnap and transform into slaves. Why did the same 'God' they brought to us alongside with them not prevent them from invading Africa in the first place? When the first human being conceived the idea of enslaving Africans, was the same 'God' sleeping or was the enslaving of Africans a commendable gesture?

An odd concern about Africans is that they are prone to emotional weaknesses and are always seeking love where they would never find it, making them always live at the mercy of others. Europeans and Asians care about their own kind, which accounts for their degree of team spirit and self-sacrifice amongst them. We should copy such positive gesture and stop seeking love from others in this competitive world. Africans have to unite in spirit to face the future. Africans must learn to unite, develop team spirit, and appreciate one another so as to become stronger.

I usually wonder whether the pharaohs of Egypt truly enslaved the Israelites as the Bible proclaims. If this biblical proclamation is true, and considering our present circumstances, should we then accept slavery as human nature and devises of achieving absolute control and at the same time fight to resist it in any manner that it comes whether with chains or with information? Should we try as much as possible to enslave others too? Was the story of the pharaohs enslaving the Israelites created to justify the fate some people would face in the future which we are facing today?

If most African Americans look down on Africa, why then do they complain about slavery since they are also products of the same scheme? Are they not supposed to accept this irreversible fate and deal with the reversible one, 'mental slavery' or stop hating Africa and return to Africa, their root? Or do they need Moses to resurrect and lead them out of Egypt (America)? I am questioning our minds at this moment.

During the spate of xenophobic violence in South Africa, I had a serious dialogue with friends from East, West, North, South, Central Africa, and a friend from the UK. I said, and I quote: 'When a man's corpse starts to rot and smell, friends, allies, and strangers will run away, but your brother will never run away, love one another. I also said, and I quote: 'When a man is bitten by a snake, whenever he sees any crawling animal around him, even if it is a millipede, he will react as if it was a snake and the extent of his reactions will vary based on the person's level of civility.' My friend from East Africa said, and I quote: 'During the apartheid era, all Africans fought for the freedom of South Africa, so why should we be chased away when we visit our brothers?'

My North African friend said, and I quote: 'Why do black people hate one another?' (I grasped this comment with mixed feelings.) I nearly thought that he meant 'black' with regards to other Africans who do not have light skin like him. My South African friend said that the problem is not African brothers coming to their country but that they are taking away their jobs, their women, oppressing and intimidating them, corrupting the police, and acting as if they own South Africa. Out of an emotional outburst, my West African friend said, and I quote: 'When I was in elementary school, I used to pay survival levy for South Africans ' (pointing a finger at my South African friend while he lamented).' Everyone exploded in laughter; then my UK friend said that we should examine properly the category of people causing the violence and find out whether they are looting the belongings of the people they attacked in this so-called xenophobic violence. He also said that we should find out the root causes of xenophobia that he thinks it is economic and political. A friend from DRC said, and I quote: 'The person causing this xenophobia is a green snake in a green grass.' After a long debate that lasted for more than five hours, we continued this discussion at my place of residence.

I told them that I would not be happy if it was in my country that fellow Africans chose to come together in the so-called unity without positive intentions and expect me to be dumb. My female friend said, and I quote: 'The problems in South Africa are not caused only by those foreigners who turned into scavengers to overcome the harsh economic realities in South Africa. Most people in South Africa have skeletons hidden in their own cupboards but will gladly enjoy talking about others.' She also said that some South Africans are only confused about the strange success of some 'foreigners' (African immigrants). They do not want to get close to them and learn from them. Rather out of pride, jealously, and prejudice, they want them nailed at the cross. But if any one of them has the slightest opportunity, he will also do whatever he thinks those foreigners are doing.

I told them that one must do unto others as he would expect others to do unto him. I went ahead to elucidate that the xenophobic incident that happened in South Africa could happen anywhere in Africa (they grasped this statement with mixed feelings). My South African friend understood that maybe there would be xenophobic violence against South Africans in other African countries where South Africans are residing. My East African friend understood it that maybe someday South Africans will start migrating to other African countries and start oppressing the indigenous, taking their women and their jobs. They understood this statement in many ways. I went ahead to tell them that the system is not equipped well enough to sustain the entire South

African populace economically in terms of jobs, let alone other 'foreigners' (African immigrants). My South African friend said that in South Africa, foreigners are working in many hospitals and universities. I finally said to them that the solution to all our problems can be found in our minds. Primarily, I see mental slavery, but secondarily, I see that we lack true spiritual unity and team spirit.

Conscious and well-informed South Africans are rarely xenophobic, and if some ill-informed South Africans chose to violently act out on their xenophobic hostility towards 'foreigners' (African immigrants) and burn people, should these few illiterate class of people also keep on crying bitterly of apartheid and racism since the architects of these anti-social ugliness are also the same people who utilised South African resources to build South Africa to the beauty and standard it is today? Without these same people, there would be no 'new' South Africa where one would see a need to be xenophobic. I want someone to think and throw away narrow-mindedness. Should South Africans move forward and forgive the errors of the past since they say 'no pain, no gain'? After all, some heroes sacrificed their lives and freedom for this 'new' South Africa. Should they be complaining all the time when they still enjoy the products of the 'new' South Africa? Should 'foreigners' (African immigrants) not forgive this xenophobic explosion and understand that the people who violently perpetrated these nefarious acts were looting the victim's properties hence robbery in disguise? I told South Africans that in as much as xenophobia is not a commendable gesture for the 'new' South Africa, if one digs deep into the archives to unravel the primary causes of xenophobia (I do not mean xenophobic violence), one would realise that in reality, it is not fear of 'foreigners' (African immigrants) but fear of the unknown and uncertainties; and any one can react on those fears depending on his level of civility, but in all, I advise South Africans to say no to xenophobia and racism, Africa is one.

One will find out that xenophobia is also related to mental slavery. We have failed to utilise our minds creatively, which accounts for why everyone is looking unto the system to provide jobs for all when it is almost impossible. If we could be creative minded and also develop a supportive culture, then we would be able to create a mini-system of our own which would sustain us, since it is practically impossible for the larger system to provide for all. The problem also is the lack of creative culture, the lack of purposeful leadership, the lack team spirit, and the lack of supportive culture. Europeans support Europeans, Asians support Asians, Africans support others and not themselves. Out of inferiority complex, they fail to consume what they produce, and it is a status symbol in Africa to be false in behaviour and lifestyle. Nigerians created the so-called Nigerian movies that are making waves all over the world, though sometimes cheaply made, but the creative ideas are still there. All that the African continent should have done was to collectively improve upon the concept and find the best ways to improve on the quality of the product so as to meet acceptable standards rather than persistently searching for faults and talking down on the product. South African music is wonderful and should be fed to the world out there for them to have a taste of real African music and in return we create wealth.

Such initiatives are stepping stones for people who want to stand on their feet and independently manage their lives, people who are striving for economic independence, self-sustenance and self-identity. It does not necessarily have to be movies, but any creative endeavours that aligns with our needs as long as it makes economic or developmental sense should be promoted and supported and not ridiculed. Sometimes if you develop an idea and put your fellow African on the helm of affairs, he would make sure that he destroys your work just to bring you down. Sometimes he wishes that he was the one who did your work. I have been a victim of this in my expedition in Africa hence I advise Africans to develop supportive culture and promote creativity.

As I said before, the truth hurts but must be told in these present times. I am not happy that Africans have no direction in life, rather we prefer to live like lower animals, and it is not as if we do not have the same brain power like other human beings. What I think is that we are just sleeping and also suffering from chronic mental slavery. If civilisation began in Africa, as they claim, does that not tell anyone that Africans possess powerful minds just like their European and Asian counterparts? Today, we speak people's languages; we dress like them; we eat what they eat; we learn what they taught us even if it is crap; we want to behave exactly like them but not think exactly like them. We have nothing to let others learn in return. Sometimes I wonder if we ever take time to understand the inference of that. Being a human being and having nothing to call your own and having nothing to teach others is a terrible disaster, and we must address this today.

Though I am one of the people who are profoundly angry that Europeans are plundering our resources every day without giving a horseshoe about how we feel; that we are indebted to Europeans amidst our economy and cultural evolution they destroyed, that they enslaved our forefathers in the past without any effort of reparation, I must also state that I frown strongly at the absurdity and frugality of our leaders who do nothing but oppress their own people and devise avenues to also loot the resources of the African nations. They are not appreciative of technology and how we could innovate or copy (clone) technology to develop our continent Africa. What are we going to do with mineral and natural resources without European technology? Are we going to eat crude oil? Are we going to chew raw gold and raw diamonds?

All I am asking is for Europeans to be impartial because without our natural resources, their technology would be worthless, and also considering the fact that they are still the same people diverting our minds completely away from the scientific realities of the day with their bogus fear-based religious doctrines introduced with guns. They are also the same people who are raising mercenaries of mental slavery in our midst every day, whose jobs are to blindfold us while our resources are looted. Europeans have to become reasonable now because their tricks are on the table. They should stop acting as if they could get into any continent and do whatever they wish while at the same time preaching against crime, dignity, preaching integrity, respect, democracy, and love. They must stop buying over the minds of our naive leaders, confusing them to gain access to anything and anywhere in Africa. This is not respect, this is not democracy, and this is not dignity. How can you systematically transform a man into a fool with inferior and expired information only to end up calling him one? In the past, Nigerians succeeded in their Advance fee fraud because they understood in time that any human being can be fooled no matter how intelligent he is, so long as you tap into his mind and know exactly what he wants desperately. Africans have been tricked for so long due to their quest for God and the unknown, and it is time that the world stops their tricks. What Africans are getting from the world is mind diversion leading to mental slavery which subsequently leads to economic slavery. The same illusion, a 'heaven' that you would only see when you are dead. Who wants to die? Nobody, yet everybody want to go to heaven.

Another complex problem in Africa is lack of mental curiosity. Some of us have refused to think. Some of us are so lazy that you begin to wonder how they can survive this tough world. Most Africans have decided to render their minds motionless (static) hence only adjust to control from others. This is a sad situation because animals do not think; rather they follow control and instincts. If you buy a dog, of course you do everything for the dog. As humans, we should ask ourselves, what it is that we are doing for ourselves. I do not believe that God created animals as human beings in Africa. We are human beings with minds and brain powers as others, but we are not making use of them, and the advanced nations are concluding that we are not exactly like them in terms of human intelligence and African leaders are almost proving them right. I am happy with myself though because I have proven that I am a perfectly normal and a creative human being, even more creative than the majority of Europeans you see today.

How come our engineers and professors couldn't build the first African car? It is because we lack the motivation to commence anything. Africans have a big problem in terms of thinking about the future. We do not think about the future, rather we prefer to wallow in the pleasures of the senses and ask the future to kiss the dust! Metaphorically speaking, of course, through our actions. Sometimes we are quick to mortgage the future for our immediate wants. We lack the ability to dream big. When we become a bit successful, we relax and start gathering ego, seeking unnecessary attention and praises. That is also a serious problem in the continent. We arrive easily and we seek little tasks and not great ones.

Back to the issue of mental slavery, today, a more dangerous form of slavery is taking place in Africa and everyone plays dumb. Maybe we do not recognise it. Take note that mental slavery is even worse than physical slavery. After reading this book, you will understand how to recognise mental slavery. Take note also that majority of the mercenaries of mental slavery today are fellow confused Africans, no longer Europeans. We live in societies where almost everything is moving in the wrong direction and everyone plays dumb. A friend of mine said that we do not know where we are heading to, what we are doing, and what we want to achieve, that we are totally lost and confused in Africa yet pretending as if we absolutely know what we are doing.

I say to the world and to whoever it is his intentions to actualise the dominance and takeover of Africa, that if civilisation began in Africa then for a cycle to be completed. Civilisation and development must surely come back to Africa and in full force, and this is the time. Everything in life is cyclical. No one can stop the development of the entire African continent; otherwise, the world would experience a shock that would bring the entire human race to a standstill. No matter how many prophets are silenced every day, no matter the number of strains of HIV/AIDS that invade Africa, no matter the quantity of mineral and natural resources looted from Africa every day, no matter the number of instigated wars and no matter the number of African leaders that are brainwashed and turned nuts every day, the truth must be told for the emancipation of the people and for the future of our children and the generations to come. I absolutely fear no persecution in saying this, for fear of danger does not prevent soldiers from going to war. Arise, Africans, for this is the time!

Africans have to learn the process of genuine love which leads to self-sacrifice. It is only through genuine love that one can render selfless services to his society and mankind just as others are doing in the advanced nations. We misunderstand love with weak emotions. We seem to lack strong survival principles; we seem to lack strength and courage to face hard situations, surmount them, and become strong; we seem to lack the ability to analyse things critically; we seem to lack patience and endurance; we seem to lack the ability to think about tomorrow and live for the future; we lack team spirit, strong will power, and an ability to persevere; we have failed to understand that we should not fail just because our ancestors failed; we prefer living in a world of fear, superstitions, wishes, and prejudice; we have also failed to understand that we have to build a better future for our children and inculcate the same culture into their lives for the future of their own children and generations to come; and in all we lack spiritual unity. It has always been easy for others to get in between us, divide us, and take full control of our lives because we do not truly understand what genuine love means.

These days, we are making matters worse when some con men in our midst, who claim to be church pastors, have transformed into mercenaries of mental slavery. Tough economic situations and unemployment have transformed them into scavengers. They have mortgaged their conscience for money and material gains. They have turned into agents of mental slavery, a more dangerous and more complex form of slavery. They are playing a more prominent role in this era, spreading adulterated information that blindfolds our people.

Wake up today, Africans, or forever sleep. When men gather together in the name of 'God' every day, pray in the name of 'God' every day, call the name of 'God' every day, yet their lives remain the same and show no trace of improvement, and they still cling to their old styles, exhibiting so much wickedness, then you begin to wonder if they are actually calling the name of the one true universal God of absolute justice and balance, the Creator of the universe, God of righteousness or some demigods. Religion which should help people build their lives spiritually is now used to arrest the minds of the people, and this calls for serious attention as the same ways and manner people gather together every weekend, dressed in their most beautiful and cleanest of all clothes, wearing the best perfumes, only to end up achieving practically nothing but mental slavery, we can also in the same manner gather every weekend to discuss the way forward for our continent Africa.

This is a time for change and mind revolution. Note that religion could work for you or against you, depending on how it is administered. Religion if rightly administered could help control crime, help one rebuild his life, help one achieve peace and harmony in life, strengthen family union, and enforce discipline in a family. I am not against religion; after all, I was born into a Christian family and some of my close friends are Muslims, but I am only against false prophets and false religious teachings that say, 'do not ask questions or God will punish you'. The universal God is not a weak God. He is logical and scientific in his ways. If Africa develops, we would be able to protect our future, our destiny, and our existence in this only world we know. I wonder why we are mostly concerned with what happens to us when we die and not what is happening to us when we are alive.

The question is why we are not making serious and collective efforts to achieve development and civilisation of the African continent as a whole. Rather out of narrow-mindedness, weaknesses, laziness, and ignorance, we are seeking an escape route, a place to go when we die, a place that has been rosily prepared for the weak, idle, ignorant, and unproductive mind; a place where beautiful naked virgins will be teasing us every now and then, a place where all that we will be doing is eating, praying, and praising God.

Let no man think that our problem is only weak leadership, HIV/AIDS, and poverty. Yes, there may be weak leadership in Africa which is not unexpected since we are still growing and practising a borrowed leadership culture, and also due to militocracy (a transformation of the politically inexperienced military class into democrats), but our major problem is mental slavery and many forms of brainwashing schemes and mind diversion which every indigenous African including our leaders are victims of. We embraced religion, but why are most religions in Africa imported? Can we ever have anything of our own? Can we challenge all religious 'Gods' to find us a practical cure for HIV? Can we just take a simple example and ask those religious 'Gods' to fill up our bank accounts with money without working hard for the money since they say these 'Gods' can move mountains. They say that the these 'Gods' can cure all diseases, fix broken teeth, heal the deaf, dumb, blind, cripple, and even restore a sterile person. The problem is that we choose to live non-practical lives. We enjoy illusions and dreams hence the world is selling them to us in various complexities. Now the world is even using our own naive brothers and sisters, false prophets to achieve their impious objectives, knowing that with money, some of us who have improper value structure, pride, self-esteem, and integrity could do anything.

One of my acquaintances is of the opinion that we should create our own religion if we truly need one and not import from others. He strongly insists that either we all agree that God is universal, otherwise every race will have its own religion and God. He says we should stop externalising God if we do not want to agree in the universal nature of the divine being. We rather internalised him, he said.

As for me, if we must cling to imported religions, then we have to refine them, extract the garbage in them, and find out which ways those religions could contribute towards our progressive developmentas well as lead us to 'heaven', as they must all work together. We must not focus on religions that tell us to go to 'heaven' alone, abandoning our natural resources on earth at the mercy of those who introduced the same religion. Any religion in Africa must pay more attention to the known while taking us to the unknown worlds.

But it is only out of ignorance that men would think that of everything in life, there is balance except in their lives. The moon is hanging in space and has never fallen to crash on us. If you throw an object up, it comes down via gravitational balance. Our blood circulates in our body in an orderly manner. Our body cells perform their functions in perfect order and harmony. Our wounds heal without our commands. Our food digests without our commands. Plants, animals, and other beings perform their activities in perfect harmony. The oceans and the seas flow in orderly manner. The planets, the stars, the galaxies, and other celestial bodies spin in perfect harmony. All these are testimonies and evidence that there is absolute balance in life no matter what religion one believes in. It is time that people start living with the reality that there is no forgiveness of 'sin' without atonement, for in life there is balance from all the evidence around us.

Whatever happens to us in life is only intended to achieve a form of balance. Whatever manner this balance takes place, we may not know. No one knows what happens to the dead; only God, death, and dead people know (wherever dead souls are if not in the grave). Let no man deceive you: the reality is that life is logical and there is balance. Whatever you sow in life, one way or the other, you must reap even if you do not know how, for the justice of life is inescapable, good begets good, evil begets evil, and life is cyclical. Arise, Africans, for this is the time!

For African Americans and the Caribbean who are not comfortable with their conditions in the American community and who crave reunification with the great continent Africa, be informed that Africa is not as ugly as she is being presented to the world. Those who wish to join the 'Zion Train' back to Africa for the purpose of reunification and not the purpose of polluting our values, those who wish to join hands in the tough and rigorous journey of developing and recivilising Africa where they say civilisation began, those who truly crave returning to Africa, would be reintegrated into the African continent with maximum ease. You would eat and dine with your brothers again. Africa is your root, and any man who does not know his root will always strive but will never arrive.

Africans must wake up today and refine what they listen to as wrong concepts, wrong education, and false doctrines morally degrading audio and visuals could result in mental slavery as they all pollute the mind. Some of them slow down the functioning of the mind and others drive the mind fast in the wrong course.

Most of us are only concerned about now, pleasures of the senses and what happens to them when they die, abandoning all that is happening to them when they are alive. We breed children every day as if we are competing with the Chinese and the Indians, yet there is nothing to show to the world as a legacy and intellectual wealth and productive capacity reserves that we are preserving for those children and generations to come except spurious traditional beliefs, strange cultural practices, borrowed strange behaviours, foreign Gods, and false religious dogmas. Behold, our real problem is the disease of the mind which I call mental slavery.

Man is only able to understand just an infinitesimal workings of the Supreme Intelligence, the universal God (simply called 'God' in English, *Chukwu* in Ibo, *Modimo* in Tswana, *Oluwa* inYoruba, *Allah* in Hausa and Arabic, *Thixo* in Xhosa, *Mungu* in Swahili, and many other names). Truly, no man has seen this God in person, and no man knows what shape or gender God is. No man knows precisely and accurately where God lives if he actually lives somewhere, whether he is the whole universe itself, or whether he lives in our bodies, (but I choose to say that we are all little intelligent beings hence gods also). No one is absolutely sure if there is life after death, no one is absolutely sure if there is reincarnation, and no one is absolutely sure if there is heaven or hell. The universal God has not revealed any of these to anyone, rather we live by speculations and what we are told by religious institutions, and their books; we live by beliefs and superstitions. I strongly believe that the world is scientific and that there could be a being who we have given the name God, but I do not know where or what shape he or she is. I do not know what gender God is; neither do I know if Adam and Christ look like Europeans as being projected in the Bible.

If you look upon the sky, you will notice zillions of worlds. How come with our minds, though limitless in their inherent capabilities, think that we can equate our wisdom and thinking to that of the infinite intelligence (God) who has made the universe which is infinite also. We have to stop deceiving others today for the sake of the unknown. For the non-liberated minds in Africa, I would prefer to advise that you live right for the sake of the unknown, which is known to no one and also live right for the fact that there is balance in nature and life. For all mercenaries of mental slavery, beware, your actions shall find you someday, for you reap what you sow.

Energy is never destroyed but changes forms. Life is logical and scientific. The universal God is also scientific and logical in his ways. He is of no race, religion, tribe, nationality, or gender. We understand just an infinitesimal and insignificant level of the energy of God, and Africans must know today that God does not belong to any particular religion. God is for all creations in the universe. God's energy, power, and intelligence is infinite hence God could not have chosen any particular religion or any particular people to run his affairs unless if there is a smaller god who is in charge of the earth and also who is in charge of a particular group of people whom they say he chose. Wake up, Africans!

Today, man has morally degraded far below expectations in so many ways that we are afraid of uncertainties now. Women sleep with dogs, men sleep with goats and call it 'safe sex'; industries are manufacturing chemicals that see the ozone layer as meal; humans are transforming into programmes and robots with no trace of feelings for anyone. Some Africans are exhibiting 'coconut syndrome' not endeavouring to exhibit European creative intelligence. Man is making diseases and making their cures. I may not wish to mention a lot of things humans have done on this planet for me not to be seen as judging anyone, but if Sodom and Gomorrah really did exist, then why would men marry men in churches today? The same churches that speak against it in their books still use the same books to wed same-sex partners. What is wrong with Africans that we do not notice all these ugliness and blindly copy, abandoning science, technology, and creativity which we should actually copy?

Why would humans think about cloning other humans? Why would man create humans in the laboratory? What kind of a human being would that be? How come man has chosen to abuse his intelligence? How come we have become like children with our over-developed intellect? How come we are turning nuts with all that we knowHow come we want to contaminate nature's creations and order? Is it not enough that in some places of the world, people prefer more proteins that they are even making chickens with three legs and more wings? Is it not enough that most food we consume today is genetically engineered? How come man wants to tamper with the greatest of all God's life creation: 'man'? Africans must rise against all these ugliness or else we would be swallowed alongside in the consequences of global errors, as we are the ones who mostly suffer the consequences of global mistakes, we have no defences against anything, HIV and global warming for instance.

Civilisation they say began in Africa, but today evidence pointing to this fact is gradually vanishing from the African continent. Impious men are trying to destroy all evidence that civilisation ever commenced in Africa through history replacement, destruction of tangible evidence like the pyramid of egypt and many others. Why is it that some humans have degenerated so low, hence acting as if they must do whatever pleases them all the time untouched, undermining all the workings of nature? Behold, Man, the justice of life is inescapable.

What is the future of the African continent going to be like? What is the fate of our children, the unborn, and generations to come if we have to sit and watch things go wrong without any struggle for changes? This task has to begin now, at least if not for us, for the future of our great continent Africa, for the future of our children, the unborn and the generations to come.

Somebody asked me what we came to this world to do, and I told him that we did not come here to prepare to go to 'heaven' or 'hell'; rather, we came to make this world a better place for our children, the unborn, and the generations to come so that they will find a better dwelling place, and in doing so, we would truly find the purpose why we came here on earth. People like Martin Luther King, Malcolm X, Nelson Mandela, Steve Biko, Ken Saro-Wiwa, and many others sacrificed their lives and freedom for others; they lived their lives serving humanity. We breed multiple children every day, yet we find no need to struggle for the future of those children and generations to come as those noble men did.

People like Albert Einstein, Isaac Newton, Michael Faraday, Alexander Graham Bell, Bill Gates, Mark Zuckerberg of Facebook and many others sacrificed their times and mental energy for the good of humanity. Why can't we copy from those people instead of copying same-sex marriage and 'coconut syndrome'?

This is a wake-up time. Arise, Africans, take up the helmet as a symbol of wisdom. Begin to emulate the thinking of the great sons of Africa like Philip Emeagwali, the computer genius. Begin to think creatively like Europeans and not just copy only their behaviours (mostly the vain ones). Begin to copy and clone technology and science in its true context and not same-sex marriage. I think that 90 per cent of Africans are under a deep mental siege and hence are deeply asleep. 9 per cent who think that they are awake but are also asleep hence fooling the 90 per cent who are sleeping deeply. These are the ones that I call mercenaries of mental slavery. Though they know just a minute working of the human mind, the problem is that they are taking advantage of others with the little knowledge they have. They are the mercenaries of mental slavery, hypocrites, fanatics, false prophets, etc. They are not completely sure of what they are telling the people, and they convince the people to believe in what they truly do not understand fully just for the sake of money, control and power. We wonder how a sheep can lead a sheep, how a cow can lead a cow, or how a blind man can lead a blind man. Only about 1% of Africans are truly awake but their voices are not heard. They are unpopular, the doors are not open for them but the false ones have all the wide doors open and are very popular, just as they say, the wrong things sell easily and are more commercial.

Behold, the only thing that can never change in life is change itself. Most people are seriously seeking the truth to unravel their missions in life, but they have been misled by teachings from mercenaries of mental slavery, whose voices are louder, spreading imported doctrines which they have not taken serious time and efforts to understand fully just for the sake of money. Information that lack both truth and facts.

Because of the quest for money, fame, power, and material gains, they are disseminating doctrines in a way and manner that impairs reasoning, doctrines that say 'do not ask questions or else God will punish you'. These people sell 'God' and beliefs for money; they sell dreams, trying to awaken others while they are not truly awake. They feed the minds of the people with stories of the past which do not add values to their present lives, stories about the lives and history of others and not that of our African ancestors, information that cannot be substantiated scientifically, accurate historic data or by any other means apart from word of mouth and books about the lives of others that it now looks like scam tricks. They disseminate expired stories and information which the originators have discarded long ago, binding the minds of the people with so many fears, fear of the unknown, fear of the afterlife, fear of death, fear of non-existent spirits and demons, fear of the anti-Christ, Satan, Lucifer, hell, beast, marks of the beast, '666' marks, etc. Many of these fears cannot be proven in any practical ways to exist.

Some 'living churches' found mostly in America and Nigeria have practically become banks and party grounds. Their pastors have become Christ, but this time around, a different type of Christ because the true Christ that we were told of in the Bible neither flew private jets nor drove limousines, never slept with his female admirers, never performed prearranged illusions with his friends acting as blind, deaf, dumb, and crippled people; never assassinated competitors, never fought over church collections, never dressed as an oppressor, never contested for the presidency of Israel just as most Nigerian church pastors are contesting for presidency, never used occult tools. (Very few churches in Africa are carrying out genuine spiritual works according to the teachings of Christ, and those few have no worries with the works of Mohammed, Mahatma Gandhi, and other great religious leaders, and from the ways and manner the leaders of those churches behave, you will know that they are not deceiving the masses. However, most churches today are run by ex-thieves and ex-con men.)

I once told a friend that if someone wakes up in the morning and decides to commit suicide, at least there is a personal decision to do that though a negative one, and if he succeeds then that was his decision, but in our case, Africans are moving towards a suicidal direction which we have not chosen for ourselves, a direction which the wicked world has designed for us.

This direction is leading us nowhere but to utter destruction, and today, this direction is led by fellow Africans who are used as tools of mental slavery and religious diversion. I call them chimps because they are not acting like human beings with minds of real human beings. They drive the best of cars, fly private jets, wear the best of clothes, and live in the best of houses, use sophisticated scientific gadgets in their luxurious churches and houses while still telling their blindfolded members to keep digging the sky with their mind for 'heaven' and forget this earth and the scientific process that is giving birth to everything that we know on earth today that is not of nature. I tell them that as many souls of African children that they diverted their minds to nowhere and turn them nuts every day, so also is the number of curses that will be upon them from the spirit of our great continent Africa. The pilots of these doctrines do not give a horseshoe about both the physical and mental needs of the people; rather, all they want is money. In reality, if the heaven they preach does really exist and is up in the sky as they say, why then are they amassing so much wealth that we do not know if they shall migrate to heaven with them? They even acquire private jets that I wonder if they shall be flown to heaven with those jets when they die.

The average African has failed to ask himself the kind of heaven Europeans designed for them with religious books and religious institutions. The only world they know, they are being displaced every day by the same people that gave them religious books at gunpoint. If such a heaven does really exist, Africans will not be allowed in there. Europeans and Asians will fight to occupy all the spaces therein.

Why do we think that HIV and AIDS cannot be eradicated from Africa? Who thinks that the world will open the gate of heaven widely for us if there are so many good things in that glorious place called heaven, when in the only world we know we are systematically being eliminated. We are systematically being reduced to the status of lesser humans, yet no one sees this. Africans have turned deaf ears to words of wisdom. Africans have closed their eyes and minds to reality. When a man finds you unfit in the only world you know, what makes you think that he would freely give you a key to heaven. Any religion that tells you not to think or ask questions, please when you run, be like the biblical wife of Lot: never look back or you will turn into a pillar of salt (lies). Any religion which tells you to be poor on earth and be rich when you get to heaven, please run away from it, for it is total mental slavery. Any religion which gives you hopes only when you are dead, please run away from it, for they are agents of mental slavery and dominance. Any religion that claims that material gains are evil when all the tools they use to function are material, please run away from it, for it is mental slavery. Any religion that is introduced with a gun and a book, scrutinise that religion and know what it intends to achieve. Religion is perfectly healthy when properly administered by well-trained minds who try well enough to distinguish between allegories and literal statements and also make their followers understand the differences. False religion, I say no, run and run as far as possible, for it is one of the greatest tools of mental slavery. I tell you today, the reason why the African continent is not fully developed up until now is mental slavery, and this is caused primarily by false religion, strange superstitions filled traditions, bizarre cultural practices, and faulty education systems. It matters not what you are told, the universal laws and golden rules 'love one another, do unto others as you would have them do unto you; whatever you sow, that you shall reap'. When you understand these laws and abide by them every day, you will not need to occupy your mind with stories of the past which inventors have discarded long ago. Endeavour to occupy your mind with a greater mission ahead, which is the mission of the development of our great continent Africa. When you read the Bible and other religious books, please endeavour to pay more attention to the wisdom therein for inspirational motivation, spiritual guidance, and empowerment. Avoid stories, miracles and heaven crave.

I must emphasise also that a few Africans are truly awake, but their voices are not heard or I put it that they are afraid to speak out for the fear of being persecuted since real messengers are persecuted by their own people whose minds have been biased and in some cases by their traitors who have been paid like the Judas story of the Bible. Also sometimes when real messengers speak, fellow Africans think that they are either crazy or have gone nuts. We would rather prefer to pay attention to those deceiving and brainwashing us, we prefer illusions. We will not want to listen to those telling us the truth out of genuine concern. A friend of mine at a point owned up that it was too late for him to live in reality.

In these present times, humans no longer feel anything for their fellow humans. People only know what is wrong when it happens to them. People have sold their conscience and majority of us are acting like programs without human feelings. When we are in serious situations and needs, we expect people to have feelings for us and assist us but the reverse is the case when others express such emotions. If humans could learn to treat others in the same way and manner they wish to be treated, then there never would be wars, crime, strange diseases spreading around, hate and disunity, religious diversions, illusions, and fantasies, and there will never be all sorts of negative existence and emotions. There would never be people exploiting the happiness of others; there would never be deceit; there will never be psychic vampires who live by sucking away the positive energy happiness of others. Today, Africans must know that the world has transformed into a dog-eat-dog, eat or be eaten world hence it is time that we stop acting like little children wearing diapers and stand up, think, and act like Europeans and Asians. The Chinese, Indians, and Japanese have proven a point that all humans are born equal with the same capacity to utilize both synthetic and creative intelligence and also innovate; they have emulated Europeans, Americans, and Jews, and now they have gained respect. It is only Africans that have decided to be backward. Only Africans have decided to be slaves of the toys made by others yet they cannot even make a toothpick.

We must today begin to create like others; we must learn to copy from others what makes them strong and stop copying their weaknesses. At least we must look up to people like Chinua Achebe, Wole Soyinka, Philip Emeagwali, Mandela, Malcolm X, Dr. Martin Luther King Jnr. and many others to see that these men ignored European weaknesses and copied their strengths. If we have up to 1,000 of such men in Africa, then think of what the African future would be like. The fact is that Africans would prefer to copy same-sex marriage, drug abuse, women abuse, 'coconut' syndrome, crime, false living, and many negative attributes.

We live in a world where men deceive others every day just to make a living. Men crave hearing that their sins become obliterated when they pray to God hence false religious warlords feed their minds with what they crave to hear. These mercenaries of mental slavery sell forgiveness to them. Men want to believe that their crimes and wickedness become obliterated as soon as they kneel down and pray to 'God', after which they go about committing atrocities again and also ask for forgiveness that sometimes I begin to wonder who this God that forgives them all the time is.

Who is this 'God' that armed robbers pray to before embarking on their wicked expeditions? Who is this 'God' that 419 men call upon to bring *mugu*? Who is this 'God' that American soldiers pray to before attacking people in Iraq? Who is this 'God' that suicide bombers pray to before sacrificing their precious lives for nothing? Who is this 'God' that allowed lunatics, chronic alcoholics, and drug abusers to divert aircrafts into the beautiful twin towers in America, killing more than 5,000 innocent people, including women and children? I begin to wonder if it has become a daily routine that the universal God's work would be to sit and wait for people to commit all sorts of carnage and come knocking at his door for their atrocities to be obliterated. Only a fool thinks that the universal God reasons like us humans.

The universal God is perfect in his justice system. The reactions of a person's actions always follow him like a shadow; you can never run away from it. If you do well, you will reap good. If you do evil, you will reap evil. Thinking that the universal God forgives your evil deeds is ridiculous because even laws made by man have no provisions for forgiveness, let alone laws that are perfect, divine, universal, and impersonal. For those given hopes of a better place to go to when they die, you had better start thinking to make your lives better here; at least you have to start from the known to the unknown. Those hopes render you inactive, lazy, and idle and unable to effect changes in your lives and immediate environments. Wake up today, align yourself with the right teachings, and learn to live in reality.

When you visit religious institutions, remember to ask questions regarding teachings which you do not understand fully and ensure that you are not brainwashed, rather be provided satisfactory answers to your yearnings. Do not be deceived, neither should you allow an illusion-filled environment to confuse you. Know today that the road to awakening and self-realisation is a very narrow one but must be followed. The first step is to learn to live in reality and purge your mind of all beliefs that you cannot prove, beliefs that you cannot independently prove one way or the other even non-scientifically without a third party, without stories and history of others.

Begin to awaken your thinking faculty, as all powers exist within. If one could be sincere to himself, everything around you, things you crave, things that make life worth living today are either created by the universal God or a man like us, a man with the same mind and body, a man with the same brain function as us. The question is why we continue to depend on the creations of others all the time, when we could actually create or are we lower humans? Why can't we let others depend on our creations the same way we depend on theirs?

Why can't it be a two-way process? Why would Africa be such a big market for the inventions of others when children of Africa are born in the same manner as others? Why can't we create and sell to the world? The only thing that may explain this is that either we are inferior to others or we are deeply asleep. I would choose the latter, for I am not inferior to anyone, and I am also soundly awake. Behold the wake-up time. Arise, Africa, for this is the time.

Man has visited the moon and is venturing other planets; he has broken the atoms, driven on land, sailed on seas and deep seas, discovered the life of metal, (electricity), and many more wonders. Humans like us have advanced virtually in all fields of life, but all Africans do every day is program their minds with inferior and expired information that lead us to the direction opposite of where others are heading to—information we have been receiving since childhood and for the past centuries; information which provides us hopes only when we are dead; information that cannot bring solutions to hunger and starvation; information that cannot provide us a direct cure for HIV and other diseases; information that cannot bring civilisation and development; information that blacklist science and technology as evil and occult practices, yet everyone makes use of the fruits of science and technology; information that tells you that those who meditate are practising occultism; information that clearly blacklists any other information as being evil, bad, or wrong; information you must believe 100 per cent without asking questions or else 'God will kill you' and if you question anything that makes no sense in it, it becomes blasphemy; information that results in chronic mental slavery; fear-based information; information that can brainwash you and leave you a moron; information which promotes laziness and lack of creativity; information intended to slow people down mentally; teachings which teachers do not practise; information that is not even controlling crime anymore; information that makes you a 'good heaven seeker' person while the people who created such information are plundering your resources every now and then on earth.

A reasonable man should be able to measure his success in respect to numerous religious stories he has been hearing since childhood. A man boldly went on TV and told his blindfolded members that a TV is a devil's box and that members should discard them. The members went ahead and discarded their TV but never asked how the leader communicated with them; of course, the leader communicated with them via TV. I ask also how a voodoo priest who abandoned herbal medicine practice to become a false medium could make you rich. You find that in some African countries, even educated people and politicians go to these empty, powerless, and deceitful people to acquire non-existent powers.

In these present times, men practise religions of convenience. People listen to doctrines that complement their lifestyles and their yearnings. Fake church pastors are now acting like voodoo priests. Fake churches (religious banks and party grounds) have so many denominations that you begin to question the truthfulness of the whole scheme. You begin to wonder if there is competition among Gods or whether God has varieties. Behold, true messengers preach reality. They do not sell false dreams and false hopes. They also preach improvement of lives which is of paramount importance. Today I preach empowerment and mental freedom just to complement their works.

We must stop being psychic vampires and sadists who derive joy from the downfall and pain of others. We must destroy the scarcity mentality, learn to support and rejoice over success rather than rejoice over failures and above all we must develop mental curiosity and imaginative abilities. We must wake up today, for this is the time. Men have become lovers of only themselves, chronic lovers of money and material acquisitions that they could go to any length to acquire them. Vicious capitalists are now controlling the earth hence it is time for Africans to stand up, begin to redesign their future and reshape their destiny, embrace their heritage, and take charge of their lives. When I speak in this manner, they presume that I am preaching against capitalism, but my message is not against capitalism. The way human beings are acting on this planet today looks as if all the wealth they amass after destroying the happiness and lives of others would be taken alongside with them to their graves, and that truly makes me wonder. But the reverse is the case: this earth is a shrine, and not even a single hair on your body would you go along with.

In the quest for money, men cause others so much pain, yet when they depart from this earth to the great beyond, they do not depart with anything. Due to poverty, unemployment, greed, ignorance, and lack of regulation in religion, men are enslaving those who yearn for the truth about the universal God and life. They end up receiving doctrines that tolerate weaknesses; doctrines that impair reasoning, rational thinking, and common sense; doctrines that promise forgiveness of sin without atonement; false doctrines that intoxicates people's senses, which accounts for the reasons why criminals and men of extreme wickedness cling to bogus religious doctrines yet find no courage to stay away from their criminal ways, because someone out there, a false spiritual comforter, sells false dreams and false hopes to them, sometimes making them believe that no matter how sinful they sink in their wickedness, they will be cleansed when they ask for forgiveness. Know today that though the truth is bitter, it must be told. Whatever we sow on earth, that shall we reap one way or the other, even if we do not know how. Balancing is the true order of life and all existence in nature. It is only out of foolishness and ignorance that men would think that of everything in life, there is balance except in their lives.

Africans are suffering today because in the past our ancestors never forecasted the future; they never thought that events in the world would be constantly changing. Africans must know today that the only thing that can never change is change itself. Today, Africans are still ignoring the need for change. Africans condition their minds with false beliefs that cannot be proven in any practical ways; we lack the will to adopt changes; we allow our entire existence to be controlled by inferior conditioning meant to control the lives of little children and lower animals; we fail to ask questions about belief systems and events around us. Right from childhood, our minds are conditioned and several images useful and useless planted therein. Sometimes we grow up with the wrong conditioning and image implants and never flee from the grip as we become adults. The most potent and fertile stage of the human mind is when he or she is young and tender, and it amazes me that it is the time when we physically assault our children in the name of disciplining them, instilling fear in their minds. It is the time when we brainwash our with stories that can never help them when they grow up; it is the time that we force our children into child labour; it is the time when we expose our children to all sorts of abusive treatments; it is also the time when we quarrel or engage in vioent reproach with our spouses in the presence of our children. For the future of Africa, let us begin to raise a stronger generation with powerful mind culturing and human conditioning, let us 'reformat' our minds and free reasonable spaces for valuable information and not the ones designed to enslave the mind; let us begin to copy science and technology in its true contexts. Let it be known to all Africans that mind is the powerhouse of the body and that the human mind is the home of thoughts and thoughts give birth to ideas and ideas result in the physical manifestations by application of rightful actions and a man becomes what he thinks.

We crave to believe that when we die, there is another place where we shall be conscious of and I have nothing against that except that it has not been proven scientifically and with tangible evidence but what has been proven is that when we die our dead bodies go back to earth but our legacy remain behind and also our progenies remain behind. We accept doctrines that bear no proof so long as they are congruent with what we desire to think and hear. We fail to accept the reality of death which is even more certain than the birth of a person. Every man shall depart from this earth someday. The question is what we will leave behind for our children and generations to come. What will be the legacy? Will it be xenophobia and tribalism? Will it be ritual killings and secret cultism? Will it be faulty leadership and wolves in power that loot national funds and hide them in Swiss banks accounts, funds that end up being confiscated when they die or end up in the hands of their unproductive children? Is it prostitution and same-sex marriages? Will it be terrorism? Will it be alcohol abuse, crime, drug abuse, sex abuse, life abuse, women abuse, child abuse, and time abuse? Will it be lack of creativity? Will it be foolishness and ignorance? Will it be illiteracy? Will it be mental slavery? Will it be spinelessness and narrow-mindedness? What will the legacy be?

Today, Africans must know that we are here on earth to perpetuate purposeful living, and when we pass on, we leave a legacy for those who shall leave after us. If we live our entire lives on this planet achieving nothing, then we have lived our lives not better than other lower animals. After all, average animals in the wild feed, breed, excrete, breastfeed their young ones, look after their young ones, hunt for what to eat, and do everything average human being does, hence what will distinguish us from animals in the wild if we live and act exactly like them? What distinguishes a human being from lower animals is the power of reasoning and the power of creativity, but how many of us are reasoning and creating today. We are just proud and shameless consumers.

Man has been given the power to control lower animals, but it amazes me today that due to our inability to ask questions in life and to follow the progressive trend that gave birth to the current-day civilisation, our entire lives and existence are being controlled by others. The food most of us eat, the general languages we communicate with, culture, religion, education, concept of right and wrong are all determined by others. I know that this part of the book will anger a lot of people that they wish I hang, but let me say this today, for it is said that the truth hurts but the revelation of truth liberates men from servitude. As I said, any part of this book that hurts you, go back there and see if it reveals a sad reality that you do not want to deal with. A Caucasian friend of mine in North America at some point told me that we are all human animals, but some people are more human, and I must tell you that this was one of the deepest reasons why I left the Western world as I preferred to go home and be creative and useful to Africa than be an unproductive entity and a slave in a part of the world where things have been made well. Let the mosquitoes bite me; let the heat of Africa ravage me; let my people act stupid before me; let the dust disturb me; let the flue ravage me, but I must be in Africa to contribute my little quota to the building of our great continent Africa. Even if I die in this course, let this message be immortalised, for I do not speak or write just because I have mouth to speak or hands to write. I speak out of deep inspiration from the universal God and from the spirit of our great continent Africa.

This is a point of deep awakening when Africans have to turn the clock around or do we wish to hand over our great continent to others because we have failed to fit since the fittest survives? How long shall we live in chronic ignorance; have we not learnt from the events of the past, slavery, colonialism, destruction of African evolving economy and culture, hypocricy of the advance nations, divide and rule, forced dorminance as it happened in America, Australia, New Zealand and South Africa; when will we think like rational human beings; when will we wake up? Today, begin to reason, for if civilisation began in great Africa, it means Africans were thinking in the past. We must become actively creative now; we must contribute to this system to gain respect. We must be 'in' the system and not just 'with' the system. We must stop hating Europeans rather copy from them. We must become critical of all strange beliefs, doctrines and information around us.

Africans are not yet free though; physical slavery only gave birth to colonialism, which is another form of slavery, and this ushered in neo-colonialism, which is also a form of slavery, and finally, a more dangerous form of slavery which I call mental slavery is taking place in the continent on a larger scale. Join the ark today and be free completely. Our mission is to bring total liberation to Africans, to free Africans from all forms of mental slavery, and not to cause trouble or confusion in their lives. We wish to bring true empowerment which is of the mind, to enforce growth, development and civilisation of Africa. We also wish to bring spiritual unity among the entire children of Africa at home and the diaspora. We do not intend to pursue a struggle for one African nation as Gadhafi was clamouring but to engineer spiritual unity both in the manner of improving trade barriers, encouraging the development of one African language for easy communication amongst Africans, improving interactions and social integration amongst African indigenes all over the globe. We wish to prepare Africans for the challenges ahead, as the future seems not to be certain, and most importantly we intend to abolish, correct, or redefine the meaning of the word *black man* as used to denote Africans all over the world.

The true self never lies, and when a man aligns himself with the true self, he begins to experience the power of the infinite intelligence (the universal God); when a man awakens his inner self, he becomes alive again and attuned with the invincible forces of creation. He is then part of this force. The divinity which shapes the destiny of a man dwells in his hands. Mind above matter, all powers exist within. The true mission of a human being on this planet is to establish oneness with this creative force, the universal God, and the only way to do this is by demonstrating the creative power which the same universal God has endowed in all humans. This is a wake-up time for Africa; let us prove our humanity before it is too late.

I am on my knees pleading to the world to remove the grip in the minds of Africans, to tell us the whole truth (including all hidden information) about this 'God' which they brought to us with guns yet the Bible is used to wed same sex couples in churches promoting Satanism yet preaching holiness, and also to free us from mental slavery. What have we done that the world feels that we should not exist? Our children were kidnapped and others bought as slaves; we are trying to forgive and 'forget', yet more evil and injustices are happening under our noses every day. Is it the creation of HIV virus and blaming it on Africa? Is it the guinea pig status of Africa and children of Africa all over the globe that are about to face endangerment because of chronic ignorance and inability to produce what they consume and consume what they produce? Why is the world so cold, insensitive and cruel towards the children of Africa? Why have they turned us into preys that they must devour? Why have they turned the minds of our leaders against us? Out of greed, quest for money, wealth and power, the world undermines the lives of children of Africa. Laws they created work against us. Sometimes I ask this imaginary 'God' they introduced to us with guns as to how come he does not look down from 'heaven', where they claim that he lives, and see the pain and tears of children of Africa? How come he does not want to help vulnerable children of Africa suffering in Soweto and Alexander with no food and health care? How come he allows the minds of African leaders to be biased? How come he does not see the plight of great Zimbabwe? How come he does not see what cruel politicians, (secret cultists, and mafias) are doing in Nigeria? How come this imaginary 'God' allows African leaders to loot the wealth of nations and hide them in Swiss banks accounts? Where is this imaginary 'God' that allows HIV to infect an unborn child in the womb? Where is this imaginary 'God' that we must always give our little hard-earned income to and he will never give us back in return, rather all we get is after-death hopes? Where is this imaginary 'God' who allows the new age churches and their false prophets to steal so much money from poor Africans and give nothing in return rather than false hopes? Where is this imaginary 'God' that rewards us only when we are dead? How come he does not see poor little children and women being killed in Sudan every day? Where was he during the Rwanda genocide? Where was he during the Nigerian civil war? Where was he during the apartheid era? Where is this imaginary 'God' that will never provide a practical solution to any problem rather than stories and brainwash from his mercenaries? How come he does not see poverty ravaging great Zimbabwe? Where are you this imaginary 'God' that has given Africa unto the hands of those who introduced him to us yet they are treating us as if we are enemies that must be crushed? How come the natives of India who are the true indigenous of America are almost going into extinction? How come the aborigines of Australia are also going into extinction, the Maoris of New Zealand are also going into extinction? How come this imaginary God allowes all of these ugliness against the weak and vulnerable. But I tell the world today that no such thing will ever happen to Africa, if it is what they are dreaming of achieving with religious diversion and HIV. Despite the brainwash and mental slavery, the world must realise today the futility of trying to mess with the great continent Africa. Any such attempt will bring another era where science would no longer be able to contend with the problems the world will face. They tried to seize the land of South Africa from the natives but today they are stuck there with no identity and not knowing what to do and where to go. The sins of their forefathers have been used to repay their children and I hope the world learns a hard lesson and stop oppressing the weak, poor and vulnerable.

Mental slavery is a more dangerous and more complex form of slavery, one which you may not notice even when you are a victim; one which you could be a mercenary yet not aware of what you are doing; one spread by mind diversion, deceptive image implant, negative habits and negative lifestyles, negative emotions, bogus religious beliefs about the unknown, old and weird cultural and traditional practices and beliefs, the afterlife story, non-existent fears, confusion, ignorance, fear of death, false hopes, non-existent heaven, non-existent hellfire, non-existent anti-Christ, '666 threats', earth that will be consumed by fire someday, non-existent beasts that will come and swallow everyone, non-existent UFO, non-existent ghosts, non-existent demons, non-existent spirits, non-existent spirits of our ancestors, what we listen to; what we believe in; what we read; what we see; what we think; what we do; what we make others listen to; what we make others read; what we make others believe; what we make others think; what we make others see; and what we make others do.

You may be an agent of mental slavery without knowing it. One way of recognising when you are an agent of mental slavery is when you are spreading expired information passed on to you by others, when you are spreading information which you cannot prove to be true and deep down in your heart you are not absolutely sure if you believe in what you are telling others.

In the game of life, there are no losers and there are no winners. Only a non-liberated mind fears the certainty of death. It is even less certain that a person would be born on earth than that someone would die; death is an absolute certainty and a reality that everyone must face. Our concern though should not be what happens to us when we die, but the good legacy we leave behind for the living. Today, Africans must run away from teachings, concepts, information, or doctrines which they cannot prove in any manner or by any scientific means available in these current times, except with references to stories, information, rumours told by others or books written by others; stories about the lives of others and not about our lives or history of our own people and ancestors, and information provided by those who have only their own selfish interests to protect.

Africans are the most confused of all the people in the world. Sometimes we even feel inferior of ourselves. Remember that civilisation which thrills the world today began in Africa and our continent is great; remember also that Africa has more natural resources than most continents of the world. We must learn to appreciate our skin pigmentation and be proud of our heritage. We must stop neglecting our history, good culture, and traditions, for those are not what civilisation means. If our culture and traditions build us positively and generate peace, harmony, and happiness in our lives, then they must be preserved, but if they promote backwardness and savagery, then they must be discarded without fear of gods or spirits of ancestors. I decree that if you are in any part of Africa and your culture still promotes ritual killings and human sacrifices, please without hesitation, burn down those shrines and whatever masks they are using to preserve those non-existent gods. I promise you that nothing will happen to you, but ensure that you stay away from the shrine worshippers and the village chiefs because they are the ones that will attempt to kill you to make it sound as if the 'gods' killed you. Let me tell you, if you do this, you have done well to save the lives of those who would have been used for ritual sacrifices.

We must also stop importing more religions into Africa and stop Christian churches from splitting into untold number of fragments. We must also ensure that Christian churches fuse together and stop contradicting one another in their teachings. Some say that when you die, you go to heaven or hell depending on your deeds; some say that when you die, you remain in your grave if you did not do well but go to paradise if you did well; some say that 'heaven' and 'hell' are all here on earth and all these teachings contradict one another, yet people are listening and following any directions without asking questions as to which direction is right. God is the one and universal. Good Christians seeking the face of God through the right means will make heaven if there is such a place that is not here on earth. Those from other religious sects seeking the face of God through the right means will also find God and heaven if heaven is not here on earth. The problem that I have is that Christians are religiously 'racists' towards all other religions; in some countries, Muslims are intolerant of other religious beliefs and that is not a welcome idea, for the universal God is not racist. They do not understand that if you are born in a deep Muslim society, you may not have a choice of religion, rather you must be a Muslim, and if you are born in a deep Christian family and society, the only choice you have is to be a Christian, so what determines whether someone makes it to heaven; simply your deeds.

You might also decide not to be religious and leave a righteous life, and I tell you, if there is a place called heaven, the heaven gates will also be open for you, as the determining factor is your deeds. There are laws in this universe and the universal God has made a few of these laws known to man, yet man calls the name of God every day while still violating those laws. However you want to put it, I remind you that if there is love as Christ preached, this world will be free from pain and evil. Other laws like the law of retributive justice, action and reaction, law of karma, law of sowing and reaping, cause and effect are all universal laws. If we understand and obey these laws, the gates of heaven will be open to us, that is, if there is a place called heaven, and we will find happiness, peace, and harmony here on earth.

We must stop searching for more foreign God(s) to worship, for God is one and universal. We must also stop seeking hopes where there is none. Know today that all powers exist within. Our ancestors were busy with demigods in the past, and now we are busy with foreign gods. Today religious priests are acting like voodoo priests. Wake up today, Africans.

The survival of the fittest has no mercy for the weak. This is a world of the strong; the weak, lazy, and ignorant have no space therein. The universal God protects the strong, but this is not to be misunderstood as the wicked that has been classified as strong in this emerging New World Order.

The weak shall be displaced one way or the other no matter how much time and efforts they waste seeking 'love', pity, and ingratiating others. We must commence active struggle to reshape our future and redesign our destiny.

We must be careful of what we listen to, for today men who do not even have basic primary education, con men, and men of the underworld have turned into priests. What are they teaching us? There is no regulation and moderation in what we hear today in most religious institutions.

Being creative empowers an individual; education empowers an individual; knowledge does the same as well as wisdom, and imaginative ability is a very important aspect of a human being that should be developed. The human mind must be developed logically and scientifically and not with stories. Remember, mind over matter, all powers exist within.

We must realise that we suffer in these current times because in the past our ancestors were busy with futile rituals to non-existent gods. They wasted time in powerless witchcrafts which have neither definite nor positive results. They wasted so much time worshipping non-existent gods which could not protect them when Europeans invaded our land, gods which do not have a cure for diseases, gods created by people and housed on carvings. They never tapped into the creative source which dwells in the human mind as the advanced people are doing every day; they believed that solutions to their problems dwell in the hands of deities and gods, not knowing that all solutions to a man's problems exist within him. Man is a smaller god as the universal God designed us with in his image and that image is ability to create.

We must reduce our pleasure levels to energise our minds for the struggle ahead. Everyone should take up his mental spears and mental shields as a soldier in this new course of fighting mental slavery and enforcing creativity in Africa. We have no time to waste abusing alcohol, drug, and sex. We have no time for religious illusions and fantasies, prearranged magical acts and illusions in the glorified name of miracles. We cannot be multiplying in our population, bearing more children every day without any plans for them and their future, giving birth to a generation of future slaves. Africans must know today that the main causes of mental slavery in Africa is religious diversion and superstitions

When foreign diseases invade our lives, there is never a cure until it comes from others. Our lives and total existence are dictated by parameters set by others that we have been treated as guinea pigs without our knowing, yet we call ourselves humans. Why can't we control the lives of others with our own creations the same way and manner they control our lives? Why must we always be the ones that are controlled? We even import other people's religion and 'Gods'. This is the time for change; this is the period of mental freedom; a mind revolutionary era for total emancipation of Africans from the grip of mental slavery, for the problems of Africans is in the mind.

The only thing that distinguishes humans from animals is the power of reasoning and creativity. The question is: are we making use of our reasoning capacity which truly dwells in us? We were told that the ancient pharaohs enslaved the Israelites and today many nations and people are enslaved one way or the other. No one knows if the story of the pharaohs enslaving the Jews was intended to encourage slavery. I am only saying that Africans must think and also make reasonable efforts to establish the truthfulness of whatever they listen to or read when it comes to religion.

If the story of the pharaohs enslaving Israelites is true, then it could mean that slavery could be a human way of achieving control and man's nature, but we must also fight against it. We must now recognise this slavery in the style and manner that they come. It may not be with physical chains but information and false religion. Hence when you recognise it, you may be able to run away from it to be able to live a fulfilled life free from the complete mental control of others.

Today, it is no longer physical slavery but mental slavery; a key and a chain far larger than the physical ones we know have been used to lock our brains and minds that we cannot think any more as normal human beings hence I tell Africans to break this chain immediately because mental slavery is another instrument of dominance. This is also an era of spiritual unity of Africans. We must choose one of the African languages and ensure that they are introduced in all schools in Africa the same way English, French and other colonial languages are taught. Also schools must ensure that Africans learn this language and know it; in this way you could see an African person and say *Kunjani* or *Kedu* and he would respond.

This is the time to bring the attention and minds of Africans to reality and the right task, which is one of developing and civilising this great continent Africa, our true home. This is the time to destroy all the fears that have hypnotised our minds and turned us into weak vessels that cannot challenge concepts we do not understand, concepts that can only make sense to little children. This is the time that we challenge imaginary religious gods to 'punish us', but we must ask questions when we do not understand teachings about those gods.

The 91 elements of this earth that we know today are found here on earth; all the resources of this earth are all abundant in Africa. The world is tilling the land for natural resources; the world is advancing every day, but the attention of Africans is directed upwards to an unknown 'sky' world they call 'heaven' which you can only visit when you die—a world designed for poor and lazy people. According to what we were told, Christ said that the meek shall inherit the earth, and I ask who is inheriting the earth today, of course the strong. Is Christ making promises to Africans that would only come true when they die? A heavenly promise when Europeans are dominating the earth! What about the unborn and the generations to come of those who will die and inherit heaven? Is it because Christ did not have children that he did not see the need for a man to be strong and fortify the future for his children, the unborn, and the future generations? How come those who are Christ-like are the ones suffering in the world today? How come children of Africa who believe in Christ are the ones suffering from HIV and poverty? What is he doing for his followers that are persecuted in Africa? Is he telling them to endure pain including the death sentence by HIV/AIDS so that they will inherit 'heaven' when they die? Is he telling them to abandon their natural and mineral resources to the same people who introduced doctrines about him? Is Christ not seeing that when we die, even if we are going to 'heaven', our children remain here and they also are going to have their own children? Is he saying that we should not protect the future of our children, the unborn, and the generations to come? Have the teachings of our Lord Jesus Christ been twisted to enslave Africans and achieve dominance? Or are we not getting the original teachings of the Bible? I need an answer before I write my next book. I am worried that maybe the Bible we are reading today is not the original Bible, as it has undergone a series of changes—from the old version to King James Version to Revised Standard Version.

When one goes to school, he acquires knowledge, and this knowledge keeps changing as one starts climbing the academic ladder. Sometimes what you learnt from the beginning becomes almost irrelevant as you climb. But how come Africans stick to information which may have expired as we grew older? It bothers me that even in these current times when the truth is no longer held a secret, we prefer to listen to doctrines that can only make sense to little children, lazy and idle men.

False religion does not encourage hard work or creative thinking; rather, they say that a poor, lazy, idle, and ignorant man would go to 'heaven' when he dies, so he should not worry. If there is a better place than earth, the advanced world would already know because we know absolutely nothing except what they told us and what we've seen ourselves. And if such places do exist, I am not absolutely sure that they would want Africans to go there because HIV is killing us in the known world; someone tells me that I should not worry so that when I die of HIV I would inherit heaven or paradise. If there is a better place than here, the poor, lazy, and ignorant would never be allowed to venture there. If there is a better place than here, then the world would not waste time in science and technological advancements. If there is a better place, the gate would surely be closed against Africans, for even in the only world we truly know we seem not to be welcome at all. It bothers me why Africans cannot get out of the box, destroy narrow-mindedness and ask themselves why NASA is investing billions of dollars in space exploration. Why they are trying to find out if life existed in Mars.

When you were a child, you were told about 'heaven' and 'hell' to prevent you from indulging in immoralities, but today, an average African even up to the age of sixty years still believes in those stories told to little children. The concept of 'heaven' and 'hell' was not explained very well to us. They were used in an allegorical sense and not in a literal sense. Bear in mind that our fear is that this heaven and hell story may be preventing the development of our minds, for any man who is truly convinced that heaven and hell is somewhere else not on this earth, any man who is convinced that there is another place where poor, ignorant, and idle people would go to when they die, then the person would be preparing to go there during his entire existence here and avoid things of the earth and even ignore his generations to come. He would see no reasons to struggle. These stories paralyse a human being's enthusiasm and make him lazy and unproductive. Yet there is no definite proof of anything. The only stories we get are stories that are constantly hammered into our heads until they glue in. This is pure mental slavery and must be corrected. My problem is that if Hitler came here and took on the Jews, George Bush took on the Arabs, who knows who would come and say that Africans are unfit to live on this planet. A Japanese government official mentioned in a public speech that Africans are inferior in intelligence, and any right-thinking person would understand that they may not be the only ones thinking that way.

Run away from crime, for it is a waste of time and creative energy, and the world knows this. The same energy and power you apply to engineer crime could be applied in advancing like others. Fear no more, for your fears do not exist. It is the eyes of childhood that fear a painted devil. Destroy laziness, idleness, scarcity mentality, hatred, disunity, xenophobia, wickedness, selfishness, tribalism and tribal marginalisation, false prophets, and religious diversions. Let all African leaders pull resources together and challenge all African engineers to develop the first African car. Let us start from there. Let African leaders make research institutions the top-most priority in their nations. Does it ever disturb any right-thinking African to ask why there are no research institutions in African countries? But they are introducing strip clubs and more liquor shops. Sometimes I ask why most African nations are ruled by unserious people who do not worry about the collective future of Africa, men who are surrounded by sycophants and political prostitutes who applaud all the nonsense they do, men who would quickly take the lives of their own people, but when there is external pressure, they chicken out.

Free your mind today, for we know that the problems of Africans are mind related. Let us start from the known to the unknown. Only a wicked person worries about where he would go when he dies due to fear of reactions of his negative existence and wickedness. The wicked goes seeking for forgiveness of sin and even pays money to those who are willing to receive money and material gifts to relay their pleas to God, when even man-made laws have no room for forgiveness.

For those who live worthy lives, fear not, for there is balance in life and do not worry about 'heaven' or 'hell'. If there is any place one would go after death apart from the grave, surely the universal God of balance would not lead you to the wrong direction. For those who live in wickedness, turn away from your wicked ways so that your life will gradually normalise.

Wasting your time worrying about where to go when you die and still continuing in your negative actions is a sick task; run away from your wicked ways, and with time, you would find peace and happiness, and the fear of death, fear of afterlife, and fear of hell will vanish. Run away from evil and wickedness, and you will be free and happy, for once you disengage from negative existence, fear of the unknown and the afterlife will vanish.

The fact that during the era of slave trade, Africans assisted in trading their fellow Africans for money greatly angers me. We even captured and sold our kinds to invaders. Sometimes I ask myself what has gone wrong with Africans.

Granted that religion could help control crime and also maintain spiritual harmony in a society if well applied without hypocricy or negative motive, but politicians must begin to look into what false religious warlords are teaching the people. Or are politicians benefiting by permitting proliferation of false religions to achieve mind control of the people and quell the anger of the people since most of them have nothing to offer? Today, we play a more dangerous role in mental slavery. It is said that necessity is the mother of invention. Civilisation was advanced because there were needs in the lives of the people, and such needs triggered creativity. Are we not seeing any needs for a change in Africa when HIV is almost sweeping us away from the only world we know? Africans must learn that everything we see on earth that is not of nature is the creation of man, human beings like us. They are all created by physical means and not by magical acts, witchcraft, or voodoo.

We wonder why our professors only boast about their academic robes and achievements when they can neither invent ideas nor transform already existing ideas into physical manifestations for the betterment of Africa. I also wonder the kind of leaders we have today in Africa. Africa needs visionary leaders, those who would understand the needs of the people and also the need to invest in research, science, and technology.

Chinese, Japanese, and Indian people went through the same process as us; they resisted mental slavery and adopted creativity, and today, they have conquered economic slavery, and I wonder why we are not making same efforts as other human beings. The future of Africa dwells in our hands, and the people need proper reorientation and reconditioning. This is a wake-up time. In Asia, young school children build sophisticated electronic gadgets as their projects while in school. We attend ill-equipped schools without infrastructures to waste time in secret cultism (Nigerian case), exam malpractices, prostitution, and parties only to come out with shiny certificates that cannot be practically defended. I asked a friend of mine how he thinks that millions of graduates of higher institutions in Africa could be employed every year when there is no mass job creation. This situation calls for a total revamp of our academic institutions so that graduates may be able to create jobs for themselves when they graduate from schools rather than sit and wait for jobs that do not exist. Also skills acquisition and talent development as veritable tools of youth empowerment are very vital in African development. We could create a mini-system of our own just as Nigerians boldly introduced their cheap Nigerian movies into the world market and they are making waves ubiquitously. All we have to do is destroy narrow-mindedness, support them, and encourage them to improve on the product standard and quality since they are gaining grounds in the world at least to bring dignity back to Africa.

Poverty is a serious problem affecting us in Africa. We are still struggling for basic needs like food, health care, shelter, etc. African leaders should intervene and help develop poverty alleviation and empowerment structures.

Our academic institutions have turned into breeding grounds for criminality. Male lecturers and professors waste their times chasing after young female students. They display so much empty pride without anything to offer in terms

237

of research, innovation, idea generation, and idea development; without any contribution to the society; without any means of measuring success regarding what they are planting in the minds of the students. Sometimes they even accept bribes from students to excel them in their courses. We go to school only to obtain a certificate, a piece of paper without any measurable success in terms of creativity.

Africans must know today that human beings are the greatest of all God's life creations on planet earth possessing intelligence, but when a human being does not utilise his intelligence, when a human being has failed to think, then he is underutilising his God-given capacities and may be seen or treated as an inferior human being by others. In this new world, only the fittest survives, and if others could think, if others could achieve extraordinary success in life, then we can do it. If men like Martin Luther King, Nelson Mandela, Philip Emeagwali, Wole Soyinka, Chinua Achebe, Chike Obi, and many other children of Africa, then I am happily and proudly African.

Every creation starts from ideas and ideas originate from thoughts and when the right actions are applied to ideas then creation occurs.

Today I spread this message to Africans all over the globe. I spread the message of true empowerment which dwells in the mind. Today, we fight the greatest enemy of our times. Today, we fight mental slavery. Today, we fight for African unification. Today, we fight for good governance. Today, we fight against AIDS/HIV. Today, we confuse the greatest enemy of our times that is deployed to displace Africans from their own lands. Behold the wake-up time.

If you want to be part of this global activism against mental slavery, please email us at *info@camareb.org* or visit our website at *www.camareb.org* to join and interact with members and the author.

www.ingramcontent.com/pod-product-compliance
Lightning Source LLC
Chambersburg PA
CBHW030306290526
45785CB00001B/236